"Rory and Ita are two good Irish people, the sort of rare, dignified souls one always hopes will move next door or take up the mantle of godparent. . . . Those interested in understanding how Irish fortunes rose and fell over the twentieth century will enjoy spending time in Rory and Ita's company."
    —*The Baltimore Sun*

"Rory and Ita's story has the feel of people enjoying themselves as they unabashedly reminisce. . . . The memories form a striking, cumulatively remarkable and memorable portrait."
    —*The Miami Herald*

"This is Irish storytelling refined to a satin finish."
    —*Los Angeles Times*

"An oral history not only of the lives of Rory and Ita Doyle but of an Ireland changing almost imperceptibly during the last half of the twentieth century. . . . *Rory & Ita* is as much a gift to Roddy Doyle's readers as to his parents."
    —*Providence Journal*

"This move into sweetness may arise partly from the genuine affection that Doyle feels for his parents, but it also comes from the sort of politics that has been central to his work from the beginning. . . . *Rory & Ita* quietly and subtly dramatizes the lure of his Dublin life and its softening effect on the nationalists who settled in the city after independence."
    —Colm Tóibín, *The New York Review of Books*

PENGUIN BOOKS

RORY & ITA

Roddy Doyle is the author of six novels. The first three—*The Commitments*, *The Snapper*, and 1991 Booker Prize finalist *The Van*—are available both singly and in one volume as *The Barrytown Trilogy*, published by Penguin. In 1993, *Paddy Clarke Ha Ha Ha* won the Booker Prize and became an international bestseller. Doyle's next novels were the acclaimed bestsellers *The Woman Who Walked Into Doors* and *A Star Called Henry*. Doyle has also written for the stage and the screen: the plays *Brownbread*, *War*, and *Guess Who's Coming for the Dinner*; the film adaptations of *The Commitments* (as cowriter), *The Snapper*, and *The Van*; *When Brendan Met Trudy* (an original screenplay); the four-part television play *Hell for Leather*. Roddy Doyle has also written the children's books *The Giggler Treatment* and *Rover Saves Christmas* and contributed to a variety of publications, including *The New Yorker* magazine, the anthology *Speaking with the Angel* (edited by Nick Hornby), and the serial novel *Yeats is Dead!* (edited by Joseph O'Connor). He lives in Dublin.

RORY & ITA

Roddy Doyle

PENGUIN BOOKS

PENGUIN BOOKS

Published by the Penguin Group

Penguin Group (USA) Inc., 375 Hudson Street,
New York, New York 10014, U.S.A.
Penguin Books Ltd, 80 Strand, London WC2R 0RL, England
Penguin Books Australia Ltd, 250 Camberwell Road,
Camberwell, Victoria 3124, Australia
Penguin Books Canada Ltd, 10 Alcorn Avenue,
Toronto, Ontario, Canada M4V 3B2
Penguin Books India (P) Ltd, 11 Community Centre,
Panchsheel Park, New Delhi – 110 017, India
Penguin Books (N.Z.) Ltd, Cnr Rosedale and Airborne Roads,
Albany, Auckland, New Zealand
Penguin Books (South Africa) (Pty) Ltd, 24 Sturdee Avenue,
Rosebank, Johannesburg 2196, South Africa

Penguin Books Ltd, Registered Offices:
80 Strand, London WC2R 0RL, England

First published in the United States of America by Viking Penguin,
a member of Penguin Putnam Inc., 2002
Published in Penguin Books 2003

1   3   5   7   9   10   8   6   4   2

Grateful acknowledgment is made for permission to reprint an excerpt
from "The Hallway" from *The Reed Bed* by Dermot Healy (2001).
By permission of the author and The Gallery Press,
Loughcrew, Oldcastle, County Meath, Ireland.

Photographs from the author's collection

ISBN 0-670-03204-2 (hc.)
ISBN 0 14 20.0360 3 (pbk.)
CIP data available

Printed in the United States of America

For my grandparents.

Roddy Doyle

For the next generation,

Elizabeth, Rory, Jack and Kate.

Ita Doyle and Rory Doyle

Life without memory is no life at all, just as an intelligence without the possibility of expression is not really an intelligence. Our memory is our coherence, our reason, our feeling, even our action. Without it, we are nothing.

Luis Buñuel, *My Last Breath*

The house is dark and silent.
The door has just closed behind me or soon will open.

What darkness! What silence!

Dermot Healy, *The Hallway*

In all of my life I have lived in two houses, had two jobs, and one husband. I'm a very interesting person.

Ita Doyle

I wanted to ask the questions before it was too late. And they wanted to answer them.

The book is about my parents, about the people they were before they became parents. But there's very little about parenting. My sisters and brother are born and named, but I didn't think I had the right to bring them into the book. Anyway, they're too short in the tooth, and too cute to be cornered by a brother with a mission and a microphone.

As for the parenting, the teacher in me gives my mother and father eight out of ten, but is it too late to add, 'Making good progress'?

Roddy Doyle, 16 May 2002

Chapter One – Ita

'The first thing I remember is the gramophone arriving. I know I must have been less than three, because my mother was still alive. It was a lovely thing. I can still smell the wood of it. It was dark wood, with a press below the turntable for the records. Slats behind the turntable, six or eight of them, each the width of my hand, opened when a handle was turned, and released the sound. It was good sound. It was beautiful. I can still remember it, and the little needles and the little box, the dog of His Master's Voice on the lid. And the needle had to be fitted in. I was able to do it myself later, and the handle turned and away we went.

'The first record we had was John McCormack, and he sang "Macushla". And there was McCormack singing "Adeste Fidelis", and that used to be played every Christmas. And there was "The Old Refrain", which is still in my mind, played by Fritz Kreisler. And a song that started, "Where are the boys of the Old Brigade?" I can remember marching around the room listening to it. And there was a record of somebody reading *The Selfish Giant*. I can remember one line: "In one corner of the garden it was always winter."'

She remembers hands holding grease-proof paper, and lowering the paper on to the surface of a pot of soup, and the paper being lifted and bringing a film of fat with it. She remembers a tiny wooden swing, with a little wooden girl swinging on it. She remembers a stuffed dog, a black and white terrier, called Dog, and a brown teddy bear. She remembers a doll with a bald china head. She remembers pale green notepaper with serrated edges.

'I was born on the 20th of June, 1925. I think I was born at home, in 25 Brighton Gardens, Terenure, which is one of the two houses I have lived in, that house and the house I live in now. There were an awful lot of home births at that time and I feel that I was probably born there.' She knows nothing about the birth. 'Not a thing. I just came. I was named Ita Bridget. I have no idea where the Ita came from but Bridget, I gather, was my mother's mother. I was the third child. The first, Mary Johanna (Máire), was three years older than me and the second, John Joseph (Joe), was a year older.'

She was Ita Bridget Bolger. Her father was James (Jim) Bolger, of Coolnaboy, Oilgate, in County Wexford. He was born in 1890. He grew up on a farm and was sent to St Peter's College, in Wexford town, to become a priest. The eldest of five children, his father had died when he was very young. 'His mother, my grandmother, was a tough old dame and if you were meant to be a priest, you became a priest, when all this money had been spent on you.' But he had other ideas. He left St Peter's when he was seventeen and didn't go home.★ Armed with a reference, he went to Enniscorthy: 'I beg

---

★ Ita: 'He didn't go home until she died. She wasn't dead when I was born – I think I can claim that – but I have a very vague memory of my father going off with a suitcase, a small suitcase, and being told that my grandmother was either dying or dead. I was very small at the time. That's my only memory of her; I never met her.'

to say that James Bolger has received a very good education in St Peter's College, has always shown great apti-
tude, and is a very good boy. I am quite sure he is
thoroughly fitted for the position he seeks in the *Echo*
Office.' He got the job, at the *Enniscorthy Echo*, the local
newspaper.

'He got caught up in the nationalist movement and
he was found sleeping in a bed with guns under it. Now,
they weren't his guns but he wouldn't tell whose they
were, so he was banished from Enniscorthy.' This happened just after the outbreak of the War, in 1914. What
the police found in the house of Larry DeLacey, where
Jim Bolger lodged, were home-made grenades – cocoa
tins filled with gelignite and scraps of iron – as well as
yards of fuse and hundreds of detonators. They also found
stacks of Roger Casement's pamphlet *Ireland, Germany
and the Freedom of the Seas*, which had been secretly
printed at the *Echo* offices. He was arrested, along with
Jack Hegarty, another lodger, and taken to Arbour Hill

barracks, in Dublin. A defence fund was quickly organised, and a campaign to have the men tried by jury.

Here is the account by Robert Brennan,★ Jim Bolger's
brother-in-law:

> . . . after two trials in which Tim Healy and Charlie
> Wyse Power appeared for the defence, the two were
> acquitted on all charges of treason, sedition, creating
> disaffection etc. They had been charged, amongst
> other things, with knowing that the seditious liter-
> ature and the explosives were in the house and with
> not informing the authorities. The jury found they
> were not guilty, though neither of the two men
> could get in or out of bed without climbing over
> stacks of the literature, and they could hardly move
> anywhere in the house without knocking over one
> of the pernicious cocoa tins. DeLacey's old house-
> keeper, shown the yards of fuse, said of course she
> had seen it. She had cut yards off a length of it to
> tie the little dog to the bed-post.
>
> Tim Healy was largely responsible for the
> acquittal. He made it appear that Hegarty was being
> persecuted, not for his political activities, but for
> his religion. His plea was based on the fact that
> one of the witnesses for the prosecution, who tes-
> tified that pro-German notices were in Hegarty's
> handwriting, was a Belfast man who had himself,
> as he was forced to admit in cross-examination,
> preached in the streets of Cork with a Sankey and
> Moody band. Hegarty, said Tim, had been hounded

★ The father of Maeve Brennan, author of *The Springs of Affection*, *The Rose Garden*, *The Long-Winded Lady* and *The Visitor*.

out of his employment and out of his native city by the bigots who had come down from Belfast to insult the people of Cork by preaching against their religion.*

Barred from Enniscorthy, Jim Bolger 'lived in New Ross for some years but he was able to send his writings back to Enniscorthy, so he was still working for the *Echo*.' From New Ross, he moved to Dublin. He followed Robert Brennan, to work on the *Irish Bulletin*, a Sinn Féin propaganda sheet which was produced daily and delivered by hand to the Dublin newspapers and to all the foreign correspondents in the city. Production and distribution of the *Bulletin* were difficult but the authorities in Dublin Castle never managed to stop a single issue. It was published every day, from November 1919 until the Treaty was ratified two years later. 'He never fought, as such. He was more an intellectual than a fighter.'

On the inception of the new State, Jim Bolger became a civil servant, at the Department of External Affairs. 'He never lost the idea of what he had fought for, but he wasn't a diehard.' His first task was to sit outside a room with a gun while the new Minister, Gavin Duffy, was inside the room. By the time she was born, three years later, he was sitting at a desk, in the Accounts section of External Affairs, and studying accountancy at night, at the College of Commerce, in Rathmines. He was also a freelance journalist, calling himself The Recorder, writing GAA† match reports for the *Irish*

---

* From *Allegiance* (1950) by Robert Brennan.
† Gaelic Athletic Association. Jim Bolger reported on gaelic football and hurling.

Independent. He also wrote for *Ireland's Own*, 'about ordinary life and things that go on. One article I found was about cutting the front grass. He also wrote a series of articles about the Young Irelanders for the *Independent*.

'My mother's name was Ellen O'Brien. She was born, I think, in 1895, in the townland of Ballydonegan, near Ferns, in County Wexford. She is a bit of a mystery to me. My father never spoke of her. Maybe it upset him too much, or maybe he thought it would upset us.'

She doesn't know how her parents met, or where. They were married in 1921, in Liverpool. What a Sinn Féin activist was doing in Liverpool during the War of Independence, she doesn't know. 'He never spoke about being out of the country. He was a terribly secretive man, you know. His right hand did not know what his left hand was doing and that is the truth of it.'

Home was 25 Brighton Gardens, in Terenure, a suburb three miles south of Dublin's centre. It was one in a terrace of small redbrick houses. 'There were thousands of them around the place.' The front door was painted

brown, with two stained-glass windows and a brass knocker, letter box and, later, when the electricity had been installed, a brass bell.

Immediately inside, there was a hallstand. It was tall, with a mirror set into its backing. It had hooks, for coats, high on its sides, and a shelf, for gloves; there was also a rack for umbrellas, and a tin pot at its base, to catch the water. There was brown lino in the hall. There were two prints, *The Laughing Cavalier* on one side, and *The Toast* on the other. Both had been acquired in exchange for cigarette coupons. 'I always loved them.' There were also two pictures in the front room, but she hated these ones. The first was called *First Love*. 'There was a man in robes that you'd usually see on a Roman, and a lady with her eyes cast down, and he had his hand on her arm and they were leaning on a kind of a marble pillar, and that was *First Love*. There was no picture of the row they must have had, but *Reconciliation* showed them actually smiling at each other, so I presume they must have had one. But I always hated them. They were eventually stolen when my father moved to a newer house. There were a few other things taken too but I was so pleased with whoever took those horrible pictures; I always thought how welcome they were to them.

'The room at the front of the house was very seldom used. Christmas Day and very odd days in between. Some people called this room the parlour and others even called it the Jewman's room; people never used it but if the moneylender came looking for his money he was brought in there. But we always called it the sitting-room. There was a suite in the sitting-room, a sofa and two chairs, upholstered in brown leather, and very cold on the behind. There was a black marble fireplace, with colourful tiles running down both sides. There was a humidor on the mantelpiece, an ornate wooden box with shelves for pipes and a china jar for tobacco. My father smoked twenty Sweet Afton a week, and a two-ounce tin of Mick McQuaid Cut.' There was a large oval mirror in a mahogany frame hung above the fireplace. There was a mahogany book press against one of the walls, packed with sets of Francis McManus, Lynn Doyle, W.W. Jacobs, Maurice Walsh and books on Irish history and literature. There were two drawers under the press, containing accounts, receipts, letters, all held by rubber bands. There was also a rosewood sideboard. The doors were beautifully carved, in a rose design. The chiffonier, on top of the sideboard, its exact width, was a mass of small shelves backed with mirrors. These shelves held small ornaments. 'I remember a glass jam or marmalade pot, in a silver holder, with silver lid and spoon. It was never used.' On the sideboard itself there was always a glass bowl, full of fruit – apples, oranges, 'nothing exotic, and refilled each week from Miss Gibney's fruit and vegetable shop in Terenure'. There was a fawn carpet with an ornate border. The floorboards along the walls were varnished.

Behind the sitting-room was the kitchen. 'Now, that was where we lived, in the kitchen. There was a table that folded up and went against the wall. There were the chairs that came with the table; they were around the walls – that's what we sat on. The one comfortable chair was my father's. If he wasn't there whoever liked could live in it, but there was always a row over it.' There was another book press. There was a big black range for cooking and heating the water. 'And then we got more refined and the range was taken out and there was an open fire, with a nice red, wooden surround, with dark red tiles and a back boiler, and the fire heated up the water.' The boiler was in the hot press, also in the kitchen, where the clothes were stored and aired. 'There was a big fender which was to keep people from falling into the fire, but it used to be draped with clothes. The lino had a red and fawn square design.' There were flowers in the pattern but they were hard to discern in each tiny square. 'It was a thick lino but nearly like mosaic, all these tiny little squares it broke into.

'Down a step, and into the scullery. There was no room for a table in there. There was a gas cooker, and a porcelain sink beside it. On the other wall there was a big cupboard. There was a hinged board that could be pulled down, you could lean on it, for cutting bread, meat and vegetables. The floor covering was stuff called congoleum.* That would have been the cheapest. You

J. E. Beckam, Rathmines Studio, Dublin.

could cut it with a scissors. It had lovely bright colours until they were walked off.'

Up one flight of stairs, carpet held in place by brass stair-rods, and there was the first of the bedrooms, Joe's. There was a bed, a dark-wood dressing table and a wash-stand. She remembers no pictures on this boy's bedroom walls. 'People didn't put things on the bedroom walls, except they were holy pictures.' Beside

---

* From *You Must Remember This: An Oral History of Manhattan from the 1890s to World War II* by Jeff Kisseloff: 'All of this later helped me in the army, because I learned how to get dressed putting on my socks and shoes fast on the cold floor. Congoleum, which I learned later was not a bad word for floor covering, to me was one of the worst words for poor people. If you had congoleum floors, that was terrible . . . To this day I don't like to walk barefoot except on my own rug at home' (Lee Silver).

Joe's room, on the landing, was the bathroom. There was the bath and 'then there was a kind of a board that went across the bath that held the wash-basin. There was room on that as well for a little dish with soap and a face cloth.' The hot water came from the boiler, below in the kitchen hot press. The toilet was outside, 'out the back, and I was always kind of nervous going out there at night.' Later, an inside toilet was installed, 'a giant step for the Bolgers'.

'And then up another flight of stairs and there were two bedrooms with a good-sized landing, that took a fine big chest of drawers for linen and towels and that kind of thing', and two pairs of old swimming togs, male and female, sleeves to the elbows, legs to the knees. Her bedroom, which she shared with Máire, was the one on the right. The sisters shared a double bed, although she thinks she slept in a cot until she was six. The bed had brass knobs which could be screwed off and on, a favourite game. There was a light-coloured, hardwood dressing table with three drawers and a good big mirror, and there was a nice centre-doored wardrobe to match it. 'And there was a small fireplace, one of those small steel fireplaces that are much sought-after these days.' It was never lit. 'It must have been cold because I remember trying to get dressed under the bedclothes, and in those days we wore things called combinations, which was a combination of vest and knickers, and trying to get dressed under the bedclothes could be very awkward because you often stuck your leg through the wrong hole and you had to keep manipulating, but we did it, nevertheless.' There was lino on the floor – 'I can't remember it but I'm sure there were flowers on it, and a carpet strip where you got out of bed, and you made sure you stood right on it, I can tell you.' The bedroom wallpaper was 'always flowers; even when it was changed it was flowers.' There were net curtains on the sash windows. There was a chamber pot under the bed, 'a very elegant one too, with all kinds of flowers and furbelows'.

The front bedroom, her parents', had a black marble wash-stand, with a delph* basin and matching jug for the water which was brought up from the bathroom. There was a dressing table in one corner, and wardrobe and double bed. They all matched and were, she thinks, rosewood and probably intended for a bigger room. There was a polished wood crucifix above the bed, perhaps a foot high, with a silver-coloured Christ figure. There was a carpet. 'I can still see it, pale green with pink roses.'

Downstairs again. Outside the scullery door, there was a passage. 'I have a vague memory that there were two windows, two sash windows, nearly together. I may be wrong in that but it was certainly a wide-ish window and the passage was the width of that window. There was a meat safe in the passage – I can't remember what the covering was made of but it kept the weather off it – and a great big mangle for the clothes. And then there was quite a nice little garden, good high walls. They must have been about eight feet high around, and little beds, garden beds, right around and a little grass bit in the middle. My father took care of that, and I was sorry for the grass because everything he did was very methodical.'

The house was lit by gas. The gas mantle, made of asbestos gauze, was attached, locked to the pipe-end; each mantle had to be lit by match. The mantles were

---

* China (from 'Delft').

very fragile; they crumbled if touched, even with a match. The gas provided good, uniform light. 'But what happened every now and again was, it would suddenly start going down and there was a rush to the meter to stick the shilling in. And if you weren't wise and had your shillings piled up you were in big trouble because you had to go searching. It was originally a penny meter which was dreadful but then they changed it to a shilling meter. The gas man used to come every month and collect the money and there used sometimes be a payback; they'd decide how much you'd used, and a lot of women were delighted when the gas man came because he would give you back a few shillings and there would often be enough for a dinner or so out of it.'

The children weren't allowed to use the gas upstairs. 'It was supposed to be very dangerous but we were given candles which I always considered quite as dangerous, if not more so.' She remembers Joe once setting fire to the curtains in the girls' bedroom, and Máire shouting, 'Look what you did!' The top of the dressing table was burnt black but was later restored.

She remembers the landlord calling for the rent. His name was Mr Pearse, a Wicklow man. He owned most of the houses on both sides of the road. 'He was very friendly; he used to bring us sweets. Maybe if you didn't have your rent he wouldn't bring any, but he always had sweets in his pockets for us.'

She liked the house. 'I don't know whether childhood has that effect on you or not, but I never saw anything wrong with it. I'm sure the sitting-room must have been freezing, but I never thought it freezing.' She remembers bits of plaster falling off the walls, and her father getting dado rail to secure them. She thinks now that the walls were rarely papered because her father was afraid that the whole walls would come down if the old paper was stripped from them. And then there was the time the bedroom ceiling fell on her. 'We were in bed and we heard a kind of rumbling. We were very quick actually, and we pulled the sheets up over us. There was no weight in the plaster. It all came tumbling down on us, and we looked up and all we could see was these little narrow laths, and the plaster gone – in a big hole, like. It just happened to come down over the bed. And I can't remember how it was repaired but it was repaired very quickly, if I remember rightly.' But she liked the house. 'I thought it was grand. And I loved everything about that locality. I was very happy with it.'

Her father wore a felt hat and he always wore black boots with toecaps, which he polished himself. 'He wore brown suits with a very fine white line; you'd hardly see the line.' When the suit became a bit shabby he'd get a new one, exactly like the old, and the old one was worn at the weekends. He always bought the suit in Kevin & Howlin, on Nassau Street. Tom Howlin was a Wexford man, an old school friend. Years later, she went with her father to buy a suit for her wedding day. 'I remember him saying, "I want a suit for my daughter's wedding," and it was the very same suit as the first one I remember him in. When he went on holidays he took off his tie, he took off his collar – and he was on holidays.'

She can't remember her mother. 'I can only remember her hands. I can't remember her face. I have no memory of her attire whatsoever. I can't remember what she wore on her feet. The only memory I have is her hands, doing things.'

She was three months short of her fourth birthday when her mother died in March 1929. 'I was told that we all had some kind of a flu, and she stayed up to look after us, and she got pneumonia and she died. I remember being carried in to see her and I remember her hands were white and I remember saying, "Mammy has new gloves."'

She remembers the priest coming to the house, with two altar boys. 'I was in the cot, in my bedroom, and, whatever way the coffin was fixed, I could see it through the door. And I thought it was wonderful, the priest coming up the stairs – he had a kind of regalia on him, and these two little boys ringing bells and going into her room. I thought it was a holiday. The priest and the two little boys and the bells ringing, and then off they went.'

She watched from her parents' bedroom window. 'I must have been still sick because I was taken out of the cot and I can remember the horses had black plumes, and there was a hearse and my father had a black hard hat. Neighbours were there, I can remember that. I can't remember relations but I remember my father had a black armband and a black tie, and all the blinds were pulled on the road. The men walked off behind the hearse, only the men.

'I never realised she was dead. I remember being told that she was coming back, which was terrible but I sup-pose it was done to shut me up; I was told she was coming back. I'm still waiting.'

A hand.
Her hand,
Winding a handle and putting a needle
  in place.

Only a hand.
I can not recall a body or face.
Later, I knew that the handle was part
   of a gramophone.
Newly arrived
And she still alive.
Later still,
When lonely and blue
I handled that handle,
Remembering she had handled it too.*

---

* By Ita Doyle.

Chapter Two – Rory

'My first memory is of the stone floor. Stone slabs. And I remember soldiers marching past the house, on the cobblestones, through Terenure, on the way back down, I presume, to the barracks in Rathmines. Soldiers marching, with their leggings and boots, and dragging cannon, guns with mules, and the noise and the screeching and the roars of the men. I can remember that; it was quite a thing. And another memory is of my Grandfather Mullally eating griddle cake in our house in Terenure, and drinking his tea out of a saucer.'

He was born in the Rotunda, the maternity hospital on Parnell Square, just north of Dublin's centre, on the 8th of December, 1923. 'My mother was very upset shortly after I was born. The midwife and nurses came down to find out what was wrong with her and she said, "Nobody brought me any whiskey." Now, my mother was a non-drinker but she had this notion in her head, listening to all the women talking, that when somebody's child was born they brought her in a glass of whiskey. So she was waiting for the glass of whiskey and it never came and that, naturally, upset her. Being deprived.'

He was a big baby; he weighed 15 pounds. And he was called Roderick Timothy. 'My mother could arrange everything and she had decided that I was going to be a girl and she was going to call me Bridget, after her mother. And when I was born and I was a boy she got a bit of a shock and she had no name for me. The usual thing then was to have three days before your christening, so my Aunt Bridge and my father arrived in a cab to bring me off to the Pro-Cathedral, and my father said to my mother, "What are we going to call him?" She said, "I don't know. Call him what you like. Call him Patrick, after your father." So he says, "That's alright," a quiet man. So on the way up O'Connell Street, clip-clopping in the cab, my Aunt Bridge said, "You're not going to name the child Patrick after that impudent oul' get"; she said to my father, about *his* father. And he said, "What *are* we going to call him?" So, they had a general argument, and then one of them realised it was the first anniversary of the execution of Rory O'Connor,[*] so I was named Roderick, after Roderick, or Rory, O'Connor, and Timothy, after my father. And that was it.' From then on, he was called Rory, although his birth cert records just his surname and the fact that he was male. He was the first of nine children. After him came Breda (1924), Aileen (1926), Nancy (1929), Jackie (1931), Patsy (1936), Rosaleen (1937), her twin, Frederick, who died a few days after the birth, and Angela (1943).

His father was Timothy (Tim) Doyle. He was born in 1893. One of eleven children, he grew up in a cottage in Templeogue, a village in south County Dublin, in an area known as the Strand, along a stretch of the

---

[*] Rory O'Connor (1883–1922): born in Dublin; wounded in the 1916 Rising; interned; IRA Director of Engineering, 1919–21; rejected the Treaty, 1921; took a leading part in establishing an anti-Treaty Republican garrison at the Four Courts, April 1922; surrendered, June 1922; executed, December the 8th, 1922.

Dodder River.* Tim's father, Pat Doyle, was a farm worker and 'was known as a good ploughman'. His father, Tim's grandfather, was a blacksmith; he ran Doyle's forge, in Firhouse. Tim's mother, Helena Thornton, was born in 1852.† Her mother came from Galway. Helena was fostered to Mrs Bridget (Biddie) Conlon, a shopkeeper and small farmer, in Balrothery, near Tallaght, and this was where she eventually met Pat, Tim's father.

When he was born, Tim was thirty. He drove the Dublin–Blessington steam tram, from Terenure to Poulaphouca, in Wicklow. The Dublin–Blessington line was closed in 1932, and after that Tim had various jobs, usually in running and maintaining boilers. He eventually became a general factotum at Baldonnell Aerodrome, and worked there until he retired in the late 50s.

He was a member of the IRA until 1922, with his brother, Johnny, in a company based around Rathfarnham. He was involved in the burning down of the Custom House in May 1921. 'My father was one of the men detailed to go down to the cellars, armed with pick-axes to stave in the barrels of lovely whiskey and brandy maturing down there. He was picked because he didn't drink. They then lit wood and paper torches and threw them into the sea of alcohol and got up the stairs as quick as they could. When they got outside the Custom House, the British troops had arrived and my father told me that he ran down the quays faster than any Olympic runner, with bullets hopping around him.' Five men were killed and seventy captured that day, so the raid was considered by many to have been a tactical

---

* The cottage was behind what is today Cheeverstown Convalescent Home.
† She died in 1952.

disaster, but 'my father got a medal for burning down the Custom House and they had, in fact, broken the back of the British establishment in Ireland. All their records were gone and they couldn't conduct the civil administration of the country. The Dublin Trades Council was delighted; all their members were employed in the rebuilding. Many businessmen and strong farmers were very pleased and forgot to pay their taxes. They were outraged when, several years later, the tax inspectors of the new Free State government sent them bills of arrears. The British were gone but the tax inspectors were Irish and transferred to the new administration with their memories intact.'

There was a British Army aerodrome in Tallaght, where the Urney chocolate factory was later built, and, if his tram was empty and other conditions were favourable, Rory's father would climb on to the roof of the tram: 'He had a big long rod and every now and again, when no one was looking, he would pull down the telegraph wire and cause considerable annoyance. He was a very observant man. If anything moved, he'd know what was happening. He was a one-man intelligence unit between Terenure and Tallaght.' He stopped fighting at the start of the Civil War. 'He couldn't face up to fighting the men he'd been with; he just couldn't do it.' Later, he joined up when De Valera founded Fianna Fáil in 1926, 'but he was still close to the Republican fellows who were causing the trouble'. Some of his old comrades were executed, first by the new Free State Government, later by De Valera's Government. He had contact with Gerry Boland, a minister in De Valera's government – Boland had been a carpenter in Crooksling Sanatorium, on Tim's tram-route – and he was able to trace the whereabouts of arrested men and then inform their families. 'I remember a woman coming to our door, to my mother, and she said, "Will you tell your husband thanks very much to Mr Boland. They took Tommy the other night and I know where he is now. He's down in the Curragh★ and I know he's alive."'

His mother was Catherine (Katie) Mullally. She was born in January 1900, in Tallaght, a village seven miles south-west of Dublin city. She was one of ten children. Her father was a coal merchant. Earlier, he and his brother had been hauliers for the numerous paper mills along the Dodder River. He knows little about the family's origins. The 1901 Census lists the Mullallys as resident in Tallaght, but he doesn't know if they came from there or if they were 'outlanders, or runners into the district'. There was a suggestion – 'remarks passed, but nothing positive' – that the whole family came from Kill, in County Kildare. 'My grandfather spoke with a different accent to the locals. He called a door a "duer", and the floor was the "fluer".' Katie's mother's name was Whitty, and *her* mother, still alive in 1901, gave her place of birth as County Wicklow. He doesn't know where Katie's mother was born: 'Nobody asked the question.' Although Katie was one of the younger children, 'she ended being the dominant organiser of the family and she organised my grandfather's coal business and that sort of thing, and did a good job. If anybody in the family was in trouble or wanted a hand-out, they came to Katie, and she obliged.'

He doesn't know how his parents met, but Tim's tram went right past Katie's house; 'he passed up and down

★ Army barracks and prison camp.

through Tallaght every day.' They were married in 1922. It was a quiet wedding. Tim's brother, Johnny, had recently died. Another of his brothers, Christy, had joined the new Free State Army. 'Like many another Irishman, he needed a job. Christy was a little man. A nice softly spoken man. But he was the toughest character. They called him Christy the Grocer – I don't know why. He joined the British Army, the Connaught Rangers, and he served in Meso-potamia and Salonika. As a matter of fact, he was a first-class sniper. He told me once, he sat up in a tree, just outside Salonika, watching for a Turkish sniper. He told me, "I got him." When he came home on furlough, my grandmother made him hide my father's and my Uncle Johnny's guns under his bed and, once, when the house was being raided by the RIC★ and the British Army, Christy gave them a tongue lashing – "Can a soldier not have a bit of rest without you bastards tormenting me?" – and they left the house unsearched. He then joined the Free State Army when it was first organised, and was involved in the artillery bombardment of the Four Courts,' which led to Rory O'Connor's arrest and eventual exe-cution – and to Rory's name a year later. 'At the same time, his brother, Johnny, was about to suffer critical and fatal wounds in Moran's Hotel, just across the city, fighting with the anti-Treaty forces.' So, it was a very quiet wed-ding. The wedding breakfast was at Katie's sister, Bridge's house, the gate lodge of Rose Hall, in Templeogue.

His first home was a house† in Tallaght, close to the water pump at the top of the town. 'My grandfather

---

★ Royal Irish Constabulary.
† Today, the house is the Tallaght Credit Union.

took that house and put half his family into it.' The first year of his life was spent there. But the first home he remembers was a whitewashed cottage, no longer standing,★ on Terenure Road North, where the entrance to *The Star* newspaper offices is today. The landlord was Mr Nolan, the local coal merchant, who lived in a large house further up the road. He doesn't remember much about the house. 'My only real memory is of one large room.' It was the kitchen/living-room. He remembers the stone floor but 'I can't remember the furniture in the room. The furniture was very basic in those days. People just didn't have the money to buy furniture.' He remembers the stairs: 'I can still see these stone stairs.' And he knows that the bedroom he shared with his sister Breda was right over the next-door neighbour's house. The neighbour was Mr Mannering, old Har (Harry) Mannering, a taxi driver, and 'you could hear him snorting and shuffling down below'. Of the bedroom, he remembers 'just a big bed, with two of us in it'. He remembers pouring the contents of a jar of Virol over Breda. Virol was 'a thing like a softish toffee, a food for building kids up. For some reason or another we were in the bed and we had the Virol and I poured it over Breda's head. That caused a bit of consternation.'

There was a small yard at the back of the house, with the toilet, a dry closet – a bucket and seat. 'Dry closets – we thought they were wet but they weren't.' There was no bathroom in the house. 'There was a kind of zinc bath that was taken down to wash the kids. When we got older, there was a stand and a basin

---

★ The cottage was a few hundred yards from Ita's home in Brighton Gardens.

on top of it. And that was it. As you got older, you went off to a more private place and wash-stand, to wash yourself down. But that was later. Washing was easily done – you licked your finger and then rubbed your face.'

There was no gramophone in the house but there was music. He remembers his mother singing 'The Faithful Sailor Boy'. And his father sang. *I dream as the hammer strikes the anvil, and I dream as the sparks fly on the floor, and my bright-eyed turtle dove, she the only girl I loved, as I stood outside the good old smithy door.* 'My father had a stock of music hall songs – *And they pointed to the spot, in the graveyard's gentle plot, where my Mary sleeps in sunny Tennessee.* And one of his favourites was [*sings*] *Jim O'Shea was castaway upon an Indian isle, The neighbours there they liked his style, they liked his Irish smile, They made him lord and master and general of them all, And called him Nabob Mumbo Jumbo Ginigo Jay O'Shea. Across the sea came Rose McGee to wed her Nabob pal, In emerald gems he decked her arms and when he kissed her hand, He took her to his hareem where he had wives galore. She started shedding a tear, He said you have no fear, I'm keeping these wives for ornament, my dear. So she had rings on her fingers and bells on her toes, Elephants to ride upon and shamrock Irishgrown, Come all the way from Ireland on each Saint Patrick's Day, To Mrs Nabob Mumbo Jumbo Ginigo Jay O'Shea.* And he played the melodeon. He played all the old dance music and he was very popular, any party on.'

He remembers the Centenary of Catholic Emancipation, in 1929. 'The bunting and yellow and white papal flags all over the place, and that kind of a general air of excitement. And the badge. There were two kinds, two levels of badge. There was a bronze-coloured one, the cheaper one, and then one with enamel. And it had a broken bell with *Saoirse Eireann*★ on it.'

He remembers his Uncle Jem, his mother's brother, Jem Mullally, visiting the house. 'He worked in Boland's bakery and he'd arrive now and again with a little sack of bread. And my memory is that there was always a caraway seed cake in that load of bread. The caraway seeds had a special taste.' He remembers eating bread and jam and eating Post Toasties for breakfast. 'They were an American cereal thing, in a packet, like the kids eat now.' He got the *Tiger Tim* comic every week.

He travelled on his father's steam tram to Tallaght, to visit his grandfather, his mother's father, Johnny Mullally. 'He was a big man with a hat, in the back yard, in the hay shed. I remember him pushing us into the hay and breaking his heart laughing. He had no teeth. He'd be laughing, a big man, and he'd take delight in knocking us down into the hay, and us getting back up again. That's my vague memory of him.' And he went further on his father's tram, with his mother and Breda and, later, sisters Aileen and Nancy, all the way to the terminus at Poulaphouca. They'd have a picnic there. 'There was a lady there who ran a tea rooms. We called her Aunty Pinchie. The place is still there but, I daresay, she's not. But that was the highlight, the tea rooms.'

His first school was the Presentation Convent, on Terenure Road West. He doesn't remember his first day and he doesn't remember the teachers. 'Just people walking in and out and green paint on the walls and drawings, on brown copybook covers, on the walls of the classroom.'

★ Freedom of Ireland.

There are stories that he associates with that house in Terenure. He heard them years later, from his mother. 'When I'd go to visit her, she'd start talking, and I learnt more in those hours than I did when I was living there. But she told me about how I'd come home and tell her about this bold boy and he was frightening the sheep and annoying the men and it was terrible. So, she said, "One day, I don't know what put it into my head to go up and meet you coming from school. And there I saw you with your coat over your head and you making flapping noises and the sheep scattered all over Terenure." Of course, there was little or no traffic then, you know, the odd electric tram. The sheep were all over the street and the drovers were using bad language and calling me all sorts of names. But I was the culprit and she found me out.' And there was the story about his mother looking for turf. 'There was a coal strike. You absolutely depended on coal, for heating, cooking, and there was no coal available. Now, I don't know why my grand-father in Tallaght, who was a coal merchant, couldn't get coal, and the landlord was a coal merchant, so it must have been a general shortage of coal. And she said she'd have to get turf, and she knew there was a turf accountant up the street and she didn't know what a turf accountant was, nothing about betting or bookies. She thought a turf accountant was some kind of a country turf mer-chant. So she went in and asked for a sack of turf, and cost, to great merriment among the locals who knew my father.' His father loved horses and greyhounds. 'He was an expert, a very shrewd operator. Small bets, and that was how he got into trouble over the Grand National. In 1929 it was, I think. My mother saw the name of the horse, Tipperary Tim, and because my father's name was Tim she decided to go wild and she bet a shilling, and she gave it to my father and told him to put it on Tipperary Tim. Now, he knew all about horses and he knew that Tipperary Tim, at 100–1, wouldn't be there. So he put it on another horse; he knew better. And the only horse that finished the Grand National that year was Tipperary Tim, at 100–1. And my mother was waiting for the five pounds. When my mother lamented her lamentations were loud. She called my father all the names.'

There is one more Terenure memory. He remembers dismantling, 'very expertly, the alarm clock. Now, alarm clocks were a luxury item in those days. An awful lot of people depended on the neighbours to be banging on the window or the door, so you were high up on the ladder with an alarm clock of your own. My father had to be up to go to work, and there was a bit of noise generated when it was found dismantled, so all I said

26

was, I was mending it. All around me, I can still see the bits and pieces; I think I did it with a knife – I was able to undo all the screws.'

In 1929, his Grandfather Mullally died. 'I remember his funeral. That was high drama. My older cousins were distraught. They made more noise, hullabalooing and screeching for my grandfather who had looked after them and they were very fond of.' The Doyles moved from their house in Terenure to Tallaght, so that his mother could run the family coal business. 'We were a self-contained family in Terenure. There was only my mother, my father, myself and my sisters. When we moved to the house in Tallaght there was the six of us, and more to come, and Aunt Lil, and Uncle Bob, and my cousins, the two Kellys, Jack and Hugh, and, eventually, four more cousins, the Poyntons. I don't know where we all slept. I do know that only a couple of years ago I started laughing; I was in the bedroom here, and I suddenly realised that this was the first time I could point at the bed and say, "That's my bed."'

Chapter Three – Ita

'There was a lady at the corner of the street, a widow, and, now and again, she'd go mad and she'd throw statues, always religious statues, out through the window and they'd land at the path opposite and smash, and nobody paid any heed to this. She'd come out the next day and everyone would say "Good morning," or "Good evening," and nobody would say, "What happened to you that you threw the statues out?"'

She loved the street. 'I don't think the winter kept me in. We just wrapped up and went out; the weather meant nothing to us.' Her great friends were Doris and Marie Sullivan, who lived next door, in No. 26, and her best friend was Noeleen Hingerty, who lived opposite, in No. 4. There were other children from up and down the street, the Kerrigans and the Fays and the Murphys. They

all grew up together. They played with wooden hoops, and sticks. They could beat the hoops up and down the street with no traffic to get in their way, only the odd milk float or coal cart. And there was hopscotch. 'We drew what we used to call a piggy bed on the path and made numbers in the boxes. Then you had a piggy. It was usually a stone but we devised a thing; you put a stone in a shoe polish tin and it slid better. And I can remember once, there was a girl who lived in the street parallel to us, Oaklands Terrace, and she was forever whining. And my brother, Joe – who, I must admit, was a bit of a brat – he took the stone from her, and she set off away, "Joe Bolger took my piggy! He took my little piggy!" She ran home screaming, so somebody ran after her with the piggy because we didn't want to get into trouble. And, of course, we had skipping ropes which we could stretch right across the street. Some could barely jump but others had dazzling performances. I was a good skipper.'

The milkman came around on a horse-drawn float. 'In those days you got your milk into a jug. You'd bring out your jug or he'd come in and fill it, whatever it was, a pint, two pints, and he'd always put in an extra bit which was known as the tilly,* and sometimes the tilly varied. But the churns were beautifully polished – everything was beautifully polished, absolutely spotless.

'And then there was the coalman, Mr Nolan.† The Nolans lived in Terenure. Quite a big house they had, beside the police barracks. They actually had a ballroom in their house and we used to go up there for dancing lessons; Lillie Comerford was the dancing teacher.' The Tontine Society also met in the ballroom, every Sunday morning. 'The Tontine was, really, to bury people. You'd see men going in there every Sunday and paying into the Tontine, and then, when anyone died – people didn't have spare cash and it was very important to have money to bury people and it would be a matter of pride to

---

* From the Irish word *tuille* – a little extra.
† Rory's parents' landlord, when they lived on Terenure Road.

bury them properly. So, it was its own form of insurance.

'Mr Nolan was a great big man and he was black, black and he always had a sack around his shoulders, and I don't know why or what it was there to preserve, because underneath it was black too. Our house had no back entrance, so he used to carry the coal right through the house and on the coal day they used to put newspaper for him to step on. I don't know what it cost; they'd pay him there and then. The milkman would be paid once a week.'

She remembers the neighbours with great affection. 'Such a mixture of people, all types, all religions and, I suppose, all social classes. There were two Garda sergeants, one right opposite, and one beside us, Mr Sullivan. There were Church of Ireland people, the Wilkinsons, on the other side of us, in No. 24, and every Sunday morning their window was open wide and hymns came soaring out. They had a loganberry which used to grow beside the wall and Mr Wilkinson used to put a branch over the wall, for us to take the berries, but sometimes his wife would come out and take it back. She was a very nice lady but she obviously didn't want to share the loganberries. Mr Wilkinson's sister was married to a man whose parents lived opposite, and they were Presbyterians. Carmichael was their name, and then further down the road there was the Holmes family and Mrs Holmes was Mr Wilkinson's sister as well, and they were Church of Ireland. He was in Guinness. And then there was a Jewish couple past him, a Mr and Mrs Matofsky, and they had some kind of a furniture factory. And two doors from them there was another Jewish family, Mr and Mrs Morris, and then back down the road, Mrs Morris's sister lived and she was Mrs Silverman.' The vegetable man called once to the Silvermans and young Sammy Silverman was sent out to get the vegetables and fruit, including a pound of plums. 'So the vegetable man weighed the plums and he gave them to Sammy and Sammy went in, and Mrs Silverman weighed them and they were light-weight, and she ran after the vegetable man and she told him that she'd weighed them and they were light-weight, and he just kept going and he shouted back, "Weigh Sammy." Mrs Silverman used to seek refuge in Mrs Morris, her sister's house, and I don't know whether Mr Silverman went and got violent, or whether he just went peculiar, but they always said that it was the full moon that affected him. It could have been anything, but the moon was blamed. He came down to Mrs Morris's house, shouting that he wanted his wife back. She always went back but, whether there was violence in it or not, I never did know. He always seemed an exceptionally quiet man to me.

'There were a mother and daughter who lived down the road. They were lovely people and they were always beautifully dressed and they always appeared to have plenty of money, and there was an elegance about them. But they just disappeared overnight. Nobody knew why, and then it was discovered that they owed rent. They owed everybody, and where they went, nobody knew. They just disappeared.

'And there was a lady opposite called Miss McGuirk and she had a maid, and the maid was in full regalia, and a cap with lace. Mary – I never knew her surname – was the "little maid". Maids were often referred to as "little maids", even when they were quite hefty lassies.

Mary was small and thin. Miss McGuirk was a really nice woman, a gentle lady. Ladies did not keep lodgers; ladies had "friends", who visited for a few days, a week, or longer. Hence the need for Mary to help out. Then Mary decided that she was going to Australia, to live with relatives who were already settled there, and Miss McGuirk decided to give a little tea party, to say goodbye to Mary. Tea parties were invariably "little". Myself and my sister were invited. We enjoyed our tea, and handed over some small gifts and Mary told us about her proposed journey. She was very young, she was only fifteen or sixteen, and she told us that it would take her six months to get there – she was going by boat, to England and then on to Australia. And then, when Mary went, no new maid appeared.' After Mary's departure, there were no more lodgers. 'But what I didn't know was that when Miss McGuirk died, she actually died from malnutrition.

'There was another couple, just the husband and wife, the Dees. They were very nice. He worked in a shop on Camden Street called Gorevan's. It was a fine big shop and he was in the shoe department and Joe always referred to him as "the Head of the Boots".

'Joe had a satirical streak in him; there were always remarks. I always referred to him as a brat, although I got on very well with him. But he was kind of wild. He was very much the favourite. He went everywhere with my father. The funny thing is, while myself and Máire felt this, we kind of accepted it: Joe was the pet, and that was it. Anything that Daddy was going to, Joe went with him; they'd go to football matches together. But he had lots of his own friends. He wouldn't have played in our group, except for the odd time to torment

us. There was a group of boys he used to play with and I remember once they got up a soccer team and they called themselves Oakland Rovers. And my father, being such a staunch GAA man, I think he'd have dropped dead on the spot if he'd known that his son was playing soccer. But they managed to get jerseys – how Joe managed it, money-wise, I don't know. They were green with a yellow stripe, and Joe's jersey was hidden under his mattress and my father never found out. Now, where they played I don't know, except that it was only on the street. One of them was Tom Hingerty, my friend Noeleen's brother. In those days boys wore short trousers until they were in their teens and even late teens. And, for some reason, Tommy Hingerty had the nickname "Pot" Hingerty – I don't know why. But they had a back door leading into the garden and when Pot Hingerty got his long trousers somebody drew a saucepan on the door with the long trousers coming out of it.

'My sister Máire was very quiet. She was very studious; she played on the road to a certain degree but not to the extent that I played. She was more sedate and always very quiet, and her head in books from a very early age.'

After their mother's death, the children were looked after by a housekeeper, Miss Dunne. 'She arrived very soon after my mother died. I thought at the time she was old but she was probably only about forty, not much more. And we also had a maid – we were spoiled. The maids came with amazing regularity but they were all lovely and they were all very nice to us.

'Miss Dunne's name was Mary Teresa but she was "Miss" Dunne. And she really did look after the four of us. She taught me lots of music hall songs, and I still remember them. Her favourite was always [sings] *Joshua, Joshua, why don't you come and see my ma, She'll be pleased to know that you're my best. beau. Joshua, Joshua, sweet as lemon squash you are. Yes, by gosh you are – Joshua, Joshua, Joshua.* And then there was another one: [sings] *I'm a hoity-toity girl, A high and mighty girl. My old stick-in-the-mud took me for a wife. Fancy me wearing bags, riding bikes and smoking fags, Showing off my bits of rags at my time of life.*

'Miss Dunne told us that she only had one brother, Willie, and Willie was killed in the War and she hadn't another relation in the world. And she had a boyfriend, and the boyfriend was Tom Dunning, and he lived in what was called the Hospital for the Incurables, in

Donnybrook. And every Wednesday, which was her half-day, she went to visit Tom Dunning, and sometimes she'd take us with her. He had a small room and we'd go in and say hello to him. He always wore a cap – I don't know why; I never knew if he was bald. I believe it was arthritis he had and he was very crippled, and quite a youngish face but, always, the cap. He used to lever himself out of the bed. And along the corridor there were alcoves and fires in them, and seats. We'd sit away from them, so I never knew what they spoke about. But he was a very nice man, very kind and nice in every way. It was very sad, really. I remember he smoked a pipe and every Christmas my father used to send him plug tobacco, even after Miss Dunne died. She died before him. She had a heart condition. I remember her coming home one day; somebody was helping her, holding her arm – I can't remember who. Her lips were blue and she was shaking. I didn't understand at the time, but she'd had a heart attack. I was three when she came, and I was ten when she left. She retired. She lived in a flat further up the street. She was in hospital when she died, very soon after. I remember somebody saying, "She reached out to get a glass of water and fell dead."'

Dottie Mulhall was one of the maids. Unlike most of the others, Dottie wasn't very young. 'She would have been in her thirties. Her mother lived in a little white cottage off Terenure Road North. She was a lovely old lady, and she had a canary and we were very fond of it. We used to pick groundsel – it's a small summer plant, a small form of dandelion – but the canary used to love the groundsel and we'd pick the groundsel just for an excuse to go in and see Mrs Mulhall. She always had lovely scones or biscuits. Joe was very fond of Dottie and Dottie spoiled him – which we were always delighted about afterwards, because when he got the arthritis he suffered so much. But at least he'd had a spoiled childhood.

'There was another very kind girl called Lillie; she was about sixteen. She came from the North and she was lovely. She was a beautiful cook and baker. For Christmas one year she gave me a bar of Palmolive soap and a small Cadbury bar, both luxuries at that time. A strange thing about Lillie; it was very sad really. By that time we were in secondary school and we had our school uniforms, and we had cases, for our books. Lillie had her half-day on a Thursday, and Lillie got a new outfit one year and it was as near to a school uniform as you could possibly buy. Black shoes, and she had the navy beret – it wasn't the kind of outfit you'd expect a young girl to buy when she had enough to buy a real outfit – because I think she got about twelve pounds a year, and her keep. So, I met her one day going off on her half-day and she was carrying a school case and wearing the outfit and I remember, I thought it was odd but, looking back on it now, I think it was sad.'*

None of the maids wore a uniform. 'They'd wear an apron, but it was more to keep them clean than anything else. Everybody wore an apron in those days, what we would have called a crossover bib.' Unlike the

---

* She met Lillie again, years later, at a friend's house. 'And there she was, married. He was a funny-looking man, but a nice little man, and they were obviously comfortably off. I don't think she recognised me. But if she did, I didn't pretend to recognise her because I don't think it would have been fair. But I did get talking to her, and she had two sons and they were attending a very good school and I was more than pleased to see how she had got on; I was delighted, because she had been very kind. I saw her death in the paper a few years ago.'

housekeeper, Miss Dunne, the maids were known by their first names. 'We didn't really think of them as maids; they were more like friends. We were conscious of who they were, not *what* they were. We would never have dreamed of asking them to do anything.'

Her first school was Presentation Convent, on Terenure Road West.* 'It had a big, high, high solid wooden gate, and you went in through that. And I can remember being in rooms, nice bright rooms. I remember being there but I can't remember my first day.' She remembers two teachers but she isn't sure which was the first. 'I remember a Miss Byrne, and Miss Byrne lived to be a hundred; she's only a few years dead. And there was a Sister Evangelist, who was the Head. I must have been a bit of a chancer; I remember, now and again, saying that I was sick and being kept at home. There was nothing wrong with me. I can hardly remember it but I do remember staying at home, and the luxury of lying in bed.†

'There was a mixture of children in the school, all statuses, types. There was a lot of poor children there. As a child you don't look at these things as poverty – but children who, in the summer, would have little short-sleeved dresses and, in the winter, they'd have a jumper with the same short-sleeved dress over it. I can remember children who wore berets on their heads. And these kids used to have sores on their heads, and it must have been

---

* It was also Rory's first school. He might have been in Ita's brother Joe's class.
† Ita: 'Sister Evangelist was still there when my nieces went to school. Máire brought her daughter up to the school and Sister Evangelist asked her was I still delicate or had my health improved.'

from some form of malnutrition, although the sores could spread to kids who were well-cared-for. But it was always a sign that they had these sores on their heads, when they had these berets on. I can't remember bare feet, but I often saw kids with shoes and no stockings. I remember, there was a scheme – free milk, little cartons of milk. It would have been means-tested, and I was never given milk, and I was livid because I got nothing. They used to get a bun and a carton of milk but we'd have to bring in sandwiches and I thought this was terrible discrimination.

'I remember a man once, at Christmas, a Mr Ryan; he might have been a solicitor, I'm not sure. But, whatever he was, he wasn't short of a few pence, because he sent in boxes of sweets to the school and they were brought around the classes. Everyone in the class got two or three sweets. We didn't get many sweets, so I went home in great delight with my sweets and I still had two left when my father came home. And he said, "Where did you get the sweets?" And I said, "Mr Ryan left in a tin of sweets and we all got sweets." "And who is this Mr Ryan?" and I said, "Mary Ryan is in my class." "Oh, I know who you are talking about," and he said, "Will you go back with those sweets tomorrow and tell that nun that if my daughter needs sweets I'll buy her sweets and we don't want anybody's charity." Needless to remark, I didn't bring back the sweets. Nor did I tell the nun what he had said.

'Another time, Máire went on a message for Mrs Murphy, across the street, and Mrs Murphy gave her two pennies. And Máire was sitting at the table playing with the two pennies, and Daddy said, "Where did you get the money?" and Máire said, "Mrs Murphy

gave it to me. I did a message for her." "And you have to be paid to do a message for a neighbour?" And Máire said, "No, I didn't have to; she gave it to me." So, Máire was taken by the hand and brought across the street and the two pennies were given back and Mrs Murphy was told that Máire would go for messages in future but payment wasn't needed.

'When Christmas came around he really had no idea what kind of a present a child might like. I think I was about five or six and I got a beautiful sewing basket. I hardly knew what a needle was for at the time but it was beautiful, padded with a high lid on it, a lovely thing altogether – beautiful threads and spools and all kinds of things in it. I was fascinated, but I didn't know what to do with it. And the following year, I got another sewing basket. I never got a doll. I never got those kinds of things. There were quite a few single ladies in his office, and I think he got advice from them as to what to buy us, and they had as much a notion about what to buy a child as he had.

'Every Christmas we were taken into Baggot's, in Rathmines. It was a lovely shop, with pens and stationery and books. So, we were taken into the shop and we could choose our present, provided it was a book. Well, to be fair, you could choose either a book or a fountain pen. So I had a good collection of fountain pens and I had a great collection of books. They weren't frivolous books either. They were books that would do your mind good. One year, when I was ten, I got *The Rubáiyát of Omar Khayyám*, and I still have it. But, I can tell you, I wished Omar Khayyám anywhere other than lying at the end of my bed that Christmas.

'My father had a dread of draughts. He seemed to find draughts where we wouldn't notice them. Dottie Mulhall's brother was a handyman, John Mulhall, and he used to come over with long lengths of felt, and the felt was hammered right around the door and the door forced closed to prevent these draughts from coming in. But, no matter where he sat, he got a draught. I think he used to attract draughts like some people attract wasps.

'He knew the words of every Irish song and he had books and books of Irish songs, but he couldn't sing them. He hadn't a note in his head, but we got "The Boys of Wexford", "Boulavogue", all those marvellous songs. But the only time he sang was in the bathroom.

'He used to catch the tram at the end of Brighton Road, in Terenure. He went on it every morning and came home every evening. I happened to be with him one day; we must have been going to town for something. There was quite a few people waiting, and the tram arrived, and they were all extremely mannerly; one would stand back to let the other on, and there was no rushing. The conductor was saying, "Hurry up, come on, get on quickly." And I still see my father: he wore black toecap boots and the memory I have is of the toecap boots standing still and the voice saying, "Do you know what? If you didn't stop to let people on, you would get there much quicker." Then he proceeded along. He was much cheered by those behind him, but I was mortified.

'He always wore toecapped boots. I can still remember, one pair replaced the other – they were replicas of each other. He had a short leg, which I was told happened when he fell off a horse as a child. He always had to get a raised heel on one boot. But you would never notice it; he never limped or anything like that.*

'He won a junior championship medal for hurling, in 1910. And that has a story too. When he reported for the *Enniscorthy Echo*, he used to attend County Council meetings. And there was one member of the County Council who sat at the top table, probably chairing the meetings, and he had a gold chain. A lot of men wore them then, a watch at the side, and the chain attached to the buttonhole on the waistcoat. This particular man had a row of medals on his chain. And before the meeting one day, one of the other young reporters borrowed all the medals he could find and fitted them on to his own chain. And towards the end of the meeting he stood up, displaying these medals to the councillors. He looked at his own watch but pretended it wasn't working, and said, "Excuse me, sir, could you tell me the time by your watch – and chain – and medals." My father had given him his medal for the chain. And then – I was about

---

* Ita: 'I had forgotten all about toecapped boots until two weeks ago, I was sitting in Coffey's, a coffee shop in Sutton, and there was a young man at the next table, his legs crossed, reading the *Irish Times*, and he had jeans on and a fashionable sweater. But he had toecapped shoes. And, immediately, it came into my vision, standing at my Uncle Bob's [Robert Brennan's] grave in Mount Jerome and looking at the feet beside me. I always say, at my height, I'm nearer feet than heads. And looking along the side of the grave, there were three or four or maybe more pairs of toecapped boots, all well-polished. And one pair belonged to De Valera, and one pair belonged to Dr Jim Ryan who was a TD (member of parliament) at the time. And I don't remember who the others belonged to but they were all fine, upright citizens.'

eight or nine — and a box came to the house, addressed to me, no note, and wrapped in cotton wool was the 1910 medal. It came from Daddy's friend, Teddy Redmond, who ran a printing place in Enniscorthy. He had come across the medal and, instead of sending it to Daddy, he sent it to me.

'In the evenings, if the weather was fine, he'd look out the kitchen window, and say, "I think I'll go for a walk on the headland." He'd go out the back door, into the very small garden and he'd do the whole thing in, I suppose, one second flat. But he'd walk up and down and up and down, and every day he'd say the same thing: "I'll go for a walk on the headland." I think he lived and died a countryman in spite of living in the city for so long.★

Sunday was her father's big day, when he travelled around the country to report on GAA games for the *Irish Independent*. St Patrick's Day was another important day, the Railway Cup Final, at Croke Park. 'I remember him going to a match down the country, I think it was Thurles, one Sunday. And he arrived back that night with a grandfather clock he'd won in a raffle. It wasn't a great big one but he was delighted with himself bringing it home.

'He wasn't a drinker. He liked a whiskey but he never

★ Ita: 'When he eventually got a slightly bigger garden, he put a fence across it and he grew vegetables, and his greatest worry was keeping the dog out. And, eventually, when the poor old dog died, he was buried with the vegetables. My father kept a diary, and in it is written: "Poor old Bouncer. He now lies in the spot I spent hours and hours trying to keep him out of." He wrote in the diary every day. Everything — going for a walk in the park, "met so-and-so", "went to so-and-so's funeral", "he lived too long, nobody knew him any more" — those kinds of comments. Some nights he wrote: "And, as another great diarist said, 'And so, to bed.' "'

went drinking. I only once in my life saw him drunk. He had been at a match down the country and he was delivered home. I didn't know what was wrong. I must have been very young because I'd never seen a drunk man before.

'He was a very, very quiet man but, sure, he must have been dead lonely.'

Chapter Four – Rory

'I remember my grandfather's funeral, and the wake. Shortly after that, we were living in Tallaght. But I've no memory of getting there.'

The house* was rented from the Dominicans. 'It had two big gates to the yard and a couple of stables, sheds for holding the hay and coal, and a big sty. It was a long, single-storey house. The front door also had a half-door, outside; when the front door was open, the half-door kept hens out and children in. The kitchen was the living space, a very large kitchen, and the rafters were open. The stove for cooking was at one end, a big dresser at the other end. And a very, very large kitchen table. There was no electricity and no such thing as running water, no flush toilet. The only luxury would have been the oilcloth on the table, and then linoleum was bought for the floor. At a later stage, my mother put her hand on some money and the rafters were timbered and closed in. The back door led to a kind of store, coal in bags for delivery, up on shelves.'

The bedrooms were off the kitchen, 'in both directions, various bits and pieces added to the house. A double bed carried four children, two at the top, two at the bottom; a double bed on each side of the room, so there would have been eight in the one bedroom. I

---

* Today, the Tallaght Centre for the Unemployed.

remember, we had a beautiful statue of the Virgin Mary done up for the May altar – a beautiful lace veil put on it, and flowers and all, and a candle, carefully burning. And Aileen it was, came along and messed with the thing and the veil caught fire. The lace was ablaze, and the screeching and roaring. My Aunt Lil came down and she had a bucket of water and she just lashed the contents into the room and put out the fire and drenched the whole lot of us.'

When he'd lived in Terenure his mother had bought him *Tiger Tim* every week. That stopped when they moved to Tallaght. 'One, it wouldn't have been available and, two, there were too many other calls, too many other voices.' There were his sisters, and more sisters and brothers on the way; there were his six cousins, the Kellys and the Poyntons; there were Aunt Lil and Uncle Bob. But he remembers no resentment at the sudden expansion of the family, 'no loss. You accepted it. You were just part of the whole thing – and it included horses and pigs.'

The Kellys, Jack and Hugh and Patsy, were the sons of his mother's sister, Nannie. 'Their father had the forge in Tallaght and when the mother died my grandmother took them in, to look after them, because she thought the father wouldn't be able to. She took two of them, Jack and Hugh. Patsy went to serve his time as a barman; he lived over the pub, Fleming's, on Trinity Street. My grandmother died in 1916 and Jack and Hugh just lived on in the house. Then another sister of my mother's died of cancer, Mary, and my mother took four of the five children into the house. The Poyntons. Tom, Frank and Seán were the boys, and the girls were Chick and Marie. Chick's real name was Bridget but she was never known as anything else but Chick.

'Aunt Lil was my mother's sister. She was with us all of her life. She was a small, good-humoured woman. She never had a job. She just lived in the house and did anything that needed to be done, looked after the children and that sort of thing. She was, generally, part of the house; she was never regarded as a poor relation. She was unique; she had an old-world sense. Nothing bothered her. I remember once, my mother sent Lil into town to get her some china; she wanted a set of delph. And Lil came back with a cup and saucer. And my mother said, "What's that?" And Lil said, "It's china. But", she added, "it's hand-painted." She'd bought it in Camden Street, hand-painted, and spent all the money on it.'

Uncle Bob was Bob Mullally, his mother's brother. 'A single brother. He worked at hitting and tipping – doing bits of jobs around the place, nothing permanent – knocking down hedges for farmers, that kind of thing. If you asked him to trim a hedge for you, he'd go at it with a slasher; he was a most unhandy man. In actual fact, he could only drive a horse and cart. But he didn't work in the family coal business because there'd been a row between himself and my grandfather, a big falling out. But he still lived in the house. He had a box with his own food in it. He sat at the end of the long kitchen table, and he went to all the Dominican services and joined in the hymn-singing, with great enthusiasm. He was famous all over the world, wherever there were Irish Dominican missionaries. Later, when we moved to Newtown, we had to erect various outhouses to hold people, and Bob, who was part of the clan, was given an outhouse of his own, a lean-to where he lived. He did his cooking outside in the back yard, on a type of brazier. He used an old perforated bucket as a firebox and, to get it lighting, he'd swing it around, and he'd be singing "Tantum Ergo" and "O Salutaris" and all sorts of hymns like that, to our irreverent amusement. Also, in later years, he discovered this amazing thing, that people threw out all sorts of treasures, threw them into the bins – the service having been recently introduced by the County Council – and he used to go through the bins, much to my mother's mortification. But the point is this: Bob was there and she regarded it as her duty to look after him.

'She kept a sow in the yard, and I remember a litter of little pigs. And then, one day, Joe the Jingler arrived. He had a sharp penknife and he performed a very painful operation on about half the pigs – neutered male pigs were less aggressive. He then poured iodine on the poor unfortunate pigs. The squeals were unforgettable. Joe the Jingler married a widow with a farm near Crooksling and set up a milk delivery service. He would juggle with the milk jug, to my mother's great annoyance, flinging it into the air and catching it just inches from the ground.'*

A stream ran beside the house, to the River Tymon, on the other side of the Dominican College. 'It came down from Whitestown – it's up near Jobstown – and it came down the field opposite our house. It went underground, under the road, culverted. I crawled along the culvert once, under the road. It was a terribly dangerous thing to do; the water level could have changed at any time. The stream then went on, behind the wall that divided our house from the College. There was a

---

* Rory: 'He also delivered milk to Ita's home, in Terenure. She didn't like him either.'

water-wheel in there, and you could hear it turning. The stream ran through the College grounds, and down into a big tank that was known as the College Pond. In Dublin, someone in dead trouble might have said, "Well, I'm going to throw myself into the Liffey," or something like that, but in Tallaght the saying was, "Oh Jesus, here's for the College Pond.'"

'Tallaght was just a village, with County Council cottages down one side of the street and the walls of the Dominican College on the other. The cottages had been built at the turn of the century, and they're beautifully built, granite, with Tudor fronts. And up the middle of the street were the tracks for the steam tram.' His father drove the tram down the middle of Main Street, until the line closed on the 31st of December, 1932. *The Battle of Ypres was only a sham, Compared to the rush for the Blessington tram.* 'There were a number of old chaps, tramps, who lived together in an old cottage. Nobody knew who they were; they weren't related to anybody. One of them was known as Straw Legs. He was an old man and he had a habit, when he had a few drinks on him, of lying across the tramline, outside the pub. And people would see him and drag him off the line. But this particular night he got himself further up the road. There was no street lighting at the time, and the stream engine came and ran over him, and that was the end of him. We were woken by my father, shouting in the window, "I have to go up to the barracks." He had to make a statement because he'd run over Straw Legs.

'As you went up the street, going south, you came to the Green, and the pump. That was where the people at what we called "the top of the town" got their water.

At the Green the road divided. One road went left, towards Old Bawn, and the other went right, towards the Blessington Road. As you turned right, there was a pub on the corner, O'Neill's.*And beside that pub was our house.'

On the opposite side of the road were the forge, the harness maker's, and Miss Martin's post office. 'And then, further along, there were cottages on the left, and the Garda barracks. And then you came to the Protestant church and graveyard, St Maelruain's. The graveyard was always part of village life. We attended practically every funeral, as something to do. But one part of the grave-yard, just near the church, was where some of the older landowners were buried. One of the Foxes, of Whites-town, is buried there, and on the headstone were chis-elled the words, "Fell Asleep". And we took this literally. Every time we passed, we'd run like hell in case Johnny Fox got up out of the grave to catch us. There was a baptismal font near the gates, an ancient font. The Cromwellians took the font and made a horse's trough out of it, which was a terrible sacrilege, and then knocked a hole in it so it would never hold water again.† We firmly believed that if you looked in one of the win-dows of the Protestant church you were likely to see the devil looking back out at you. I believed it. I was a grown man – in fact, it was just a few years ago – before I saw the inside of that church.'

The Dominican College dominated the village. 'It was a noviciate. There's a church there, a rather beautiful

---

* Today, the Dragon Inn.
† Rory's brother Jackie tells a different story: the hole was drilled in the font when fifteen Catholic horses were blinded after drinking the Protestant water.

small church, and the noviciate was built, like a triangle, around it, and all the Dominicans for the missions and for the Irish Province would have trained there. It had originally been a monastery, going back to the ninth century. But it was all lost with the Reformation. Tallaght eventually became an outpost against the native Irish, the O'Byrnes and the O'Tooles. So, the Protestant Archbishop's summer palace was built there, on the spot of the original monastery. It was then sold to a Major Palmer, who sold it on to a man called Lentaigne, and Lentaigne sold it to the Dominicans, in the 1850s. The famous Father Tom Burke built the noviciate and church; he was renowned as a great preacher.

'Now, that was the church we attended. It wasn't our parish church but we went there every Sunday, and every time there was Benediction. The monks sang the order of prayer, from matins in the morning, through vespers in the evening, to compline at night. We attended the Rosary, anything that was going.' The parish church was in Rathfarnham, about five miles away, but 'I never went to Rathfarnham, except for my Communion, my Confirmation and my sisters' weddings.

'Down the street from the College, towards Dublin, there was another pub, the Fox's Covert. The Foxes and the McClashins owned it, a Mrs McClashin – she was originally a Miss Fox. They also owned the Oaks, the Templeogue Inn – the Morgue – and the pub which, by then, was called John Clarke's, in Jobstown. All part of the Foxes' domain – and one day they were evicted. I saw them evicted. It was the only eviction I ever saw. All the artefacts, furniture and all, it was all on the side of the road. I saw amazing things that I never knew existed, like stuffed birds in glass domes. There was just the mother and the two sons and the general servant who worked for them and lived with them, and they all moved down to the doctor's residence, where Mrs McClashin's sister was married to Dr Lydon, the local doctor.

'Dr Lydon was the dispensary doctor and he had been in the British Army during the War and he'd picked up strange habits, like drinking excessively. Medicine wasn't practised as an exact science in those days; if you went to him with something, you got a blue bottle or a green bottle. But, invariably, old Lydon was jarred. Katie Coombes was his factotum; cleaning the place was, in fact, her job. But she gradually took upon herself the role of dispenser, and when you went to the doctor, she'd say, "What do you want the doctor for?" and you had to describe your symptoms to her. "Oh," she says, "the doctor gives a blue bottle for that." There was no getting past Katie Coombes.

'Seán Dempsey lived with his family in Tallaght, on the Greenhills Road. He was a good-looking, curly-headed young man and he was a good player of the uillean pipes. He toured Europe in the 30s, and played in Germany. The story goes that Herr Hitler – he was always *Herr* Hitler – wanted to hear Dempsey play. When he arrived in the presence of Hitler, everybody had to stand around while the great leader sat and waited for the music. Seán explained that he had to sit while playing the pipes and, according to Seán, Hitler ordered a stormtrooper to get down on his hands and knees and Dempsey sat on his back and played *Carolan's Concerto*. Seán was one of the numerous victims of the dreaded TB that I knew. There was also Mary Manning, the teacher's daughter, Teddy Corcoran, a Jordan boy, and neighbours, Jimmy, Mick and Kathleen Mullally, and others I can't bring to mind. I had over eighty first cousins but none of my clan caught the disease.'

He went to the local national school.★ 'There was an old one, with diamond windows, boys on one side of the building and girls on the other. But, in 1932, a new school was opened.† It was built on the ruins of the old Tallaght Courthouse that had been burnt down by the local heroes during the War of Independence. And we moved into that school, boys on one side again, girls on the other, but each had two rooms, one each for infants and seniors.

'The master's name was Mr Manning, who lived in one of the County Council cottages in the village. Half the day you sat and half the day you stood; there wasn't room for us all. Mr Manning had six classes to teach, from First Class to Sixth, all in the one room, all in the one day. And he did rather well, considering. When you were standing you read your book or recited and you wished your turn would come to sit down – there was no particular hardship about it; that was just how it was.'

Many of the children came to school without shoes. 'Half of them, at least, were in their bare feet, even in wintertime. I once took off my shoes and carried them. And I came home in my bare feet and got a walloping from my mother.'

There were maps on the classroom walls. 'A map of Ireland, a map of Europe, and a map of the world. I don't remember a crucifix. I'm sure there was one but

----

★ State-funded primary school. Tallaght's school was on Greenhills Road.
† Today, St Basil's Training Centre, also on Greenhills Road.

I don't remember it. The desks were wooden, two of them side by side, with inkwells. The ink was made up by some of the older boys; they'd mix the ink in a great big stone bottle. We used to put bits of carbide into the inkwell; carbide was the fuel for bicycle lamps and such. You put a piece in and it reacted; it would start fizzing and fill the place with gas. It was a horrible smell.' The desks weren't assigned to the pupils. 'I never carved my name on a desk. I was never in a desk long enough to be able to do it.' But he was in the school long enough to earn a nickname. 'I was the Professor, because I read the school books. I was good at school, good without killing myself. It was a badge of erudition – Professor.

'The toilets were at the very back of the yard. Just a long row; they called them privies. Little compartments – no doors. Just a long flat piece of wood with holes cut into it; everything went down into this pit. So, occasionally, some of the lads would stick their heads and shoulders down and look, and they saw the sights – the board went right into the girls' section. And, now and again, one of them slipped and fell into the pit and had to be dragged out. Consternation and hullabaloo, and a couple of the bigger fellows – always the bigger fellows – were given the job, and they lugged the lad out, up the road, up the middle of the town, to the pump. And one of them would hold him by the scruff of the neck and the other started working the handle of the pump, and they'd drown him until he was reasonably clean and he didn't smell too bad. But he was screeching and roaring, and then they brought him home. They knocked on the door and the mother opened the door, and they said, "There you are. Mick fell into the lavo." And then they skipped it, because – it's an extraordinary thing – but when you bring a fellow home drunk, out of Christian charity, you're likely to be blamed for getting him drunk, and it was the same with this; they brought him home covered in you-know-what and they'd be blamed for it.

'Mr Manning handed out the punishments for blaggardism and bowsieism, or for gross neglect of lessons, or for being stupid – or, not so much being stupid, as stupid enough not to do the work, particularly when he knew you could. You put your hand out and he used a kind of pointer, like one of the rungs on the back of a chair – but never excessively.

'I remember reading a story about a drummer boy, by Standish O'Grady.★ There was a secret attack planned on the Irish chiefs in the Wicklow Mountains and the drummer boy felt a kinship with the rebels and alerted the neighbourhood. It has stuck in my mind ever since. I think it was called *The Bog of Stars*.'

The girls' section of the old school became the public library, 'a great boon to Tallaght. There was a huge lot of Zane Grey – *Riders of the Purple Sage* – and lots of other cowboy stories. Max Brand was another one. I read anything I could get my hands on. I read copies of the *Century Magazine* that were lying around the place, at home. Bound copies. Bret Harte, Mark Twain, George du Maurier – they were all in that magazine. I still hanker after it. I read *The Ascent of Man*; it was in the house. And Dr Madden's two-volume history of the 1798 Rebellion. And I read another marvellous

★ Standish James O'Grady (1846–1928): a major figure in the Irish literary revival, he popularised history and the sagas: *History of Ireland: Heroic Period* (1878–81); *Early Bardic Literature of Ireland* (1879); *The Bog of Stars* (1893); *The Flight of the Eagle* (1897).

book that had found its way into the house, *The Sexual Mores of the Kanakas of Melanesia and Micronesia*; I was dead safe reading it because neither my father nor my mother would have known what sexual mores were, let alone be interested in the Kanakas. The book gave graphic descriptions of their sexual behaviour and what they got up to. I was about ten or eleven when I read it.'

The books arrived by an unusual route. 'The O'Neills, who owned the pub next door, had an older brother, William O'Neill, and he opened a big shop nearly opposite our house. But William lost his reason; he just got more and more peculiar and, eventually, he had to be put away – it was the horrors of drink. And Mrs O'Neill just wound up the business. Now, my mother bought a piano from her and, in the transaction, Mrs O'Neill says, "Sure, you might as well take these things as well" – a big, big bundle of books. And that's how they came into the house.*

'At the back of the school was a place called the Courtyard, where the County Council had their depot. A mysterious place, I never went down there. But then, when the family coal business went,[†] there was a mare and a cart left over, and they were leased to the County Council. My cousin, Hugh Kelly, drove it; he did work for the County Council, and I was given the job of taking the mare away up to the commons of Tallaght,

---

* His Aunt Lil burned the books during the Emergency (elsewhere known as World War Two), when there was no coal, and turf supplies were low. 'Dr Madden got burned and Charles Darwin got burned and the Kanakas got burned. Anything she could burn, she burned. A philistine.'

[†] Rory: 'The business died gradually, in the early 30s; hard times. Debts weren't paid or followed up, and my mother wouldn't chase anybody.'

about a mile up the road, and to let her into the field for the night. And then, the next morning – quite a nice job – I'd go up and collect the mare. It got to the stage where I was able to trot her along the road beside the bicycle.

'And, then, further along the path from the school was Cunninghams'. The Cunninghams had a triangular-shaped piece of land at the junction of Greenhills Road and the road to Terenure, and a house with a galvanised roof. On the way home, a couple of the lads would get a handful of stones and throw them up on the roof, because they always got a reaction. Thomas Cunningham would come running out, swearing imprecations after them, and what he wouldn't do to them. And this one particular day, I learned a great big lesson. I hadn't thrown stones, so I stood my ground. And Thomas Cunningham ran out and gave me a kick up the backside. So, from that I learned: in future, right or wrong, run.

'The Cunninghams were wheelwrights but they were originally descendants of a Cromwellian grant.★ They got this land, but ended up in poverty and died out. Beside them was Poyntons', who had a substantial farm called Bankcroft. There was a castle there, the remains. These were all lots of land that came out of Cromwellian grants. There were practically no native Irish with farming land in the area, very, very few.

'Most of the local women and some of the men

★ Oliver Cromwell (1599–1658) arrived in Ireland in 1649, massacred the populations of Drogheda and Wexford, oversaw the Protestant settlement of eastern land and the transportation, west, of the Catholic chiefs who had rebelled – divine retribution against the 'barbarous wretches'; he spent only nine months in the country but is fondly remembered.

worked in Urney's factory,★ and a handful would have gone into town† to work – they'd be, say, the sergeant's children or the doctor's children, into the Civil Service or into professions or trades. As for the rest, some went working for the farmers, but that was the last resort. And there would have been a handful who worked for the County Council, three or four permanent men, and the rest would get occasional work; they'd be taken on to tar the road and that kind of thing, a few weeks' work – it was almost like Famine work. The older fellows, late teens, early twenties, unemployed, they'd be hanging around the Green, maybe whistling at the girls going up to the factory or coming back down for their lunches. But in the evening time, they'd collect a few dogs and go off chasing rabbits. And, invariably, there'd be a knock on the door and, "Mrs Doyle, would you like a couple of rabbits?" and she would. No money passed hands but the price for the rabbits would be a packet of Woodbines, and they were set up for the evening. They were local footballers, and some of them would have been IRA lads, but they had no work. They disappeared, lots of them, when the War broke out. They went to England, never heard of again in lots of cases. There was a well known Tallaght footballer, Jackie Doyle, a cousin of mine on my mother's side. He was a fair-haired, tallish lad; his nickname was Lackery. Anyway, Lackery drifted off to England during the Emergency, and was eventually forgotten.'

★　★　★

★ A chocolate manufacturer, established in 1924, by Henry Gallagher, on what was known as the New Lane, then the Urney Road and, more recently, Belgard Road. It was the first factory to be built in Tallaght.
† Dublin.

Playing with marbles was popular, especially in spring-time. Hoops, using bicycle wheels, were also popular. He remembers playing handball 'with a real handball with an Elvery's* elephant on it'. There was no handball alley in Tallaght, so they played against the College wall. 'Nobody played tennis, except a few people who were better connected.' He never played soccer. 'Soccer was for Dublin gougers and gurriers. Shelbourne, James's Gate, the Bray Unknowns — I didn't know the structure of the soccer world at all, until I went to work in Dublin. Gaelic football was the game. The local club was Thomas Davis's.† I was never what you'd call a first choice. I could never get it into my mind that it was important enough to die for. My two brothers, Jackie and Patsy, won county championship medals.'

His close friends were Noel Mullally, his cousin, Seán Poynton, Francis Colleran, Joe Kelly, J.J. Hughes. 'Right across from our house were Doyle's Fields — no relation — but we could walk into the fields, through the gates, and then we took off. We roamed, up as far as Killinarden, through all sorts of marvellous fields and ditches. We'd even eat young turnips out of the ground. We went miles and miles, and we discovered all sorts of things. Once, we came across some ditches and it only came to me in later life, thinking about the structure of them, that they must have been part of the outer defences of the Dublin Pale, a part that hadn't been ploughed away, a big double ditch and, then, further ditches. We used to

---

* A sports shop in Dublin; today, on Suffolk Street.
† Named after Thomas Davis (1814–45): born in County Cork; co-founded the *Nation* (1842); a leader of the Young Irelanders (1842–5); author of 'A Nation Once Again', and other popular songs.

run up and down these things and they were quite substantial earthworks.

'There were slight divisions between the fellows going to school. It was the top of the town against the bottom of the town, that kind of rivalry. And then there was the rivalry between the town of Tallaght and Colbert's Fort – it's up the back of the Urney factory. There were the Finnegans; Billy Finnegan – Duck Egg – was a dangerous customer to get mixed up with; there were the Redmonds, Joe Stynes, and Paddy Brady, a big bruiser of a fellow.'

He wore white on his First Holy Communion Day, in 1930. 'It was a very fine, cashmere-type, woollen jumper, with white short trousers and white shoes. My

mother was also keen on sailor suits. It caused me terrible grief; I had to wear the sailor suit to school. I was much resented by the lads, all cocked up in style like that, and I was beaten up. My mother would say, "Don't you have anything to do with those fellows," but I had to go to school with them. So, the result was, my father took me down to a boxing club, down in Terenure somewhere, where I was taught how to box. Shortly after I'd acquired some skills, a row over the sailor suit blew up again and I had a fight in the schoolyard, and I knocked the mallarkey out of Paddy

Brady from Colbert's Fort. I had all the skill now, like Nel Tarleton,★ the boxer, straight left and a right cross, hopping around. In any case, I hit him enough to sicken him. And, after that, I was accepted, no more persecution, one of the lads.'

★ Nel Tarleton (1906–56): born in Liverpool; British Featherweight Champion, 1930–45.

Chapter Five – Ita

'I had no idea where we were going. We went on a train and we were met at the station by this strange man; I didn't know who he was. He turned out to be my Uncle Watt. We were taken out to a pony and trap and we sat in, with our cases. It was raining and there was a tarpaulin put over us all, and off we went – the first time I was ever in a pony and trap. Daddy, Máire, Joe, myself and Miss Dunne. And we arrived down at the main road. It was cement, and the pony and trap was lovely and smooth, and I loved that – I was really sleepy, I remember. And I remember the noise of the hooves. And then we turned up a laneway and it was rough and we were hopping along, and I'd doze off and I'd be hopped awake again. But I remember arriving at the house. It was dark, so I couldn't see what it looked like, and there was another strange man, Uncle John, and a strange woman who was my Aunt Bessie. I didn't know who they were; I'd never heard their names mentioned before. But we were brought into the sitting-room,★ and the fire was lighting and the wet things were taken off. And I remember sitting on Uncle John's lap. I didn't know who he was, but he was very nice. Very quiet, very little to say, but he rubbed

---

★ Ita: 'I knew later that the sitting-room was very seldom used, but it was used for special occasions and this was obviously a special occasion.'

my hands and heated them. And then I remember going to bed.'

She had just arrived at Coolnaboy, her father's childhood home, a mile from Oilgate, about eight miles south of Enniscorthy, in County Wexford. She was, she thinks, four years old. Watt and John were her father's younger brothers and Bessie was his sister.

'At the top of the stairs, there was a little room, and lying in this room was a very old lady, and she turned out to be my father's aunt, Mary Kate. I had no idea what was wrong with her, but she never got out of the bed, and every time we went down to Oilgate we had to get her peppermints. Years later, I asked what had been wrong with Mary Kate – she was dead by then – and I was told that, really, there was nothing wrong with her. She just went up to bed one day and she didn't get up again. She took to the bed. I suppose it was a form of depression. My cousin, Maeve Brennan, told me that when she was a child and she'd lived in Coolnaboy because her father was on the run, herself and her sister used to go up the stairs and they'd torment Mary Kate. She'd pick up her stick and she'd say, "Ah, ha, if I get you," and they'd say, "But you can't, sure you can't?"

'Another memory I have, and I was very young – all the water from the house was drawn from a well, and the well was just past the back door. It never dried and it had beautiful water. In the summer, little flies used to dart across the top of the water. They fascinated me, and I was kneeling at the edge of the well one day and I was trying to catch them and I toppled in. The water was whirling around my head – my head, my shoulders, and a funny sound in my ears. And the girl from the next farm, Eileen Parker, grabbed me. As I was toppling in. She was only about three years older than me but she grabbed me and pulled me out. She had an apron on and I can still remember my foot catching in the apron. She was trying to pull me and my foot was caught and impeding her but she still managed to lug me out. Miss Dunne came running and I was dried off and put to bed and there was a great fuss, but Eileen saved me that day.'

At the time of her first visit, Watt (Walter) Bolger, Bessie (Elizabeth) Bolger and Mary Kate Whitty lived in Coolnaboy. 'Uncle John was living in Pouldearg,★ a farm, down in a place called Balnaslaney, right beside the Slaney River. It had been my father's mother's original home.'

Watt was her father's youngest brother. He had ownership of the farm because 'my father was looked upon as the smart boy of the family; he was extremely bright. Very often, the smart boy was picked to be a priest. So, my father was sent to St Peter's College in Wexford, to become a priest. That was him fixed up, as far as his mother was concerned. And Uncle John was given his mother's farm, at Pouldearg. It was the richer farm, way ahead of Coolnaboy. So, then there was only one boy left and that was how Watt fell into possession of Coolnaboy.

'Aunt Bessie was what was termed "doing a line" with Mike Parker, of Kilmuckridge.† And Mike Parker had two old – I think they were cousins, the Miss

---

★ The Red Hole.
† Also in County Wexford, on the coast, about twelve miles north-east of Oilgate.

Byrnes, and they had a house and farm in Kilmuck-ridge. Mike★ was actually a pig buyer for Buttle's, Buttle's Barley-fed Bacon, a very big business in Enniscorthy, and he lived with the Miss Byrnes and took care of the farm for them. And Uncle Watt was doing a line with Katie Doyle, who lived in Coolamain.† She was a good deal younger than Watt. But nobody could move, because each move depended on the demise of the two Miss Byrnes. Watt couldn't marry Katie and bring her in, and, sure, she wouldn't have wanted to move in, with Bessie there.

'Now, I was too young to know what was happening but, when I was ten, everybody moved. The Miss Byrnes had died. And Mike had the farm. So, Bessie and Mike got married and Bessie moved to Kilmuckridge.‡ Máire was the bridesmaid, and Daddy was the best man. And less than a year later, Watt got married and Katie moved in, and that was the best thing that ever happened to Coolnaboy.

★ Ita: 'Mike won an All-Ireland hurling medal, in 1912, and Wexford didn't win it again for years after that. The ball that was used that day, the *sloightir*, was put into a little case. It was like a religious object. If there was a function on, part of the attraction would be that ball. Then somebody stole it. It was done as a joke but, at the time, Mike didn't realise that. And he was heartbroken, he was absolutely shattered at the loss of that ball. Because he was so proud of it.'

† Near Oilgate.

‡ Ita: 'I remember Aunt Bessie saying that she was never interested in men, which I found hard to believe. She was a particularly good-looking woman; she was lovely, tall – what they used to call in Wexford "a fine girl". They had no time for the little ones; I was a dead loss. If she wasn't interested in men, they were surely interested in her. But she said she wasn't inter-ested, and it was only in later years that she met Mike. But my cousin, Maeve Brennan, said, "My eye"; she'd been going with Mike for years, just waiting for the opportunity to get married. But the sad part of it is that, by that time, she was too old to have a family.'

'It had always been very quiet, and Katie brought great life to the place. She had eight children and I'm sure there was never as much life and love and laughter in the place, because the grandmother had had the name of being a very severe and strict woman. Katie was wonderful; I used to love going down to her, in the summer. Everything about the place, I loved. I was made one of the family, immediately. You felt that you were *the* person there, whereas, back home, you were, kind of, just someone who was in the house. But in Coolnaboy you were always treasured and taken care of and chatted to and talked to and considered as good as anyone else. And there was great freedom – the fields. I loved all the farm work.

'It's a very special place. It's a very large, long house, with a thatched roof. There was a small hall, as in most farmhouses in Wexford, and, to the left, there was this huge kitchen. And there was a big open fire; you could look up the chimney and nearly see the sky. And the usual fixtures of an open fire, big, black cooking pots and kettles. The fire was always lit. It had bellows and you'd turn the handle – it was like a big wheel – and the pipes were under the grate, and the air flamed the fire. I don't remember it ever going out; they used to bank it down at night – slack at the back of the fire, very fine coal, and it smouldered away.

'Every night, they used to say the Rosary. But there were crickets in the fire and they chirped and chirped there – I could never see them during the day. There was an oil lamp on the wall. It was over the table, so if you wanted to read, you had to go and sit under the lamp. But we'd be at the Rosary and, the next thing, one of these crickets would make a beeline for the lamp, and there'd be a great bang and the cricket would nearly explode; sometimes he'd be dead but sometimes just stunned and he'd run back home. And Joe and I got into the habit of counting the explosions and saying, "There's another one gone." And I remember one night, we were saying the Rosary, and this big beetle was crossing the floor. Joe had a plain pin. It's funny, because my father used to have a plain pin stuck in his lapel, and this was for cleaning his teeth, like a toothpick. And Joe had a pin that night, maybe copying my father, and he stuck the pin in the beetle. The pin went down on the creature and it started to go around and around, trapped by the pin. It ran away when it got free.

'Through the left, from the kitchen, there was a small dining-room and, beside that, there was another room which had no window. It was very dark but there was an oil-fired stove in there, and my aunt used to bake on it.

She'd make griddle bread, done on the fire, and scones and tarts. And then you went down a few steps, to the dairy. The dairy had the churns and the separator, which always fascinated me. You put milk in one end, and you turned the handle and the skim milk came out one spout and the cream came out another. It was fascinating; I just couldn't understand how it worked. The separating was done every morning, and the cream was put into pots. And then, once a week, the cream was churned and butter was made. Bessie had a name for being a great butter maker. She had a set of customers and I used to deliver for her. One lady in particular – I used to have to go along the bog road to deliver the butter to her. She was very old. She always gave me biscuits; she'd have these two-penny packets of Jacob's biscuits, and she'd give me a penny. But she had a beard that fascinated me, and a bit of a moustache.

'There was the yard and then there were outhouses, to the left and right. There was a barn and a very big milking shed. In the barn – one thing I remember from my very first visit there – they had a greyhound called Coolnaboy Lass. They had pups in there as well. There was a shed to the right, with a cart and the trap. And straight across the yard, before you got to the haggard, there was a pigsty. To the left of the house, there was a small gate into the garden – the kitchen garden. There were nice flowers there but it was mostly vegetables, and a big monkey-puzzle tree. They told me that Daddy had planted that when he was a young boy. They had apple trees too, "Lady Fingers" and "Beauty of Bath". The apples were never quite ripe when I was there but that didn't put me off.

'I used to go roaming over the farm. And, of course,

it never rained – I can't remember it raining. One particular day, Katie was making jam – I think it was blackcurrant – and she let me scrape the pot, and I scraped and scraped and ate and ate, and I was sick after it, and tucked up in bed. It was all one year merging into another year and, as I said, it never rained and everything seemed marvellous. I'd go across the fields to Parkers'. They had different names on the fields and the Park, as I remember it, was the name of the field I crossed to get to Parkers'. There was a field called the Haggard Field. There was another one, nearer Oilgate, called the Racecourse, and at the back of the house there was one called the Bog Field. There was a bog hole at the end of it; they had fish in that – roach. My father used to go there with Joe. They both had fishing rods. Mere females were never allowed to go fishing, but I wasn't particularly interested, anyway. I remember, a cow got stuck, near the bog hole. There were a lot of men around, trying to pull the cow out. There was one extremely fat boy, fifteen or sixteen years of age, and he got to the front of the rope, pulling and pulling. Then the cow slipped a bit and the rope went forward. And I remember someone saying, "Don't let Pat fall in or we'll have twice the job getting *him* out." It raised a laugh, and it didn't seem to bother Pat.

'And I'd sit with Mrs Parker. She'd make scones and no one ever made scones the way she made them. She used to use currants, which was unusual, and she rolled them out flat, cut them in squares and they were cooked on the griddle pan. And I used to sit in the corner and read the religious papers, *Far East*, the *Madonna*, and little religious magazines. Work would be going on all around me but, again, I was accepted as part of it.

'I hated the thought of going back home again in September. I remember once, I was brought up to Oilgate by Katie, to catch the bus for home. And the bus was full; there was only room for one and I think there were two or three others there. I was ever so polite and let the girl before me get on the bus. I was delighted; I had to go back to Coolnaboy for another day. And Katie remembered that day, up to the very end; she spoke about that day, when she brought me back to Coolnaboy, and how delighted I was.'

Chapter Six – Rory

'My mother set off with my Aunt Lil for the Eucharistic Congress, in her high-heeled shoes, most elegant, and she came home with her shoes in her hand; she couldn't walk any further. I wasn't allowed go because I wasn't old enough. But Sergeant Nyhan just up the road had a wireless. He turned it on and opened the window, and that was how I heard John McCormack.* It was marvellous. I had never heard the wireless before. McCormack was one of the very few singers we ever heard. Very few people had a gramophone, and the result was that when you heard music, it was local, almost accidental, a passing band. So, to hear that voice coming out, it was like a miracle; it was such a beautiful voice.'

The Eucharistic Congress was held in Dublin in June 1932, to celebrate the 1,500th anniversary of Saint Patrick's return to Ireland. 'It was decided to have this great display of faith, a coming together, after ten years of statehood, a big celebration of what was the Catholic Church and Ireland. There were men's nights, and women's nights, and the children's. It lasted the best part of a week but it seemed to go on for ever. There were banners put across the street, all the way down the town.

---

* John McCormack (1884–1945): Irish tenor; his record sales rivalled Caruso's. He sang at the Eucharistic Congress mass, in the Phoenix Park, Dublin, June 1932.

Some of them were supposed to have been blessed by the Pope and one of them, I remember, said "Cod Save The Pope". There was an old tramp called Jack the Rant. He had a stoop. He famously tried to straighten up, to read the banners, and toppled over backwards in the middle of the street. There was bunting everywhere. But we had special bunting put up on our house, and my mother got butter boxes. They were square boxes, about eighteen inches square, and the same height, and they were very useful. You could buy the butter boxes and they made stools, seats, presses. My mother and my aunt painted them green, and shrubs were put into them, to decorate the place, outside the door.'

His father was a member of Fianna Fáil.* 'He had a song that he sang quite often, almost like a mantra, particularly at election times. *De Valera bowled them over, As they marched along Mount Street, De Valera bowled them over, And the Sherwood Foresters were no more. De Valera bowled them over, De Valera and his gallant little band, De Valera bowled them over, And he was transported to a foreign land.* I worked in the 1932 election. I was only nine. Seán McEntee and Miss Pearse† were the candidates for Fianna Fáil. I addressed envelopes and I made paste, for the posters. The Guards‡ had a very low opinion of Fianna Fáil, as being dissident, little better than the IRA. When some of the posters were torn down, the Guards just wouldn't see it happening. So a complaint was made to Seán McEntee, and I was very young but I still remember

---

* Founded by Eamon de Valera, in November 1926, after he resigned the presidency of Sinn Féin.
† Margaret Pearse; sister of Patrick Pearse, commander-in-chief of the rebel forces during the Easter Rising in 1916.
‡ Garda Siochána: the police.

this [*imitating McEntee's accent*]: "Let ye get a sack and some bottles and jam jars and a loan of a hammer from the blacksmith over opposite." In other words, you put the bottles in a sack, broke them into smithereens and you mixed them in with the paste. I broke the bottles – I was involved in politics from an early age. And the first time anybody tried to tear the posters down, they got the fingers cut off them. The paste was so good that, years later, in the 50s, I went out to visit my mother, and I saw a 1932 election poster, faded but still there, under the arch of a bridge.'

Fianna Fáil won the election and McEntee and Miss Pearse were elected. 'There was a torchlight procession. You got a stick, and you nailed a B.B. Toffees★ can to it. Then you got two sods of turf and put them into the can, and poured in paraffin. When you lit it, you had a good torch; it burned fiercely and for a good long time. Anybody who had a horse marched it through Tallaght that night, the riders dressed in the Thomas Davis jerseys, green and an orange sash – very patriotic jerseys. I don't know where the Fine Gael† people were. They certainly didn't arrive to object. Some of them may even have marched.

'My mother took us into Dublin one day. I don't know what the occasion was; she must have fallen into some money. We had our dinner in Woolworth's on Henry Street, and it was wonderful. And then, she brought us to the pictures, the Metropole. I don't know what the name of the film was but there were a lot of these French

---

★ A popular brand, sold in cans.
† Fianna Fáil's main, often bitter, opposition; actually still called Cumann na nGaedheal at the time of the 1932 election.

officers with pillboxes hopping around, gesticulating and talking. I didn't know what they were talking about, but I remember the theme music. And I remember, quite graphically, on the Pathé News, the assassination of Alexander of Yugoslavia and the French Foreign Minister, in Marseille.★ That was the first time I ever saw a film. The next time I went to the pictures was to see *Snow White and the Seven Dwarfs*, some years later.† In actual fact, we never went to the pictures, because that would have meant the wasteful spending of money. Money was for food‡ and clothes; anything else was frivolous. So we didn't go, although some went who had a damn sight less than we had. Regular goers would tell me about Buck Jones and all those characters and I remember someone describing *Hell's Angels*§ to us. I thought I'd never grow up till I got to see *Hell's Angels*. I never did get to see it but it was a great story.'

★   ★   ★

★ The 9th of October, 1934.

† Released in 1937.

‡ Rory: 'There was literally an open door for cheap imports, and food, in general, became very cheap. A tin of Black Eagle salmon from North America, about five inches high, cost threepence. Australian butter, very yellow in colour, was considerably cheaper than Irish butter, and cheapest of all was the Chinese ham. I remember seeing them hanging from a window in Dame Street. These hams were not the same shape or colour as Irish hams; they were more rounded and they certainly stirred some primitive instinct in my young teen's sensibilities. But some vested interest, no doubt, put out a rumour that the Chinese had so many women that they were slaughtering the surplus and selling it off as bacon, and that would have accounted for the distinctive shape of the hams. The sales of the Chinese bacon declined, and stopped. No doubt the unsold stocks were donated to orphanages, along with the unsellable fruit and vegetables and such like, the donation of which, in the minds of the donors, advanced their standing on the heavenly ladder.'

§ Directed by Howard Hughes (1930) – 'Celebrated early talkie spectacular, with zeppelin and flying sequences that still thrill' (*Halliwell's Film Guide*).

He changed schools when he was twelve. 'I went to live with my Aunt Bridge, in Inchicore.* Tirconnell Park; it was a newly built housing estate. They called them utility houses; I don't know why. I think, first of all, my mother wanted me to go to the Christian Brothers, and Bridge's house was near the school, but I also think that there might have been a question of crowding. The house was very packed and she was expecting again, although I didn't know that at the time. She was expecting Rosaleen – the twins.† Bridge had plenty of room – so few people in the house; it took me a while to get my head around that – and there was always the prospect that I would be fixed up with a trade. Her husband was works manager of a printing place and had already got an apprenticeship for my cousin, Tom Poynton.

'Bridge was married to a North of Ireland man, Jack O'Hagan, from Tandragee, who started life as Jack Hagan, a Protestant, and then converted. He met my Aunt Bridge. She was a very good-looking woman, as are all my female relatives. And, in spite of his great belief in King Billy and all that background, he wanted to marry her. So, he turned around and changed his name to O'Hagan. And he became more Catholic than the Catholics themselves, very dogmatic. When they met, he was a good-looking man; he had black curly hair and a full set of teeth. When I knew him he had neither. He

---

* Suburb of Dublin, about two miles west of the city centre. Rory: 'Inchicore was a foreign country, compared to Tallaght. People had totally different outlooks and attitudes. It was an industrial suburb, physically and socially dominated by the GSR (Great Southern Railway) engineering works. Hundreds of small houses were occupied by railway workers and, strangely, when the GSR changed the colour of their rolling stock, this change was reflected in the colours of the doors and windows of many of the houses.'
† The other twin, Frederick, died a few days after the birth.

had lost his hair through enteric fever and he lost his teeth through pyorrhoea.

'Living there was persecution; it was terrible. They didn't know how to handle young people at all. They were terribly dogmatic and I think they were dedicated to the belief that, no matter what you did, you were doing something wrong. It was a most horrific time. Child abuse was what it was – nothing physical at all but constant, constant carping; you couldn't do anything right. If I came home and said, "I got a first prize in school," that achievement would be degraded – that kind of thing. I had come from a house full of people, where nobody ever rowed* in any real sense. But in the O'Hagan household there was a constant bickering that never rose to anything like violence, but constant sharp interchange. If one said, "That's a fine day," the other said, "Not as fine as all that," just for the sake of making a disagreement. But they were made that way; they knew no better.

'Jack himself had a peculiar make-up. He loved to dominate, to be the boss. He loved to be the organiser, so he organised the tenants' association in Tirconnell Park. And then, before it had gone too far, he had fallen out with several of the other people. When Jack O'Hagan fell out with somebody it was a hanging matter. He became a pioneer.† So nothing would do but that everybody in sight had to become a pioneer, and if you didn't, he positively blaggarded you. He could get quite vicious at it.

'I was living in that atmosphere, and I felt it rather

---

* Argued.
† A member of the Pioneer Total Abstinence Association.

difficult. But it didn't break me. I could have done without it, but it didn't break me. I put up with it.' He didn't resent his exclusion from the Tallaght home. 'It never crossed my mind. It was a family thing; I was going to be taken care of, later on, with an apprenticeship. At home, after me, there were three sisters and they had a common partnership of their own. And Jackie was seven years younger and Patsy was twelve years younger than me, so there was no male partnership there. My older cousins were at least twenty years older than me. So, I didn't feel any particular alienation from home. It was a house that was dedicated to the upbringing of girls. Any favours that there were, would go to the girls – unquestionably. I never harboured resentment about it.' He didn't miss his mother, 'not particularly', or his father. 'He would go to his work and come back, did some gardening, had the odd chat, went fishing and, generally, he wasn't an intruding kind of person. My mother did the lot. So, I – kind of – didn't miss him either. But, at the back of my mind, he was there.'

His new school was St Michael's, the Christian Brothers' primary school on Keogh Square, on the site of the old Richmond Barracks. 'It was an uneventful time, which I rather enjoyed. Maybe because I had a couple of scuffles early on, the lads decided to leave me alone; they'd roughed the culchie,* you know. But I did quite well there, and I did exceedingly well in the Primary Cert.† But I didn't excel at sports. I remember one sports day, sitting on a bench just looking at everybody, most of them running

---

* Anyone from outside Dublin.
† Sat by final-year primary students, to determine level of secondary education and scholarships.

around in shorts, killing themselves sweating, and Brother Brady it was, gave me a book to read. The book was called *The Boys of Benn Eadar*, a most remarkable book. The writer described helicopters, auto-gyros, as they were known then; the boys went in this auto-gyro across the bay, from Howth to somewhere near Dalkey, or some salubrious place like that. And when one of the boys wanted to communicate with his father, the writer described a video-telephone. The boy lifted the phone and pressed a button, and he slowly saw his father materialise on a screen. Now that, remember, was in the 30s. People talk about the Christian Brothers and their behaviour but, in this case, Brother Brady just reckoned that I wasn't going to move from one place to another with any particular speed just to get in front of the other fellow, so he gave me the book. I read it sitting on the sideline. That's my happiest memory of St Michael's.

'They were competent teachers. Now and again, there'd be a half dozen★ handed out for obstreperous behaviour. There was a lay teacher called Johnny Roebuck; he gave the whole class six of the best, lined us all up. He didn't ask who was making the noise; we were all making the noise, so he didn't waste his time. Apart from that, he was a good teacher. He was a tough, rough Kerryman but he didn't go around beating people up.† The only time I remember getting really afraid was during the run-up to a religious instruction exam. We

---

★ Slaps on the hand.

† Rory: 'I remember the night myself and Ita were out celebrating our engagement, and we were at the lift in the Metropole and out of the lift walked Johnny Roebuck with a lady. And I said to him, "Mr Roebuck, we're celebrating our engagement." And he said, "Be the hokey, so are we."'

were being taught the Papal Encyclicals, *Rarum Novarum, Quadrogessimo Anno*, and one of the gospels – I think it was Saint Luke. *Rarum Novarum* was about the rights of the worker; it's a very great social document. What *Quadrogessimo Anno* was about, I haven't a clue. Now, some of the fellows were careless about learning, and the head brother, Brother Hourigan, got anybody who wasn't doing well, and they were taken up and beaten across the backside, in front of the whole class. It was terrifying. I very quickly became quite a learned Catholic, theology and all the rest of it.'

He was eventually rescued from Aunt Bridge and Jack O'Hagan. 'I met an older cousin of mine, Patsy Kelly. He was one of the sons of Nannie, my mother's eldest sister. When Nannie died Patsy and his brothers were taken into my grandfather's household. Patsy was my mother's pride and joy, apart from her own family.* She arranged for him to go to Synge Street.† Then one day, she was going into town and she saw him walking along the street. He was on the jair‡ most of the time, mitching. So it was decided that Patsy would be put into the bar trade, and he was sent to Fleming's, a pub on Trinity Street. He was a likeable man, good looking, easy-voiced. He always had a good suit and the latest gadget from Dublin. Anyway, I don't know why he was there in Inchicore, but I met him on the street and he knew

---

* Rory: 'Nannie was very kind to her younger sisters, particularly my mother and Lil. When their mother died, she looked after them. She didn't live too long after her mother. So my mother looked after her children, even though they were nearly as old as my mother. There wouldn't have been more than ten years between them.'
† A Christian Brothers school.
‡ Mitching; playing truant.

Bridge of old, what Bridge was like, and he asked me
how I was getting on. I told him a few things and he
went, post-haste, and told my mother what was happening. And the upshot of it was, she arrived and there
was a terrible bloody row – and I went home. I'd been
there for a year or so.'

He left St Michael's and moved to secondary school,
James's Street, which, like St Michael's, was managed by
the Christian Brothers. 'James's Street was dominated
by the Guinness set-up. The brewery was on both sides
of the street. On the left side, beyond the gate of
Guinness's headquarters, was St James's church. And, just
beyond that, you turned on to Basin Lane. Basin Lane
ran from James's Street, up around by the canal basin,
an unloading bay for the barges bringing the hops and
barley up from the country. The school was near there,
on Basin Lane. And the smell around that area was always
of hops and malting barley.

'It was a good school. They were good teachers. There was an old chap called Breen, history and geography; I can still see him – moustache, glasses. He was very keen. He told us a great amount about Mary Queen of Scots and the association between Scotland and France. The history of Ireland didn't figure much. I think it ended somewhere around the Wyndham Land Act.* And it was vaguely mentioned that there'd been a rebellion in 1916. It wasn't history yet, I suppose; it was almost current affairs.

'I was good at history, geography, English – particularly English. With the encouragement of the Brothers, I wrote a couple of articles for *Our Boys*,† but they weren't accepted. However, I had that ability – it was recognised, to write essays and things like that. Individual books weren't on the curriculum, as such. It was general literature and poetry. There was an Irish anthology, *Blátha na File*,‡ and it had all the well-known Gaelic poetry in it, *Cúirt an Mhean Oíche*,§ and such like. The English poetry book was *Flowers from Many Gardens*, an anthology of all the better works, Keats, Chesterton, all of them. Of course, we did Shakespeare; *Hamlet* sticks out in my mind. Mention would be made of a book in school and I'd go to a library, mostly Rathmines library; I'd dig it out and read it. I remember reading *A Shropshire Lad* by your man, Housman. It was remarkable. I read Mary Anne Hutton's translation

---

* 1903 – allowed tenants to buy out landlords with Treasury loans.
† Magazine, published by the Christian Brothers.
‡ Flowers of the Poets.
§ *The Midnight Court* by Brian Merriman. Published in 1800; a satire on Irish sexual life – with certain passages that were suitable for a Christian Brothers' anthology.

of *The Táin*. I remember reading *The Canterbury Tales*.'

He remembers no violence or cruelty at James's Street. 'That's one of the reasons why I found it difficult to take on board the recent complaints about the Christian Brothers. I'd gone to primary school in Tallaght, the Christian Brothers' primary school in Inchicore, then James's Street. They weren't what you'd call very salubrious neighbourhoods and yet I don't remember seeing anything, except for that one time the Head Brother made an example of the boys who didn't know their Christian Doctrine.' He enjoyed school. 'And I learned another big lesson, about doing the obvious thing. It was during another Christian Doctrine examination, the Archbishop's examination. I had a very good retentive memory and wrote down a good account of what was in the book. I did notice some peculiar things happening at the back of the class, lads copying from the book, but nobody was paying much attention to it, including the reverent gentleman who was supervising us. In the heel of the hunt, I got 30 per cent in the exam. If it wasn't literally the same, a word-for-word copy of what was in the book, it didn't measure. You had the book on your desk and you copied everything, and everyone around you was at it. So, I was reprimanded. I think the Brother was surprised that I was so stupid, that I didn't cop on. But I had standards in those days. I couldn't bear the idea of not having a go on my own.'

He cycled to school from Tallaght, and home, a round twelve-mile journey. 'I came down through Dolphin's Barn and then cut through a lane called the Back o' the Pipes, on to James's Street. I cycled along there every day and, every day, the south wind blew and I'd stand on the pedals and battle hard against it. And I once had the bright idea, to get out of the main force of the wind along the Crumlin Road. So I went on to the Windmill Road. This was the time when the Behans, Brendan Behan and his brothers and all, had just been shunted out there★ – and there they were. I was ambushed, and I never cycled faster – I'd have won the Tour de France. The music of the stones hopping off the spokes of my bicycle was, quite literally, unbelievable. If I'd been caught I doubt very much if I'd have lived to regret it. I never went that way again.

'I had a habit of reading a book while cycling. Not to be recommended. I was going along the street one time, oblivious to everything, reading the book – and I came to a sudden stop. I ended up on the roof of a van with the book in one hand, the driver shouting; I'd frightened the life out of him. I think the book was *Glenanaar* by Canon Sheehan.

'Now and again, I'd cycle towards Terenure and up to Templeogue and drop in to see my Granny Doyle. She was a bright little old lady who wore a black bonnet and a little black cloak when she left the house. She once told me that her husband's grandfather – my great-great-grandfather, Myles Doyle – told her that he had escaped from Wexford in 1798, after the Battle of Arklow. He made his way through the Wicklow Mountains and eventually arrived at Firhouse, where he set up a forge.† She also held very deep Fenian leanings and was generally of a radical outlook. She said that Garibaldi was "a proper bowsey" for annoying the Pope. Tim Healy was "a

★ The Behans had moved from the inner-city to the new Corporation estate of Crumlin.
† Rory: 'It was finally closed in the 1940s when the last of the line, Joe Doyle, died. He was a bachelor.'

sleeveen rat" for betraying Parnell. My Aunt Bride said, "But, Ma, Parnell married a divorced woman." My Granny said, "He was a Protestant and didn't know the differ." Her opinion of William Cosgrave★ was close to unprintable and she thought that "that fellow" Hitler in Germany was up to no good and should be watched. My father was amazed when I told him about the forge in Firhouse. He said, "My mother never told me anything like that." I said, "Did you ever ask her?" He just looked at me and shook his head.

'My father was a smallish, quiet man. He was accorded a high level of respect by my mother; they never fought or argued. He never raised his voice or his hand. He was fully supportive of most of her ideas. If my mother thought that she wasn't getting her way, she could turn on the waterworks; big tears would roll down her beautiful Grecian nose, and my father was gone.

'He was incredibly neat. He always had shining shoes and could literally walk across a ploughed field and they'd still be shining. He had a stud box and a collar box and always wore a trilby hat when dressed. In my earliest memories, he also had a bowler hat in a hat box. This was worn on important occasions. He also had two beautiful cut-throat razors, and sharpened them with a strop. My mother occasionally used them for cutting up lino, and he eventually threw in the towel and began using safety razors, Mac's Smile and Gillette; the blades cost a

---

★ William Cosgrave (1880–1965): born in Dublin; attended first Sinn Féin convention; fought in 1916; Sinn Féin MP for Kilkenny, 1917–18; supported the 1921 Treaty; President of the Second Dáil and Chairman of the Provisional Government, after the deaths of Michael Collins and Arthur Griffith, 1922; founded Cumann na nGaedheal, 1923; leader of Fine Gael, the main opposition to Fianna Fáil, 1935–44.

penny each and their life could be prolonged by rubbing them around the inside of a glass tumbler. Fly fishing was his favourite hobby. He was a master of the River Dodder and would tie flies for each particular area of the river. He had beautiful greenheart and split cane rods. He taught me how to fish but I didn't have the patience. Many times in summer, he'd arrive home at breakfast time with a bag of brown trout and, sometimes, a bag of mushrooms. I only remember him being vexed whenever he heard of somebody catching fish with a net. He hated any suggestion of cheating. His sense of patriotism was total and he believed, without any reservation, that de Valera personified the spirit of the nation. He was devastated and actually shed tears when de Valera lost the 1948 election and a Coalition Government took over. His regard for his neighbours was kindly and charitable, except where he encountered overt opposition politics; then his charitable instincts would be somewhat dulled. He had played football and was regarded as a knacky wing-forward. In his last games, he played for the Seán Doyles, a team named after his brother, Johnny, who was fatally wounded during the Civil War. He often took me to boxing tournaments in Portobello Barracks. I saw the great Ernie Smith box.'*

'I don't remember being particularly interested in women; I had more things on my mind. In any case, by the time I got to school, got through the day, got back home on the bicycle, there wasn't much time left for frivolities, you know. Any of the fellows I knew who

---

* Rory: 'He was a great amateur Dublin boxer.'

got involved with girls, it meant an awful lot of their spare time. You couldn't do what you liked. If you wanted to go into Dublin★ or you wanted to go anywhere, you were tied up: "Oh, I can't go now; you see, myself and Mary are doing this, that and the other," and that, to me, was slavery.'

Women might not have distracted him but other things did. 'I was about fourteen or fifteen at the time. Dan McCabe lived up the road, up near where the High Street in Tallaght is now. He was a very kind, stern man with one of those eagle-type faces. And then there was young Dan. He was about a year older than I was, but wise beyond his years. We used to ramble the fields together but I never saw him laugh; everything in life was dead serious for Dan. He was in the Fianna,† and he organised a troop of us.

'I think, looking back, that the McCabes' house must have been the centre for dissident Republicans. I saw people; there were a couple of brothers from Howth, well-spoken men, George and Charlie Gilmore. They were engineers, in fact. One of them engineered the blowing up of King Billy in College Green,‡ and the other fellow actually had a plan to drop a bomb on Leinster House,§ to hire an aeroplane to do it. I met these mysterious people in McCabes'. And they were all gentlemen. So, anyway, I joined the Fianna Boys and we were drilled in the essentials of rough street combat, how to set up ambushes, and things like that. And all

---

★ Rory: 'We always referred to "going into Dublin"; it was never "into town".'
† Fianna Eireann – youth wing of the IRA.
‡ The statue; the real lad died in 1702.
§ The house of parliament.

of this was happening under the eyes of the powers-that-be, my own family and everybody else.

'The Fianna had a uniform; they dressed in slouch hats and a green jacket and, depending on your age, either shorts or britches, the britches with the leggings – it all looked very, very attractive.* So, eventually, it came to the time when I asked my mother what were the chances of me getting the uniform. So she said, "What uniform?" And I said, "The Fianna Boys." "What Fianna Boys?"; whereupon I explained about the Fianna Boys and Dan McGabe, and there was a terrible row and my mother made a visit to McCabes', where she left them in no doubt as to what she thought of them leading young boys astray. So I was drummed out of the Fianna Boys and that ended my flirtation with the IRA. My father was a member of Fianna Fáil, and that was what incensed my mother, but I didn't realise it at the time; I didn't fully realise the differences between the Fianna Fáil men and the IRA. The subtleties were lost on me. They were essentially the same kind of people, friendly to each other, but deeply divided on the question of the legitimacy of the State. Fianna Fáil came about when men realised that fighting and shooting wasn't going to advance the cause, but the diehards refused to fall in, and set about creating trouble. But the distinction was often very muted. When it came to election times, the diehards would often join in and canvass for Fianna Fáil, even though they'd be calling us names for the rest of the year. My mother was incensed because

---

* Rory: 'Years later, I saw groups of them, from the North of Ireland, and I found it a bit off-putting that, after so many years, they hadn't advanced the style of the uniform.'

my involvement with the Fianna Boys was a slight on my father. He never found out.'

He remembers the Blueshirts.★ 'Tallaght was crawling with them. I was too young to be involved but I remember my father mentioning the blaggards and my mother nearly nailing the door to stop him from going out to a meeting; they were going to sort out a few of the local Blueshirts. I can remember my mother almost forcibly stopping him from doing his duty.'

They moved house in the late 30s. 'The house was pretty crowded by then, shortly after Rosaleen was born, and we moved to a new house. We moved down to Newtown Park and the only one who came with us was Lil.' And then he left school. 'One of the apprentices at Juverna Press, a lad called Raymond, died of TB. That left a vacancy and Jack O'Hagan spotted it for one of his own. And that is how I became a compositor.'

★ Founded in 1933; a Fascist organisation, linked for a time with Fine Gael.

Chapter Seven – Ita

'I was very annoyed because I wasn't let go. I was too young. I can't remember if Joe was, but I don't think it would have perturbed him a lot if he hadn't been. But I wasn't let go to the Mass in the Phoenix Park.* I remember going out to the back garden and kicking the wall. I had to get it off my chest, that I couldn't go to this marvellous thing that was happening. I remember my patent leather shoes; the wall was very solid, not very good for patent leather. I think they realised how frustrated I was. Máire came home full of stories about it.

'Máire did the Primary Cert and she was due to go on to Eccles Street,† and I was taken out of national school and sent there with her. I think it was to keep us together. I was too young for secondary school, so I went into the junior school. I loved Eccles Street from the day I started. I literally never missed a day. I made friends straight away, and I felt at home. There was Sister Alvero, and a Sister Acquin. They were very nice, gentle people. Everything was lovely there. I can't say it wasn't in the other school too; it's just that I don't have such strong memories of it. I can't remember any difference between the junior school and secondary – I just moved

---

* Part of the Eucharistic Congress celebrations, June 1932.
† Dominican College, Eccles Street, north of the city centre.

up. I had all the same friends, the same girls in my class, and a few extra ones who came in from the national schools. We had classes for a half-day on Saturday but that didn't bother me, because I was happy at school. Extra hours meant nothing to me.

'We went to school on the bus, from the end of our road to Eccles Street, and it brought us directly home. And it was two pence, each way. If we got out at the Pillar* and walked the rest of the way we could save a ha'penny. And if we did it on the way home we saved another ha'penny. There was a cake shop on Dorset Street – I think it was called the Rutland – and you could buy a cream slice for a penny in there. It was worth the walk. And I enjoyed the walk back down to the Pillar because there was always a group. We always had a laugh and a chat.

'I made my Confirmation from Eccles Street, in the church on Berkeley Road. I can recall having the most awful velvet dress. It was made by a dressmaker; an awful lot of work went into it. It was a green velvet, and tiny buttons up along the front – and I just hated it. I don't know why, but I thought it was a disaster. And I had a navy coat, which was part of the school uniform, and a navy hat, known then as a riding hat. I was quite happy with the hat and the coat. There were these two unfortunate sisters – they were twins; I can't remember their names – and they were dressed up as if for their First Communion. They had white dresses and white veils. I felt so sorry for them, but then, maybe they didn't feel sorry for themselves. All I can remember then, after the Mass, is that my stepmother met me and

* Nelson's Pillar, on O'Connell Street; blown up by the IRA in 1966.

we went straight home, and that was it. I have no memory of going anywhere or doing anything special.'

Her father had married again. 'I remember her coming to the house the first time. She brought sweets. They were awful sweets but they were better than no sweets. We didn't know why she'd arrived, or why she was introduced to us. We had no idea that it was going to be a full-blown romance, or anything like that. But she came a few times. We used to play cards. She seemed OK, and then it was announced that they were getting married.'

She was introduced as Mrs Byrne. 'She'd been married before. She'd had rather a sad life. She was married very young – I think she was only eighteen or nineteen – and she had a little girl. Then her husband died when she was in her early twenties and the baby died from meningitis. When my father met her she was the housekeeper in a house in Fairview,* for a widower who had a young son. I never met them but she spoke highly of them. I can't remember the surname; the boy was called Ted.'

Her name was Pearl. 'Her real name was Margaret. Pearl was kind of a pet name.' Green was her surname before she'd married. 'Her mother was still alive; her maiden name was Kearns. Pearl had two brothers. John was the elder of the two, and he went to America. He was well-gone by the time we became acquainted with her. He'd disappeared; no one heard from him.† And the

---

* Suburb of Dublin, two miles north of the city centre.
† Ita: 'Many, many years later, a daughter of his managed to get in touch with Pearl. She was in her fifties by then, this woman, and her name was also Pearl. And she told Pearl Sr. that her father, John, and his next-door neighbour had both cleared off one day, deserting both wives and families.'

other brother, Frank, was left at home with his mother. He was a pathetic man, really. I remember going to Mass with him in the pony and trap, and the old lady looked and acted like Queen Victoria. She barely nodded to neighbours. And when we'd come near the church there was always a line of men on both sides of the road, and Frank always said, "Here we come to Gawk Alley." He was a very nice man, and had a miserable life. A dull, dreary old life. He was doing a line with a girl called Chrissie, whose father was a postman. A really nice girl, a very nice family, but not nearly good enough for Ma Green. I remember one day, she was the worse for drink and she said, "Little did I know when I was rearing you and putting you into your little sailor suits and driving you in my carriage to Mass, that you would end up with the postman's daughter." But I always liked Frank. He was very kind to us.

'She also had two sisters. One was Minnie. She lived in England, in Birmingham, I think. She had been married and had a family but the marriage had broken up. Then there was Baby – they all had funny names. The story about Baby was, there'd been a family row, after the father's will was read, and Baby went off and hid and that was the last they heard of Baby. She just disappeared. That was years and years before I came into contact with them.'

She doesn't know how her father met Pearl in Dublin, but 'the strange thing I do know is that he'd met her years before he met my own mother. He met her in New Ross. Her father was an RIC man at the time, based in Rosbercon, outside New Ross. My father had been banished to New Ross. I think she might only have been a schoolgirl; I'm not sure, but I do know he met her. And then they lost touch; he moved back to Enniscorthy and then up to Dublin. How and when he met her again, I have no idea.

'Her mother's people came from Avoca.* They were farmers. And her father had a very nice place in Aughrim,† after he'd retired from the RIC, a pub and grocery.‡ It was a beautiful place and I believe that, in their day, they were quite wealthy but they'd lost it all; her father drank himself out of it. And her mother moved back to Avoca, to live in her home place.

'I heard my stepmother described as a fine girl by a man in Wexford, when I was a teenager. She was tall, rather heavy, and very heavy legs. She had a preference for ankle-strapped shoes.§ She was able to drive. And she was a marvellous pianist.¶ She had been educated but, for some reason or another, it didn't rub off on her. She was an amazing woman – but I don't want to speak too ill of the dead; it doesn't seem fair.

'I thought that this was going to be great, that it would be great to have a mother. Joe resented it bitterly, because

---

* In County Wicklow, south of Dublin.

† Also in County Wicklow.

‡ Ita: 'I didn't see the place until a couple of years ago. Myself and Rory went into the pub for a sandwich and I was sitting there, and I remembered her giving out about the people who'd bought the place, as if they hadn't paid for it, as if they'd no right to it. But when her father died, they were bankrupt – that I know – and the place had to be sold. But she was quite venomous towards the people who'd bought it. And I was sitting there, and I was waiting for a claw to come out and grab me for even paying them for the price of the sandwich. I had this awful feeling, that somehow she'd appear and say, "What are you doing?"'

§ Ita: 'Years later, a friend referred to ankle-strapped shoes as "hoorin' boots".'

¶ Ita: 'She came out to us one Sunday, and she hadn't touched a piano in years and years, and she sat at our piano and played jigs and reels, and I couldn't believe it.'

he was such a pet. Máire more or less accepted it, without much enthusiasm. But I thought it would be great. And, I suppose, looking back, there were good times and bad times.'

The wedding took place in Avoca but the children weren't at it. 'We went to school. My father gave us each money, to buy a present. I think it was ten shillings, which was a fair bit of money. I remember buying a condiment set on the way home from school, in a jeweller's shop called Lawrence, on Henry Street. Salt and pepper and mustard; they had silver tops and a kind of flowery base. Joe bought a glass jug and six glass tumblers. I can still see them; they were yellow and blue striped. I can't remember what Máire bought, but we each had a bit of change, which was great, because he let us keep it. And that was our celebration, keeping the change.

'The wedding was, I gather, very private. Pearl's brother Frank was the best man.* I don't know who the brides-maid was. I think they came home on the same day and, if they didn't, it was very soon after. Lillie, the maid, left soon after that. And Miss Dunne left, although she was still living on the same road. And I was told that my father still paid her; he didn't just cut her out.

'And life changed completely. From being waited on hand and foot, from being rather cosseted, I was left to do everything by myself. From the age of ten, I had to wash my own clothes. Bed things were sent to the

---

* Ita: 'Frank got married years later, to Chrissie. The mother died and Frank finally got married, and my father and stepmother travelled down to the wedding. I was married myself by then. And the next time I went over to visit them, I said, "Well, what did the bride wear?" and my father said, "A scowl from beginning to end."'

laundry but personal things I had to wash myself. I've no idea how I managed, but I did. There was a big mangle outside the back door that you could run the clothes through but they had to be hung on the line to dry, and I have absolutely no recollection of how I did it, but I did – it had to be done. And the cooking deteriorated rapidly. She used to do a good steak, in the pan; that used to be grand, but she'd do a pile of potatoes and mash them and reheat them, and you'd be sick of them by the end of the week. She wasn't a good cook but, there again, we didn't die of starvation. We got our meals. And my father seemed content. That was the main thing, really.

'She was alright, as a rule. But there was nothing warm about her. And we always felt that she'd have preferred if we hadn't been there. She never touched us; she never hit us. I suppose, mentally, she could be cruel, and I don't think she really meant to be; it was just the make of the woman. She was very mean. When we were finished our tea in the evening, we weren't allowed to eat any more. I remember taking bread and butter and putting sugar on it, and putting it up my sleeve and going upstairs to eat it. You can imagine the state of my cardigan by the time I got up the stairs. But I never felt hard done by. We'd talk about what she did and what she didn't do, what she should have done. But I was always resilient and happy by nature. I kind of accepted it; I could have been worse off. I also had a great way of keeping my mouth shut. Máire gave the odd answer back but it did her no good. And Joe was very unhappy and hated the situation. He went very much into himself. He was a very jolly, cheery fellow but he became kind of sullen around the house; it completely changed his character.

He shook it off later in life but, to put it mildly, he hated her guts.

'But there were lots of things that happened. She was a bit fond of the drink and that, really, was the cause of a lot of the trouble. She managed to cover it up for quite a while. We used to get the groceries delivered from Findlater's, in Rathmines, and there was always a bottle of whiskey in the order. Maybe a friend of my father's would call at the weekend and they'd have a drink. And the rest of it would disappear. But she kept it well-hidden. Saturday was the usual day, when we were older; when we came home from school she'd be intoxicated. She'd go up to bed, and get up perfect. I don't think she ever had a hangover.

'I got a fountain pen one year, for Christmas. I had it a few months, and it went; I thought I'd lost it. It was very nice, speckled black and white – I can still remember it. The following year, when my father asked what I wanted, I said I'd like a pen. He said, "I gave you a pen last year and you lost it." He was a bit cranky but he got me the pen, the same type, but green and white this time. But that pen also disappeared. And, years and years later – I was well-married – and there was a robbery in the house in Terenure and Máire phoned to tell us, and we drove over. When we arrived we went upstairs and the place was in chaos. There must have been about fifty handbags lying on the bed. She must have had a thing about handbags. Even the Guards came in and said, "Jesus, missus, you had enough handbags." Anyway, there were loads of things lying on the bed – including my two little fountain pens. We often felt she liked to see Daddy annoyed at us.

'There was another Christmas, and he came in and,

as he often did at Christmas, he put four or five little things down on the table and said, "You decide what you want there." And one of them was a pen – again; I always loved fountain pens. And I said, "I'd like the pen." And Mum said she wanted it. So that was it; she got the pen. But the following Christmas my friend Noeleen was given a present, and it turned out to be the pen. I said nothing to Noeleen and I didn't say anything to Mum, but I thought it was awful; it was terrible.

'She used to go down to Avoca for a few weeks every year, to stay with her mother, and that used to be like a holiday for us. She adored her mother. She was heart-broken when she died. Her mother used to come up every year for a few days, after the harvest was saved. I would say she'd been a handsome woman in her youth; she was rather blocky in build.* They'd go off shopping together. I remember fur coats being bought; her mother had a thing about fur coats. Clery's was the place for the fur coats. That can't have been every year, but I remember a few fur coats.

---

* Ita: 'We met a sister of her mother's years later. She was the image of the mother. Her married name was Kavanagh. And she was a great char-acter. She went out to Montana; she actually went in one of those covered wagons. It was during the Gold Rush days. And I met her great-great-granddaughter years and years later, Kathy, and she told me that this lady had set up a bakery, making pastry for the miners. She told me that the pastry was diabolical but that it was better than no pastry. And she opened a little shop and she sold everything and anything – a dry goods store. And she really flourished, and opened more shops. If any of the miners misbehaved she'd get them by the scruff of the neck and throw them out. She ended up with a whole row of shops called Kavanagh Groceries, in Butte. She was known locally as Bow-Legged Biddie. Her name was Bridget alright, but whether she was bow-legged or not, I don't know because she was very old by the time I met her and her skirts cov-ered her knees. She was also very fond of the drink.'

'I can remember going in and out of town with Pearl on a few occasions, and she was alright. And a few trips to Bray.★ I remember her pointing out this big hotel on the sea front where she had worked in some capacity, I don't know what. But she was always eager to come out and look at it again. Maybe she had happy memories of it – I don't know.

'There were times when it was OK but, on the whole, it was pretty dull and dreary. And loveless. It was just, when I saw the mothers in other houses and the affection they had for their children, I never got any of that. And I always felt a bit in the way. She had her good moments, but they were scarce. I'm glad to say that, at this stage, I never do anything, only laugh about it. It wasn't funny at the time but, looking back, I think it stood to me; when you have things hard early in life it makes you appreciate all the things you have later. My sister and myself often discuss it, and both of us feel the same. We just got on with it. You didn't rebel; you just accepted it. That was your life, and that was it. But it was an awful shock when it happened. But I suppose, there were a few good times, and we were kept pretty comfortable. There were people who were hungry and cold but we were OK. And the neighbours around us were very nice and I had lots of friends.

'And my father was a very good man. He was completely undemonstrative, but he was a very good, straight man. He was always looked on as a pillar of the community. I remember my aunt saying that she had never

---

★ Seaside resort, south of Dublin.

met such integrity. He was a very methodical man.★
And the job was so important to him. He didn't take
his holidays sometimes until it would be pushing into
the winter. He had this silly idea that they couldn't get
on without him, things might go wrong; he'd wait until
all the others had had their holidays. He worked in the
Department of External Affairs, on Stephen's Green. He
had the key to the wine cellar, and they couldn't have
given it to a better man. There was no chance in a million years that he would rob a bottle or touch a bottle.
I remember invitations coming to him for this function
and that function, but he never went. They'd be stuck
on the mantelpiece and he'd say, "I'm not getting into
a monkey suit for anybody." But he loved going to the
Abbey.† Every first night, he was there. And the very
odd trip to the pictures. He loved Laurel and Hardy.
And the one who really impressed him was Clark Gable.
He thought *San Francisco*‡ was wonderful.

★ Ita: 'When he died, he left lots of papers. They were all very well-organ-
ised, and held together with elastic bands. But among these papers was a
memory card to a Bernard Ryan, and it said: ". . . who died for Ireland,
on the 14th of March, 1921, interred in Mountjoy Jail." Myself and Rory
put it in the glass case in the front room and it was there for well over
thirty-five years; why I kept it in the first place, I don't know – the fact
that it was historical, I suppose – I didn't want to tear it up. Anyway, last
week [end of October 2000] I read an article in the *Irish Times* about the
removal of the remains of Kevin Barry and others who had been executed
in Mountjoy Jail in 1921. And, lo and behold, there was the name, Bernard
Ryan. Rory remembered the name and went in and took out the memory
card. I couldn't believe it. I don't know why my father had it. I don't know
whether there was a family relationship – he had Ryan second-cousins –
or whether he was a Wexford man or a GAA man; they would have been
his connections.'
† The Abbey Theatre; the national theatre.
‡ Released in 1936. 'The loves and career problems of a Barbary Coast
saloon proprietor climax in the 1906 earthquake. Incisive, star-packed,

'I remember the first film I was at, *Babes in Toyland*,⋆ with Laurel and Hardy, and I had my head stuck under my father's coat from the beginning to end; I was terrified. Every now and again I'd peep out and I'd see these things moving around, and back my head would go. I remember my father laughing and Joe and Máire laughing, but I have no recollection of the film.'

She overcame her fear. 'We used to go to the Stella in Rathmines every Sunday afternoon. Four pence in it was. I loved the cowboy films. I went with my friend Noeleen and, of course, we were beginning to move into the romantic era and the two of us would come out with tears rolling down our faces. And we thought it was great value; anything that made you cry was marvellous – if the heroine died at the end or got TB, or if they split up. Jeannette MacDonald in *Smilin' Through*,† with Brian Aherne – he was good, handsome; he was mostly a cowboy – and she died at the end. That was smashing; we loved that. And we went to the Classic when it opened in Terenure, where the old steam tram‡ had been. There was an actor in one of the films and

---

superbly-handled melodrama which weaves in every kind of appeal and for a finale has some of the best special effects ever conceived' (*Halliwell's Film Guide*).

⋆ Released in 1934; also called *The March of the Wooden Soldiers*. 'Santa Claus's incompetent assistants accidently make some giant wooden soldiers, which come in handy when a villain tries to take over Toyland. Comedy operetta in which the stars have pleasant but not outstanding material; the style and decor are however sufficient to preserve the film as an eccentric minor classic (*Halliwell's Film Guide*).

† Released in 1941. 'Three generations of complications follow when a Victorian lady is accidentally killed by a jealous lover on her wedding day. Flat but adequate remake of the 1932 original' (*Halliwell's Film Guide*).

‡ The depot of the Dublin and Blessington, where Rory's father had worked.

he was bald; I can't remember who he was, but someone shouted, "Hey, you, head of skin!" And someone else shouted, "Do you comb your hair with a towel?" The little boys; the noise used to be dreadful. When the cowboys and Indians were fighting or the sheriff was pursuing the gangsters, the boys would tell them where to go and what to do and what not to do. It was all part of it, great fun.

'Our road was full of boys our own age and we knocked around with them, but there was no real pairing off or anything like that. Really, teenagers didn't exist; there was no such thing – you were thirteen, fourteen, fifteen, but never a teenager. I suppose, we kind of eyed boys and men up and down but, other than that, we used to go around in a crowd of our own age. You'd prefer one to the other, but that was as far as it got. Young people were the same as anyone else; you did what you were told.'

She continued to enjoy school. 'I always enjoyed English. I can still remember nearly every poem I learned. *Oh, to have a little house, To own the hearth, the stool and all, The heaped-up logs against the fire, The pile of turf against the wall.*★ I have dozens. And, of course, Shakespeare; I was happy with Shakespeare.

'I remember once, we did a play, *The Admirable Crichton.*† And one of the teachers, I think it was Miss Burgess, was Crichton. She was very good. She was the only one who was allowed to wear trousers on the stage.

★ 'The Old Woman of the Roads' by Padraic Colum (1881–1972): born in Longford; author of poetry and plays; *The Saxon Shillin'* (1902); *Broken Soil* (1903); *The Land* (1905); *Thomas Muskerry* (1910); *Collected Poems* (1953).
† By J.M. Barrie; gentle satire on the British class system, first staged in 1902.

There was another play we did – I can't remember the name of it – but there was a grocery shop, and I was the grocer. I was playing a man's part but I had to wear an apron over my skirt. I had to stand behind the counter with my apron on. I had a cap, and my hair was stuck up in the cap. I wasn't allowed to wear trousers, but the admirable Crichton was.

'We also did "The Hound of Heaven", by Francis Thompson.* *I fled Him down the nights and down the days, I fled Him down the arches of the years, I fled Him down the labyrinthine ways of my own mind, And in the midst of tears I hid from Him, And under running laughter.* I can't remember the rest, but it's not too bad. Anyway, we were all kinds of things, and my role – there were rocks and chasms, and I was a rock and chasm. I had a purple robe, and all the rocks – there were three or four of us – we had to sit at one side and drape these purple robes over ourselves, to give the appearance of rocks. And we were asked, "Rocks and chasms, whom do ye seek?" I can't remember the answer; I mean the official one – we gave a different answer every night. But I do remember, the highlight of the whole thing was that de Valera attended.

'I hated maths. To this day, I hate maths. And I started off great guns with Latin, but it went. There was an A class and a B class, and I was in the A class. In the A class you did Latin and in the B class you did Domestic

---

* It was a favourite of Eugene O'Neill's. 'When the mood struck him, in Jimmy the Priest's or in the Hell Hole, he was given to reciting Francis Thompson's "The Hound of Heaven", a lachrymose and somewhat hysterical account of God's remorseless pursuit of a soul strayed from grace. It was the hypnotic versification and giddy imagery that drew him, though, and not any possible resemblance to his own circumstances' (from 'Master of the Misbegotten' by Barbara Gelb and Thomas Flannagan, *New York Review of Books*, 5 October 2000).

Economy. I'd have preferred Domestic Economy, the cooking, but there was no way I was going to be demoted to the B class. So, I managed. I didn't shine in exams, but I never failed. I was quite happy with Irish. History, I loved, and was happy enough with Geography – it was different then, just mountains, rivers, places. I was fairly good at art. I was good at design, and I could draw a still life, a few apples in a bowl.

'My closest friends at school were Aileen Cusack, who lived in Howth – she's a Dominican nun now – and Brenda McDunphy, who lived in Clontarf. Her father was Douglas Hyde's secretary.* They were my best friends, along with Noeleen. Brenda and myself and Máire went to the Gealtacht,† to Ballinaskelligs, in Kerry. It was great – different. I think it was an old army barracks we stayed in. They called it a college. It was pretty basic, bare boards and miserable beds. But that was no problem. We used to have Irish lessons in the morning and, in the afternoon, we'd have trips, to places in Kerry. We went to Skellig Rocks, by boat, and Daniel O'Connell's house, in Derrynane. And we had a *céili*‡ every night, and that was grand. We had picnics, and a sports. I remember coming second in a race and getting half a crown.

'I read an awful lot – for two reasons. I loved reading; the house was full of books. But, secondly, when I got a bit older I was never allowed out in the evening, but a library opened in Terenure and it was a blessing to us

---

* Douglas Hyde (1860–1947): co-founded the Irish Literary Society, 1891; co-founded the Gaelic League, 1893; first President of Ireland, 1938.
† An area where Irish is the predominant language; most of the Gaeltachts are in the west of Ireland.
‡ A dance.

all, because it was the excuse we needed to get out. If there were no evening devotions on in the church, there was always the library. You met your friends *en route*, you went to the library, you picked your books. You couldn't delay too long – you might be timed – but you had a chat with your friends as you all walked home together, and you had the new book. You read it as quickly as you could, so you could have another night out. When the Miraculous Medal Novena started every Monday night, we were in our seventh heaven. We all got a great devotion to the Virgin Mary. We felt the Holy Mother was on our side. She had given us a copper-fastened excuse to meet.

'Nearly all of my father's books were of Irish interest. I remember going along the quays with him, the second-hand bookshops. He'd root through the books, and he always ended up buying one or two of them. I read all of Annie M.P. Smithson's books.★ I thought they were lovely. I couldn't read them now; terrible things. And I loved Maurice Walsh.† *The Key Above the Door*, *The Small Dark Man*, *Blackcock's Feather* – I thought they were wonderful. Again, I couldn't read them now, but they were great stories in their day. And, of course, we had all the

---

★ Annie M.P. Smithson (1873–1948): born in Dublin; midwife and district nurse; converted to Catholicism; took part in the siege of Moran's Hotel during the Civil War; secretary of the Irish Nurses' Organisation, 1929. Works include *Her Irish Heritage* (1917); *Carmen Cavanagh* (1921); *The Walk of a Queen* (1922); *Nora Connor: A Romance of Yesteryear* (1924); *For God and Ireland* (1931).

† Maurice Walsh (1879–1964): born in Kerry. Works include *The Key Above the Door* (1926); *Blackcock's Feather* (1932); *The Road to Nowhere* (1934), and many others. The rights to his story 'The Green Rushes', first published in the *Saturday Evening Post* in 1933, were bought by John Ford, and the story eventually became *The Quiet Man* (1952).

P.G. Wodehouse books. My father loved poetry. And I did too. And he also had – you don't get them any more – things called broad-sheets, with the words and music of Irish songs. I think they sold them outside Croke Park. They were only a few pence each, published on paper like newspaper, a rough kind of paper. They were different colours, not very bright pink and orange, yellow and pale blue. I still have them.'

She was fourteen in September 1939. 'I was in Coolnaboy the day war was declared. And I can still remember – whether it was that day or a few days after, I don't know – but I was being brought to Oilgate, to get the bus home, and myself and Katie were talking about refugees and children in England being sent down the country. And I asked, if I was a refugee could I come down to Coolnaboy. And I remember, Katie laughed and said, of course I could.'

Chapter Eight – Rory

'We left the old house, with a horse and cart loaded with furniture, and a hand-cart, and we walked down through the town, a short mile down the road to Newtown, and into No. 8. An empty house, bare floor-boards. That was a novelty, after the hard cement floors in the old house, the wooden floors and the general air of space. We started lugging in the furniture, and decisions were made as to what was to go where, decisions on how to light up the new range, how to make sure we had enough water for washing. A water barrel had to be put under the down pipe from the roof. The pump had to be located, where'd we'd get our fresh water – it was just up the road. Then we surveyed this huge expanse of garden, nearly an acre. We'd had a yard before, walled in; this was open.'

The landlord was Dublin County Council. The house was brand new.★ 'I didn't like it. It lacked that homeliness, or the inclusiveness, of the old house, where everything was so familiar. This place was bare, and I didn't like it at all. I never did like it. I tolerated it.

'In summer, I often spent the holidays with my Aunt Lizzie, my father's eldest sister. She lived in a very large

---

★ Rory: 'There was no electricity. It had been installed a few years before in the old house, so we had to get used to candles and oil lamps all over again.'

house down in Balrothery.★ And I was walking home from Mass in Balbriggan, which was a mile and a half away, and I heard the wireless; I came in the door and Aunt Lizzie said, "Do you know, there's going to be a war." Then Chamberlain came on and made that famous speech, that our ambassador has informed Herr Hitler. I felt a certain excitement but, the funny thing is, nothing exceptional happened for the rest of the year. A lot of things were being done and decided that nobody knew about, like a realisation that there'd have to be rationing – we didn't know that. And a realisation that we weren't going to get all that wheat from Manitoba. All of these things lay ahead, but only really began to happen around the middle of 1940.'

'My mother brought me to a tailor at the end of George's Street, a man called Newman, and a suit was made for me. And a new bicycle was bought, from McHugh Himself. And a raincoat. I also had a white apron, to keep the clothes clean. A white cotton one, like a shopkeeper's. I had no particular feelings about leaving school. It was part of life. I'd got a job, a scarce commodity. And I liked the thought of what I would be doing; I'd found an old book and read about printing, and I liked the idea.

'I went in the door of Juverna press at 8 am, on the 8th of July, 1940. The first person I saw inside the door was Frank Bowers; he was running his machine, which I found out later was a Cropper Platen.† Then, surrounding

---

★ In north County Dublin.
† Rory: 'He worked his foot up and down and that gave the power to the machine; there was no electrical motor or anything like that. It was generally used for small jobbing work – cards and menus.'

me, there was this huge deluge of deafening noise – the other machines. And then, up the wooden winding stairs. This was a funny, converted building, three-floored, in Proby's Lane, off Liffey Street, down at Arnott's back entrance. I went up the stairs, and into the heart of the printing works, the case room. The engine room of control and power. And all that noise. My uncle Jack O'Hagan was there, and he looked at me and said, "Go and learn the lay of the case." I didn't know what "the lay of the case" meant. But one of the fellows pointed out a frame, where the cases of type were mounted; "You learn each letter."

'Case, in printers' terms, was a tray thirty-two and a half inches long, and fourteen and a half inches broad; it was divided up into tiny little compartments, each one and a half inches deep. Each compartment held a different character – capitals, lower-case, numerals, all the commercial signs. They all had a place and you had to learn where exactly they were because, when you were setting type, you didn't look at what you were taking from the tray; it would have taken too long – you'd never have got the job set. You couldn't operate as a compositor if you didn't know the lay of the case.

'So I started learning. And, behind my back, there was a big linotype, or inter-type, machine. It was going away there, and I was fascinated, looking at the matrices,★ flowing across the bar and down the shoot, to produce

---

★ Rory: 'Each font of type, every letter in the font had something known as the matrix; it was a brass, stamped-out piece of metal, and it ran along a matrix guide, which was a ridged metal bar. When you pressed a key on the keyboard, the matrix fell out of the magazine, down a shoot, into an assembly, which would allow a line of type to be cast. On each matrix was a stamp-reversed image of every character in a font of type.'

metal slugs of type characters. And then, further down, there was a monotype caster — it cast single pieces of type — and it made a noise like a thousand guns, all the time, and, behind it, Jimmy Ward sitting at the keyboard. The caster was driven by a punched paper roll which was created by Jimmy, the keyboard operator. It was a multiple keyboard; it had an alphabet for every form of character you could use. Capital letters, small capitals, lower-case, capital letters with bold face, lower-case bold face, capital letters for italics, lower-case italics; then the numbers and other assorted characters for commercial use, like @ and £, all on this one keyboard, which worked away and punched the paper. All very fascinating.

'The first day, I also went into Millar's, on Abbey Street, and bought myself a composing stick. It's the compositor's basic tool, for setting up type, and I bought a brand-new one, my pride and joy, my initials stamped on it by old Millar. I still have it. I also bought a type-scale, for measuring type on pages, and a tweezers, for picking up single type while doing corrections. So, now I was equipped.

'I spent a few days learning the lay of the case, and Jack O'Hagan came up and asked me if I knew it. And I said, "I do." So he said, "Where is — ?" and he asked me where each particular character was. Capital *I*, lower case *g*, and, generally, he asked me to find the tricky ones around the perimeter of the case, the ones you might be inclined to slip over, like diphthongs and ligatures. To do it properly, you looked to where the box of letters was; then you put out your hand and picked up the character — you didn't look at it. You picked it up and placed it in the composing stick. That was the real skill.

So, I got through the test and I was given bits of things to set up – lines to fit into chapter headings in magazines and books. Then I graduated to setting up raffle tickets. The technical side to that job was, you had to put in a piece of perforated rule, a very thin band of metal, slightly higher than the type, to allow people to tear the tickets. And you had to put in a numbering box. Sometimes, numbering boxes got stuck and caused trouble, by being too tightly locked in the forme.★ I was delighted with myself. I liked the job, and quickly mastered the simpler techniques.

'I served a seven-year apprenticeship, working from eight o'clock in the morning until six o'clock in the evening. I was paid ten shillings a week. About seven or eight weeks after I started there was a general pay rise, and I got another shilling. So I had eleven shillings. And every year I got a rise of five shillings. Seven long years, but I didn't feel that way; all life was spread out ahead of me. I was very pleased, because I got a shilling for myself out of the ten shillings. I did marvellous things with that shilling, including bringing my sister, Breda, to the Wolfe Tone Café, just around the corner from Clery's, on Christmas Eve, where we had sausages and mashed potatoes. Breda was delighted and I felt very proud about the whole thing. To have any money at all was marvellous, because I'd never had money in my pocket before. Now I had a shilling to do what I liked with.

★ Rory: 'The forme was the final printing surface; it is the type all laid out in pages. It was the metal, the type and the blocks for making the pictures, all put together, all contained in a strong steel frame. The page was locked into the frame by wedges called quoins. When it was done properly the whole lot lifted and could be carried down and put on the machine for printing. If it wasn't properly done, it would fall out and cause chaos.'

'I learned to set type, arrange book and magazine pages, carry large formes of metal pages, mostly sixteen pages of crown quarto,★ down the winding stairs to the printing department, then back up the stairs to be broken up. The used type metal was carried by zinc bucket – by me – down the stairs, down Proby's Lane, on to Liffey Street, and down the stairs at the head office, to the basement, where there was a large metal pot, fired by gas. The type was melted at great heat and the dirt and impurities scraped off the molten top, and thrown into a box outside the door. This was called dross, and it hardened into a most colourful mass of peculiar matter. The clean metal was poured – again, by me – by ladle into moulds, to form ingots of metal, to feed the monotype and linotype machines. I had to carry these ingots back up the stairs, out on to Liffey Street, up Proby's Lane, up the stairs, and stack them beside the composing machines. That work really belonged to the general worker, Paddy Keating, but, somehow, he was always importantly engaged elsewhere.

'Juverna Press had originally been the Gaelic Press, which had printed much of the seditious literature for Arthur Griffith† and Sinn Féin. Griffith's *Scissors and Paste* was printed there, and *Nationality*. And I once discovered a couple of anti-conscription pledges, from 1918. When I went there, they specialised in the printing of religious magazines: the *Lourdes Messenger*, the *Redemptorist Record*, the *Cross*, and others.

★ Rory: 'This was a paper-size, seven and a half inches by ten inches.'
† Arthur Griffith (1871–1922): born in Dublin; apprenticed as a printer; active in the Gaelic League and IRB; fought for the Boers, 1897–9; edited the *United Irishman*; founded Sinn Féin, 1906; headed the Irish delegation in the Treaty negotiations, 1921; elected President of the Dáil, 1922.

'There were three floors, and about twenty-five people worked there. The ground floor housed the printing machines; a Cropper Platen, just inside the door; a German Quad crown self-feeder; two Wharfdale hand-fed machines; and a Heidelberg Automatic Feeder Platen.

'The second floor was the case room, the intellectual heart of the printing works – home of the compositors. The compositor, in those days, was considered the *crème de la crème* of industrial society; no other trade and very few professions were comparable in status. When the type was set, we'd send out the proofs, and the editors would come in with the proofs and tell you how they wanted the pages arranged. It reached a stage where I could nearly read their minds and I'd have the pages arranged before they came back. These were eminent scholars, some of them, doctors of theology; they'd been seconded to do the magazine. Another man I met was Dónal O'Moráin, subsequently head of Gael-Linn. He was probably in his first job, as editor of the retail grocers' magazine. He was very young and innocent, and some of the compositors gave him a terrible fright one time when he inadvertently lifted up four or five slugs. They immediately started a hullabaloo, saying that this man had broken all the rules, he had handled type, he wasn't a compositor – it was sacrilegious. They went through the motions of demanding his removal – he nearly died of fright – and then they let him off. In fact, for some of them, it wasn't a joke. They regarded it as almost sacrilegious, like picking the Blessed Sacrament up with their hands.

'The third floor was occupied by the bindery, where magazines were folded and stitched, and trimmed by the cutter, Peadar Murphy, a veteran of the 1916 Rising. One

of the ladies of the bindery, Bessie Gorman, who lived
on Dominick Street, declared one day that her mother
was broken-hearted because Bessie's brother had left the
Holy Name Sodality and joined the British Army. Most
of the women worked in the bindery, but there were
two more on the printing floor; they were machine
feeders – they fed the sheets of paper into the printing
machines. They could be grumpy. They did their jobs
and, when the machine wasn't working, they sat at the
back of it, knitting. There was another apprentice,
Michael Doggett, the same age as myself but with two
years' seniority. He was a nice, decent lad. And there
were various men, mostly from Dublin, with all that that
entails – the teams they supported, the cynicism about
political life, and suchlike. It was an eye-opener for me,
like being in a different country. The philosophy was
profoundly anti-Republican, anti-Gaelic, almost anti-
Irish. As far as they were concerned, they were Dublin
men, not Irish. They bought and read English newspapers, while I read the *Irish Press*.* They spoke of nothing
but soccer, all the Dublin and English teams, and they
jeered at Croke Park,† called them all culchies. And there
were other characters. There was Paul Hughes, who was
the monotype caster and an ex-Dublin Fusilier; he'd
been out with the British Army in 1916; a very taciturn,
grumpy old fellow. Then we had Paddy McBrinn, who
was a Republican from Belfast. And every now and again,
there'd be a shortage of ingots and a row over who had
to go and get them. They were always ripe for a row, if
they got the chance.

---

* The Fianna Fáil newspaper, founded by de Valera in 1931.
† GAA stadium and headquarters.

'Occasionally, a traveller would call to the works door. Ostensibly, he'd be looking for work. He'd be carrying a composing stick wrapped up in an apron. These itin-erant printers rarely got work. All they'd have was a grimy and creased union card, and they'd be helped by a donation from the chapel fund,★ held by the father of the chapel for that purpose. One regular caller was dressed in a dilapidated frock coat, a battered tall hat and a ragged trousers, a proofreader who had fallen on hard times. His accent was quite cultured and he was known as "the Knight" or "the Knight of the Shattered Arse".

'One day my guardian angel took his eye off the ball and the devil whispered an idea into my ear. It was a day when the directors had their meeting in the front office. I was toiling in the bowels of the basement, as befitted a printer's devil.† When I'd lit the boiler, I took a large piece of rain-sodden dross and placed it on top of the metal, and went to attend to my other duties. I think I was making the point that I was fed up with what I was doing; and I knew that if I complained, I'd just be told off. So, half an hour later, the whole office building was filled with a lung-corroding, poisonous black smoke. The directors staggered into the street, coughing and yelling. The fire brigade was called and the whole of Liffey Street came to a standstill. Jack O'Hagan‡ located the cause of the smoke and, when all was cleared,

---

★ The union was the Dublin Typographical Provident Society (DTPS).

† Rory: 'The name went back to medieval times, when the printing industry was first organised. The metal had to be boiled – dirty work – and always done by the unfortunate apprentices. They were covered in muck and dirt and smelling of smoke. Somebody named them the printer's devils, and it stuck.'

‡ Rory: 'He was known as Jacko by the staff.'

I was escorted into the august presence of the general manager, Mr Hennebery. It was pointed out, heatedly, that I was, not alone incompetent, but stupid as well, and I was sacked.

'I went down the lane to the works and told Jimmy Ward, the father of the chapel, and I reminded him that I was an apprentice and should not have been doing labourer's work. Jimmy hated any hassle but felt obliged to point out to the management the error of their ways. I was reinstated but my mother was sent for and had to endure a lecture from Jack O'Hagan on my shortcomings. When she got home I had to endure a re-run, but my father said nothing and just winked at me. Later, I heard him refer to Jack O'Hagan as a "right get" – strong words from my quiet-spoken father.

'Every man walked in dread of Jacko, who tyrannised the staff worse than any Russian commissar. To say that I was persecuted would be an understatement. You'd never, ever be told, "That's a good job"; it would always be wrong. Anything at all, no effort was made to dodge a chance to belittle you. But it all rolled off me, and my work was always accepted by the customers.* I won the William Rooney Shield for best apprentice at the School of Printing, which I attended every day for two years; a half-day in the works and a half-day at Bolton Street Technical Institute. Each year the firm whose apprentice won the award would display it in the public office. I brought the shield into work and Jacko told me not to bring things in, as they went missing from time to

---

* Rory: 'The other apprentice, Michael Doggett, never got the abuse that I did – not that he deserved it either. I suspect it was because he was related to one of the company directors.'

time. The staff were horrified, but they were afraid of him – with good reason. If they lost their jobs, it was the boat to England.'

In early 1940, the Government announced the formation of a civil defence force, the LDF.★ 'My father and myself walked up the road and joined up. We had no arms or equipment at first. We drilled with pick-axe handles and shovels. Then my father said, "I know where there's a gun." The next day, he took me off, with a spade and shovel, to a place he knew, near the bottom of my granny's garden, and he walked up and down, then pointed: "There. Commence digging." And what we dug up was an old sack and, in it, a heap of rusted metal and the butt end of a rifle. He'd buried it when de Valera had given the order to dump arms in 1923.

'We were eventually issued with brown overall uniforms, consisting of trousers, short leggings, blouse and forage cap, web equipment and a terrible pair of boots. The cap was the inverted V-shape, the same as worn by Franco's lot in the Spanish Civil War. The boots were very hard in dry weather; they'd cut the feet off you. And they were completely porous in wet weather. We paraded for drill one evening a week and on Sunday mornings. Our parade ground was the old aerodrome in Tallaght. The district leader was Tom Watkins, a veteran of the Civil War, and he arrived at our first parade armed with a parabellum. The gun was a large pistol which was housed in a scabbard which also acted as a rifle butt. He looked most impressive and warlike.

'Eventually, we were supplied with American

★ Local Defence Force.

Springfield rifles. They were at least as old as the Great War,★ or even the American Civil War. They were very long and heavy. But I remember holding the rifle and experiencing an extraordinary feeling of power; if anybody came near me, I could take care of myself. We were now required to patrol the mountains around Killenarden, and also guard Tallaght Garda barracks, where the arms were housed. My companion-in-arms on these occasions was always Gerry O'Neill, a very decent, sincere and conscientious man. He was always on the *qui vive*, always on the lookout. He constantly imagined IRA or British or German attacks and would attempt to debate the likely outcome of any such attack. I never got a minute's sleep, and had a day's work to do the next day. The mountain patrol was harrowing. Gerry saw danger every step of the way. Every bush housed a likely enemy, and many a poor devil strolling home from John Clarke's pub was petrified when Gerry shouted, "Halt! Who goes there?" The language was unedifying and frequently cast doubt on our parentage. I later found out that everybody else had been leery of Gerry's enthusiasm, and that was why I was stuck with him.

'We were lectured on the making of explosives and booby traps by a Professor Bailey Butler; the most lethal and horrible booby traps for any invader who came along, including an ingenious one – considering there weren't any flush toilets in the country – where, if you pressed the handle, the whole bloody lot blew up. He even demonstrated it, and it was very spectacular. He also instructed us on the manufacture of Molotov

---

★ Rory: 'We referred to the Great War, not World War One; we didn't realise we were witnessing the start of World War Two.'

cocktails. These were, basically, a mix of petrol and creosote in a bottle, and a rag and bung put into it. You struck the match, set the rag on fire, and threw the bottle. We were eventually issued with new, green Army-type uniforms and short leggings, and a Glengarry cap or beret. And, after several alerts, weekend training camps and other activities, I eventually reached the exalted rank of Company Adjutant.

'I was interested in the progress of the War and, usually, when I started doing something, I took more of an interest. I discovered, in a bookshop down the quays, *On War* by Count von Clausewitz, translated into English. I bought it and read all about it – how to arrange manoeuvres. And I also found an old British Army training manual, and I read that too. We had no wireless at home in the early days. And the funny thing was that, even when we got one, we weren't really conscious of it in the house. It was either barely audible because my mother couldn't stand the noise, or else there was something going on that precluded listening to it. So, the news came mostly from the *Irish Press*. My father wouldn't buy any other paper. They were loyalist or unsuitable for an Irish household. But the *Irish Press* carried the stories, and the slant on them, that he liked. It was our Bible. The outlook was, the British were getting a flaking from the Germans, and we thought that was great; they deserved to be taken down a peg. Probably, at the back of our minds, we were hoping the Germans wouldn't be *too* successful. Because, while we really knew nothing about what was happening, we had our doubts about the Germans. We didn't really hate the British, just the establishment. But the average English person, we had no bad feelings about. And we'd heard the story about Mickey O'Leary, the great veteran and holder of the Victoria Cross; he was brought around on a recruiting drive, and he said, "You've got to join the British Army, or the Germans will come here and they'll be worse than the British ever were."

'We just got very basic information. The censorship was very efficient. We didn't know, really, what was going on. There couldn't have been more than a handful of people in the country who did know. And there was never any word of those horrible atrocities being perpetrated by the Germans. In any case, remember, it was only twenty years or so since the British Army and the Black and Tans had been committing atrocities in Ireland.

'Towards the end of 1940, coal was no longer freely available.* It was quite common to see women going out and coming back with bundles of sticks that they pulled out of the hedges around the farms, just to keep the fire going. My father secured a bog cutting from the County Council, up the mountains at Castlekelly. *Sleáns*† were made; Jack Kelly, the Tallaght blacksmith, hammered them out for us. The bog was seven miles away and I spent most Saturdays and Sundays turning and footing turf. I can still remember the aroma of the tea and black-pudding sandwiches that sustained us in our toil. We eventually accumulated a rick of turf, and a lorry was hired to haul it home. When we arrived, the turf was gone – stolen. My father afterwards discovered that the thief was from Terenure. During the War of Independence, the same man had been in danger

---

* Rory: 'One solution to the shortage in our house was wet turf, primed by every book or periodical my Aunt Lil could get her hands on.'
† Turf-cutting blade; a double-sided spade.

of being executed for blathering secret information in pubs. But my father had interceded on his behalf, and had saved his life. Later in life, when most of the likely referees were dead, the same man claimed and was awarded a pension for Republican activities – and he stole my father's rick of turf. We had to return to the bog.

'Again, towards the end of 1940 – I think – the German U-boat campaign increased, and all the wheat that we used to get from Canada and the US became very scarce. So it was decided, in the milling of the Irish grain, not to separate the husks. The result was a new kind of brown bread – they called it brown bread but it wasn't wheaten bread, just a dreadful imitation. It tasted appalling.

'The O'Reillys lived opposite us, in Newtown Park. Nan went to school with my mother and she married Michael O'Reilly, a fine big man who always seemed to own a decent-looking mackintosh coat. During the War, Michael took the boat to England, along with many others. But, invariably, he visited us at Christmastime, carrying a white loaf. For anybody who experienced the brown bread made from Irish wheat, this bread really was manna. There was a parody of a wartime song which went: *Bless 'em all, bless 'em all, Bless all the lads in the Dáil, Bless de Valera and Seán McEntee, Who gave us brown bread and a half ounce of tea.* People had to stretch the tea ration by reverting to the habit of drying and re-using the tea leaves. My grandmother told me that, in her young days, the tea was so dear that the first making was reserved for important people like the parish priest or the schoolmaster, and that the leaves were used again and again. The taste of the re-run tea was diabolical.

Some people tried to make tea with shell cocoa, a derivative of the chocolate industry – the husks of the cocoa beans. The result was terrible; nobody knew how to make the brew properly.* My mother solved the matter by buying black-market tea, at £1 per pound, in Moore Street.† Anyway, during one of his visits, Michael O'Reilly described a form of heating called a Benghazi – so-called because it was devised by the British Army in North Africa. It consisted of two petrol cans, each equipped with a small tap, one containing water and the other containing engine oil, or even used oil from the sumps of cars. These cans were connected by copper pipes to a large frying pan, housed in the firebox or the kitchen range. The flow to the frying pan was controlled by the taps – three drops of oil to one drop of water. It worked on the principle of the explosive nature of the oil-and-water mix on a hot surface; it generated fierce heat. Our engineer on the project was my cousin, Jack Kelly,‡ who was regarded as the mechanical genius of the family. It worked – and there was no more turf cutting.

'Shortly after that, the owners of our old home, the Dominican Fathers, requested possession, and Jack and my Uncle Bob were now likely to be homeless. My mother couldn't contemplate such a thing, so several

---

* Rory: 'I've recently seen shell cocoa used as a garden mulch. It took fifty years to work that one out.'

† Rory: 'That was very, very expensive, but it was considered almost essential; a working man couldn't get through the day without a cup of tea, and my mother liked it too.'

‡ Not the Tallaght blacksmith, also called Jack Kelly. Rory: 'My cousin, Jack Kelly's father, known as Skin Kelly, was the original blacksmith. When he died, his brother, Jack Kelly, took over the running of the forge. So, Jack Kelly, the blacksmith, was my cousin, Jack Kelly's uncle.'

large car containers were purchased and a wooden bungalow was built out the back.★ Jack was the builder, and there was a lean-to for Uncle Bob. Jack and myself occupied the bungalow and it was festooned with rifles, bayonets, and Jack's Sam Browne belt – he was an officer in the local LDF company.

'One night, the Germans dropped a bomb on Rathdown Park, in Terenure. We felt the shock three miles away, in Tallaght. Mrs Cunningham, next door, ran up and down the road in her nightie, screaming at the top of her voice.† Jack and I sat up in our respective beds, and I looked across at Jack, and asked, "Is this war? What should we do?" Jack replied, "We'll wait till we're mobilised," lay down and went back to sleep. I did the same and, while terror and turmoil raged in the civil population of Newtown, their brave defenders slept the sleep of the just and awaited the trumpet call.

'I think it was in 1942 that General M.J. Costello – General Micky Joe‡ – led a great manoeuvre from Cork to Dublin. He brought his army over and through the Blackwater River, losing two or three soldiers by drowning. However, the Baldonnell Command was ready and waiting for him, and the Tallaght Company was deployed at the Featherbed Mountain, in an attempt to thwart an advance along the Military Road, from Wicklow.

★ Rory: 'The only cars assembled in Ireland were Fords, in Cork. All the British cars were imported in wooden crates. The crates were terrific for timber. If you had a few of those crates, you had the makings of a wooden hut or a bungalow.'

† Rory: 'My mother also had a bad night.'

‡ Rory: 'He was later the boss of the Sugar Company, but at that time he was OC of the Southern Command of the Irish Army.'

'We set up base camp and acquired several coopers of stout and a couple of bottles of whiskey. This was the canteen, and Fred Alsop was in charge of it. Fred was a Londoner. He'd served in the British Army in the Great War, had been stationed at Tallaght Aerodrome and had married Katie Ford, another schoolmate of my mother's. I was ordered to assist Fred in the peeling of several sacks of potatoes. I was also to keep an eye on the canteen, because I didn't drink at that time. I was saving myself for later.

'At about five o'clock in the morning Micky Joe's boys struck, an hour ahead of schedule; the mountain was swarming with soldiers. They'd outflanked the mountain and come at us from behind. My abiding memory is of hearing the agonised cry of our district leader, Tom Watkins, "For Jaysis' sake, save the canteen!" Fred and I promptly dumped the liquor into the nearest boghole and, afterwards, we couldn't remember where. At least, I couldn't. But I wouldn't have been too sure about Fred — he was very resourceful. But, in the scramble to dump the canteen, I struck my shin against the iron band of one of the coopers. I was wounded in action; I still have the mark to this day. I wasn't awarded a medal, a citation for valour, or a pension. Of such is life.'

'There was a day during the War when Dublin was blanketed by the most appalling fog. No buses, trams or bicycles could move. I set out to walk the seven miles home. I reached Christchurch Place and literally bumped into my cousin, Patsy Kelly. He suggested we get some chips, and he led the way down Werburgh Street, to Burdock's. That was actually the first time I ever ate chips, although

I'd heard the lads in work talking about going for a "wan an' wan",* and I'd heard it alleged that so-and-so's vinegar was really horse's urine.

'In the New Year of 1944 or '45, I took my sister, Rosaleen, to the Moving Crib, in Inchicore. It was a nativity scene, a great moving tableau, with full-sized figures and animals, and rich, very attractive costumes. I remember the cold January day and travelling on the upper deck of the No. 21 bus. Rosaleen was enthralled and, at one stage, she turned to me and said, "Are we in Scotland?"

'Clothing was rationed but I knew nothing about this since my mother controlled the coupons.† But the clothing shortage was never a problem in our house, since my mother and my sisters had a natural skill at needlework and a garment underwent many transformations before it was exhausted. But, really, what my sisters did and what they got up to, I hadn't the foggiest idea. It was part of a feminine thing, secrecy, which a man didn't enter. They had their own world.

'Shoe leather was scarce, and leather was of such poor quality that people nailed metal tips or hob nails to the soles of their shoes, to save the leather. The sound of a crowd of people walking down O'Connell Street was a unique experience – there wasn't a heavy roar of traffic to mask the sound. It has stayed in my memory.

'Sometime during 1943, we made a technological leap. We didn't know about technology at the time but that was what it was. Tom Watkins became the distributor

---

* Rory: 'A bag of chips and a piece of fish, usually ray.'
† Rory: 'I never saw a clothing ration coupon until the week I was married and my mother handed over my ration books.'

for small wind turbines, called Wind Chargers. Jack Kelly erected the mast and device, and when the wind blew, the turbine charged a car battery. This provided power for lights and for the wireless. But when the wind was low, the battery went low, the lights grew dim, and the wireless became almost inaudible. The matter wasn't helped by the fact that neither my mother nor my Aunt Lil had the slightest idea of how the process worked. No amount of advice on rationing the use of lights made the slightest difference to them. When the power was on, all the lights were blazing. When the wind became very strong, it was necessary to run outside and turn the turbine out of the wind. Apart from the danger to the turbine, the noise it made was as loud as a fleet of aeroplanes. However, the ESB★ finally arrived – I don't know precisely when since I had other important things to occupy my attentions. But I did notice that we were no longer dependent on either turf or the Benghazi, and that we had an electric cooker, an electric kettle and an electric iron.

'Cigarettes were particularly scarce. People would often queue for hours to buy five cigarettes and they could forget about brand preference. Naturally, there was a thriving black market. The inconvenience was more than I could tolerate, and I never smoked cigarettes. But, in 1944, I won some prize money in the exams at the School of Printing, and I went to Lucky Cody's on Dame Street and bought a Riseagle briar pipe and an ounce of John Cotton's Edinburgh mixture, for two pounds, ten shillings. I filled up the pipe, lit up, and strolled back to Juverna Press. Half an hour later I thought

---

★ Electricity Supply Board.

I was dying. I turned green, saw sparks and got violently sick. My first instinct was to dump the pipe in the Liffey but, on reflection, I reckoned that there'd been a lot of money involved. So I kept the pipe.*

'During the summer evenings, my friends, Desmond Sharkey, Michael Kennedy, and myself. strolled out in Tallaght, smoking our pipes, in search of recreation;

we'd discuss things, tell each other lies, make up more lies. The local lads called us the Bruno Boys, and several other names. I knew Des from living in Tallaght and, later, he got an apprenticeship in the Juverna Press a couple of years after I did, courtesy of Jack O'Hagan again. Michael I got to know when we moved down to Newtown, because he moved in with his family. One thing we shared was, we didn't have much in common with the other lads of the village. We just gravitated towards each other.

'In those days, small travelling circuses often came to Tallaght and set up their tent in Doyle's field. I was in a front seat, enjoying the show, when I thought the end of the world had come. One of the go-boys at the back of the tent had dug up a strip of sod and flung it at me. He hit the pipe, jerked it out of my mouth, and I thought

---

* Rory: 'A few years ago, I tried to smoke some plug tobacco – a fit of nostalgia – and it nearly blew my lungs asunder.'

the top of my head was gone with it. I turned to where the lads in the back were hysterical laughing, and I believe I offered to fight the lot of them. They kindly refused the offer.

'During our rambles, we hatched a brilliant idea for having some fun at the weekend dances. We'd pretend to be RAF officers, on leave from England. I became Ivor Doyalski, a Polish count, Michael became Lieutenant Montfonstaff, a New Zealander, and Des Sharkey was an Australian. We acquired suitable accents, and a lot of the girls believed us. It never crossed their minds that I, a Polish count, had a tweed suit on me.'

He liked women. 'I rather liked the look of them, the way they were made. And I liked going to dances with them. But I was also very wary of getting into any entanglement. There were also vague warnings being issued by my mother; she was adept at laying down principles: "Mind those ones; they're after your good job." That wasn't bothering me, but the trouble of disengaging, if you got entangled; that worried me.

'The other two lads went a step too far. They hired uniforms from Ging's★ and set off for Sutton Tennis Club. They were very well-received, had a good time and were invited to spend the night at the home of the Club Secretary. They enjoyed their breakfast, and were brought to visit the famous steeplechaser, Caughoo. They were photographed with the Grand National winner, and strolled down to the bus stop at Sutton Cross. The boys in blue were waiting for them in a squad car. They were arrested, very severely questioned, held in custody, and appeared the following Monday before District

---

★ A theatrical costumier.

Justice Reddin. It turned out the Club Secretary was an Army officer, serving in the Intelligence Branch, and that morning he'd noticed that Des was wearing brown shoes with his uniform, and the penny dropped. They were very lucky, because Reddin was a learned liberal gentleman who took a lenient view of their escapade. The matter was serious, since it was forbidden, under the Emergency Powers Act, to wear foreign uniforms in the State. Reddin gave them a lecture and a small fine. But they could have been jailed. I was glad I'd resisted the temptation that time, because I was older than the other two and the outcome could have been different.

'VE Day was a special day in Dublin, because some fool, a student, burnt a tricolour at Trinity College. I was in town that evening. I was coming down Trinity Street, and there were huge crowds and tremendous noise and what I subsequently learnt was that Charlie Haughey★ and a few boys from UCD had come down and set fire to a Union Jack. And a riot started. I saw this senior Garda standing up on a car, and I heard the words, "In accordance with the Riot Act . . ." I said, "I'm getting out of here," and I did. It was just as well, because there were dozens of people flattened by the Guards. Once the Riot Act was read, there was no discretion; if you were in the way, you got belted. The Guards were all worked up.

'I'd heard the news earlier. Someone came into work and said the Germans had surrendered. It wasn't unexpected. We didn't immediately fall into a bed of roses; there were still years of shortages and rationing. I didn't

---

★ A future Taoiseach, and gourmet.

see any newsreels in the following weeks; I didn't go to the pictures in those days.

'I'd got over the first years of apprenticeship, and I was getting a bit older. I was working in town, I had a few bob in my pocket, and my world was getting bigger. Then I entered the College of Art, and I entered into a completely different world.'

Chapter Nine – Ita

'We didn't look on the War as hardship. I suppose we were insulated against it. I'm sure there were awful shortages, but I have no memory of them; so I can't have been too deprived. The kitchen was always heated, because there was a back boiler. There was no coal, but we always had turf. It was usually wet but it seemed to work alright. And the next-door neighbours, the Sullivans – Mr Sullivan was a Guard; he was the sergeant up in Terenure – he used to cut turf* and every load that came back, there was turf put over the back wall for us. People helped each other.

'And, of course, there was the black market. I don't remember ever being short of tea or sugar or butter, or any of those other things that people seemed to be short of. I didn't know how the black market worked, but I do know that bags of sugar and tea managed to come into the house. My stepmother wasn't a great organiser, and she seldom went out the door; I did a fair bit of the shopping, as did Máire. So I think it was the neighbours who managed to get the sugar and tea, and she just paid for them.

'And I remember this awful thing that people still talk

---

* Rory: 'On the matter of the bog-cuttings, the Guards were especially active. They knew all about them, where they were and who was in charge of them. So when the County Council decided to open up the bog-cuttings, the Guards were in like a flash and had the best bits taken.'

about, this brown bread; I remember when it came in
– maybe I'm a bit peculiar, but I thought it was alright.
Denis Hingerty was working up in Belfast, and he'd
come home every now and again, and bring white bread.
And Mrs Hingerty always gave us some of this white
bread, and it was absolutely beautiful – it was better than
cake. But the famous brown bread★ – people complained
that they'd had problems with diarrhoea, but I can't
remember anything bad about it.

'I think the fact that he was drinking black-market
tea went right over my father's head. He handed out
money every week for groceries, and they materialised
in the kitchen; a little pixie could have arrived and
brought them, for all he knew about it.† He knew
nothing about prices. The tea was put in front of him
and he, literally, didn't know where it had come from.
And he loved Irel coffee.‡ He had it every day, after his
dinner.§ But he wouldn't have known where that came
from either. Things were put on the table, and as long
as they were paid for, he was happy. I remember coming
home with a new coat, and saying, "Do you like it,
Daddy?" and his answer: "Does it fit you?" My answer

★ Ita: 'I remember Rory talking about it for ever and a day.'

† Ita: 'Years later, in 1948, I was down in Wexford, on holidays, and my
stepmother had to go into hospital. Gallstones or kidney-stones, I can't
remember – someplace where there shouldn't have been stones. I knew
that my father and Joe were alone in the house, and two more useless men
for housework were never invented, so I decided to go home. When I got
home, there was no sign of any food. They came home from work, so I
said I'd go and get a few things; I said we'd need bread, and my father
took out £1 and said, "Is that enough?" Remember, this was 1948. When
I got married, in 1951, £1.10s was enough to feed the two of us for a
week.'

‡ Ita: 'It came in a bottle, and was made on milk.'

§ Ita: 'Dinner was eaten at about 1 pm, and "tea" was in the evening.'

was, "Yes." "Then it'll do," says he. And toeless shoes – I arrived home with toeless shoes; I thought I was the bee's knees. And he looked, and said: "How very nice. If I went around with the toe out of my boots, they'd be talking about me."

'I didn't really feel anything about the War at all,★ except this awful fear of the glimmer man. You weren't supposed to cook by gas, between the hours of this, that and the other – some time in the evening. But I remember the gas being lit to heat the kettle, and it was all very surreptitiously done; we were put to the front door, on sentry duty, to make sure the glimmer man wasn't coming. He was from the Gas Company, and if you were caught with your gas on, it was fearful – ter-rible retribution, altogether. And, of course, if the gas had been used, you had to be very quick in cooling the ring. Because the glimmer man would come in and put his hand on the ring and, if it was the least bit warm, you were in trouble. Everybody was afraid of this glimmer man but, actually, it turned out – we found out years later – there were only two or three glimmer men for the whole of Dublin.

'I wasn't particularly interested in what was happening. But the News was on every night, on the radio. Radio Eireann. My father would have thought that the BBC was biased. It was on a par with rugby and other for-eign games, so you didn't listen to it. Radio Eireann, though, was like the GAA. We did listen to some English programmes, a few comedy programmes. There was *ITMA* – *It's That Man Again* – he loved that. "Can I do you now, sir?" this charwoman used to say; I think she

★ Ita: 'Remember, I was only fourteen when the War was declared.'

was called Mrs Mop. But, for news, it was Radio Eireann. We talked about the "War", not the "Emergency". And I never heard my father say the Emergency; it was always the War. But he was the kind of man, no matter how strong his opinions, he'd never voice them. He was a very secretive kind of man. If he heard you saying something that he didn't approve of, he'd check you, but he never would have said something like, I side with the Germans or the British. That would be kept to himself, maybe discussed with friends his own age, but he never discussed such things with us.' He worked at the Department of External Affairs but, 'there again, he kept his mouth shut. His brother-in-law, Robert Brennan – my Uncle Bob – was the Ambassador to Washington during the War. And he came home, certainly once, maybe twice. I can remember one occasion, he came with little wooden ornaments, brightly painted, "A Present from Washington" written on them. We thought they were the last word; they were lovely. One was in the shape of a little clog, and one was a clock; I got the clock. I was in Kilmuckridge, and Uncle Bob came down to visit Bessie and Mike. He came down in an army lorry, and, I remember, we went up to the village in the lorry, to Boggin's, the grocery and pub. Walter Boggin, the owner, was a second cousin of my father's. There was great excitement, having a well-known visitor down there, and a Wexford man to boot – that made it better still. I don't know what they spoke about; it really went over my head. I'm sure they were momentous things he was talking about, but I was more interested in sitting in the back of the lorry, and being treated to lemonade and biscuits. He was an extremely polite man; he would never ignore you just because you were a child. He spoke to me, even in the midst of all these adults. Another time he came home, he had his daughter Emer with him. She was a lovely person, very gracious, tall and slim. I still remember her magnificent coat. It was beautiful, tweed, completely lined in fur, real fur. It was absolutely beautiful, and she was so slim – it was gorgeous.

'I remember being down in Wexford, in Kilmuckridge, and my Uncle Mike had the only radio in the district – he was an extremely forward-looking man – and lots of the neighbours used to come at night to hear the news about the War – which always amused me, because I didn't think it had an awful lot of effect on people down in Kilmuckridge. But every night, the kitchen was packed, and all listened intently. There was this old man called Andy Byrne, and he had been a seaman, but he had a farm up the road. He used to come over every night, and I only heard afterwards that he actually had money invested in Australia and his great worry was that

the Japs were going to invade Australia and his money would be gone. Andy smoked a pipe with no shank. Now and again, he'd take the pipe out of his mouth and put it in his dog's mouth. The dog always held the pipe firmly for a minute or two. Andy, and all around, would laugh heartily, and then Andy would retrieve the pipe and put it straight back into his own mouth.★ I also remember, when I was in Kilmuckridge and my father was with me, he went down to the creamery in the village with Uncle Mike. He was standing around, chatting to the men and listening to them, and this one particular man said, "It's going on too long. Why don't they just sit around the table and lay down their specifications?" And my father came back chuckling; it was the greatest cure for a war. I remember, we were at Mass one day and everything was dead silent. And a man was walking up the centre of the church, walking slowly; he was fairly elderly, and his shoes were creaking very badly. I remember looking at my father, and he looked down and said, very quietly: "They'll stop creaking when they're paid for."

'There was one time, my Uncle Bob Brennan was home from Washington – I can't remember whether it was during or after the War – and he took Daddy to Jammett's restaurant for lunch. It was *the* restaurant in Dublin at that time. We were all agog, because none of us had ever darkened the door of Jammett's restaurant, and we never expected to. So, of course, we were all dying to know what the food was like, when he got home. But we were met with a hum and a ha. "Did you get soup?" "Oh yes; I had soup." "And what did you have after that?" He couldn't remember. "It was nice," was all he said. The only thing he remembered, and he spoke about it for years, was when the waiter handed him the bill, Bob glanced at it and paid in dollars. The waiter never batted an eyelid.

'My cousin, Maeve Brennan, was living in Washington, and she bought a yearly subscription to the *Saturday*

★ Ita: 'This had no adverse effect on his health because he died of old age.'

Evening Post for my Aunt Bessie. And Bessie used to keep them all for me. I can remember sitting on the steps, at the barn, and going through the *Saturday Evening Post*; these marvellous, healthy-looking American kids with white teeth, teeth you'd die for. And slip-ons and white socks, and loving parents and beautiful motor cars, with two or three kids sitting in the back, with wide grins on their faces. The best-cared-for kids in the world, and I thought America must be an absolutely marvellous place. And all the stories about the wonderful things that happened in America. And the covers were by Norman Rockwell; they were absolutely wonderful. Between the *Saturday Evening Post* and the people we saw in the films, I thought America was the place to be.*

'I can remember the bombing of the North Strand;† the school was very close to the North Strand. I was at home that night, but I heard it, even though it was a good distance from us. Some of the boarders in school had to be sent home; they were shattered with nerves and they were home for a few weeks. It was very bad. The bomb on the South Circular Road was much nearer. I could hear it very clearly. The South Circular Road, and nearby Clanbrazil Street, were very much Jewish areas at that time. They'd started off there, when they came to Ireland, and, as they started to do a bit better for themselves, a lot of the Jewish people moved out to a place called Rathdown Park, in Terenure, with very nice houses. When the bombs fell on the South Circular

---

* Ita: 'It was only years later that I realised that not everyone in America had lovely white teeth and white socks.'
† 31st of May, 1941; twenty-seven people were killed.

Road, many of the people were convinced that the Germans knew that the Jews lived there, so anyone with relatives in Rathdown Park moved there. And, lo and behold, didn't a bomb drop on Rathdown Park and, God help them, they were convinced they were being followed. That bomb would have been very close to us, but I can't remember ever thinking or worrying that we were going to be invaded. And, of course, we'd see the newsreels in the cinema, all made from the British perspective; they were our nearest neighbours and they were winning the War – so what problems could we have? From the newsreels, the British were winning hands-down, and when the Americans joined in, sure, between them, Hitler was going to end up in Kingdom Come. We believed that – I did, anyway. I believed that we were quite safe. I slept at night.

'We had blackout curtains; actually, they were blinds. They were roller blinds, black on one side, canvas on the other, not as heavy as tarpaulin, but like it. And there were ration books, for tea, sugar, butter and clothing. They were little booklets, for all the world like ticket books. No matter where you went, you had to have your ration books.* I remember, it was a very big bonus for the men who worked on my uncle's farm: Aunt Bessie never took their ration books. They were what

---

* Ita: 'I only discovered last week [January 2001] that ration books for sugar and tea were introduced in 1942; both myself and Rory had the idea that they were brought in earlier. It goes to show you how wrong your memory can be. I found this out when I was given a photocopy of a page of the *Irish Times*, dated Tuesday, June 16, 1942; there was a photograph of Maeve Brennan on it. She was working as a librarian in the National Catholic School for Social Services, in Washington D.C. Right underneath the photograph, there was an article about the introduction of the coupons, and another article about three warships sunk by Italian planes.'

was called "dieted"; they came to work before breakfast and left after supper – they were fed, as part of their payment. On other farms, they had to hand over their ration books, but my Uncle Mike knew the right people, and there was a big chest of tea upstairs, on the landing. I remember it, a big box, lined with silver paper, a strong foil, and it lasted the whole of the War. And Bessie was a very generous person; if she heard of someone being short of tea, they'd get tea out of the chest. Mike had served his time in the grocery trade,★ in a shop in Wexford. So, while he'd left the shop years previously, he'd continued contact with them. He still knew people who owned shops, all very straight, good men, and they all managed to get black-market tea. And he also had a big sack of sugar, up on the landing. It was easily reached; it was just up there for storage – it wasn't hidden. Certain things were short, and you'd never see bananas or oranges, or anything like that. We'd always had fruit when we were small children, in what we used to call the good old days.'†

'I was aware that I was growing up, but things didn't change that much for me. There was no such thing as teenagers, so it was up to yourself how you got on between the ages of thirteen and twenty. We grew up a lot slower; we were, I suppose, more innocent. We were quite well on in our teens and still playing with dolls. You had a coat and you might be fortunate enough to get another before the first one fell off, so then you had a good coat and an everyday coat – but there was no

---

★ Ita: 'My father used to call them "counter hoppers". There was a lot more to the job than hopping counters, but he spoke about counter hoppers.'
† Also referred to as the B.M. days – Before Mum.

such thing as the latest trend. But I do remember, when I was young and clothes were bought for me, and later, when I was working and bought my own clothes, if any of my friends bought, say, a red coat, there was no way in the world I'd be seen in a red coat. Or, if they bought a green coat, there was no way I'd be seen in a green coat. So, in a way, while young people might be much more independent today, to me they're more like sheep – I don't mean that in a derogatory sense, but they do copy each other, whereas we tried to be more distinctive. We had our own styles, and while the hairstyles might have been more or less the same – such as a wretched-looking thing called 'the shingle'★ – we tried to make it our own style.

'There was one great hairstyle, when I was younger – the imitation of Shirley Temple, a mass of little ringlets all over the head. My friend Noeleen actually looked like Shirley Temple and had beautiful curly hair; her mother used to do it. People remarked on how like Shirley Temple she was. But then they had a Shirley Temple look-alike competition in the *Herald*; there were rows of photographs of girls every night – they all had the hair in curls but very few of them looked like Shirley Temple. Noeleen didn't enter; her mother had more sense. One girl arrived into school with the Shirley Temple perm – she'd had very straight hair. Oh, consternation – the nuns didn't like it one bit. Terrible show of pride; so the mother was sent for, and she arrived in the next day with the hair all frizzy, because

★ Ita: 'It was straight at the sides and bare at the back – like a boy's behind. Having read in the paper that brushing your hair made it grow, Máire brushed her shingled head for hours. It didn't accelerate growth; it just made her head terribly sore.'

it had been permed, but no longer quite like Shirley Temple's.

'I have a photograph of myself in my school uniform, and my hair was fair and I had a clip holding it back on one side. I always wanted to grow it long but it was never thick enough. It would grow so far, and you could see daylight through it, so it was better a bit short. Then

there was a style where you let it grow a bit and then turned it in. That was the style for my last few years in school; I can't remember what we called it. I put in rollers at night in the hope that I could turn my hair in, in a thick roll around my head. Again, that style was good for people with thick hair; it used to bounce – it was gorgeous. Mine wasn't quite there; it held fairly well, but nothing like the girls with the thick hair. I always had a bit of a curl in it. It had the same texture as my father's.

'Mother Enda taught us Irish in my last years at school. She was known as the Bull. When things didn't go her way, she'd just sit at the top of the class and you knew when she was going to roar, because the red would start from the bottom of her neck and spread slowly up to her face and when it hit her temple, she'd roar. So the name suited her. But she was harmless; she was actually quite nice and pleasant. The rumour was that she had been the girlfriend of Patrick Pearse, and that was why she'd taken the religious name of Mother Enda.★ But, checking the dates, there was no way she was Patrick Pearse's girlfriend, or, if she was, there must have been something wrong with his eyesight, because she was no beauty. There was a Mother Madeleine; she taught us English. She was lovely – she was tall and slim and very gentle. We had a Miss Fitzpatrick, for French. She was a very pretty woman, blonde, but she was very stern. She lived in Terenure, but I didn't take to her. And there was a Miss Tierney, who used to teach us, I suppose you'd call it gym – exercises with skipping ropes and all that kind of thing. She was good, she was fine, she was mannish in her way, which, I suppose, was called for. There wasn't much to it. I was a good skipper, and I had a top-grade skipping rope, with ball bearings in it. We had teams of skippers, and we had a Parents' Day, once a year. And dumbbells; it was very strenuous – you put your arms to the front and back, and to the side. That was about the whole of it. You just kept it up for about five minutes, in unison, of course; there was no grace to it. Then, of course, we marched to music and did a few formations – Irish marches. It was nothing very professional but we thought it was great. We wore a gym dress and a white blouse. When we were small, ankle socks; when we were older, long woollen stockings.

★ Pearse founded St Enda's school in 1908.

There was no display of knickers or bare bottoms; we were well-covered-up. Those black woollen stockings were the bane of my existence. I hated them. They were warm, but you had to wear them until school ended in June, and the itch of them in the summer was dreadful. And, every now and again, I'd get a hole in them. They had to be darned, and I had to do the darning myself, so I kept putting it off. If the hole was small, it didn't show if you put ink on your leg, under the hole; you just made sure the ink was fairly well-spread. That was great, until you had a bath and had to wash the ink off, or there were so many holes that you had to darn them. Then lisle stockings came in. They were pure cotton, more refined than the woollen stockings, and they kept their shape. And, once they were black, you were allowed to wear lisle stockings; they were much finer, much more comfortable, cool and smooth on the leg, and they didn't tear as quickly. But they were more expensive, so you had to wait your turn to get them.

'I left school in June 1943, after I did my Leaving Cert. I was eighteen. I've a vague memory of the last day. We all brought in cakes, or sweets, or lemonade. We had our party, and the nuns came in and we treated them to cakes. I remember saying goodbye to my own close friends, promising we'd see each other again.* But most of them lived on the northside and I lived on the southside, so there was that big distance between us. Some went to college, some went into nursing, a lot of them became nuns, some served their time in the

---

* Ita: 'Some of them I only met again after fifty years, at a reunion. I was very pleased, because everyone knew me. I didn't know everybody, but when I looked hard enough, I could see the younger face behind the older face.'

drapery business.★ Sometimes I'd read about somebody in the paper: she'd qualified for this or that, or a wedding announcement, and the writer Val Mulkerns[†] was in my class, and I'd read about her now and again. But that was it.

'When Joe left school, my father was keen that he go to university; he certainly was bright enough. But he went off one day and joined the Army. He just went off and we didn't know where he'd gone, and he arrived back in an Army uniform. He wasn't a tall man, and I thought he'd never lift those boots, but he did. He sat the cadetship exams and passed, with flying colours. But he was an inch too short, and he didn't get the cadetship. He was told that they might relax the height rule later, so he sat the exam again, and he got it again, but he hadn't grown any – and that was it. But he seemed to be very happy. He certainly made a lot of friends. And, of course, he was out of the house, which suited him down to the ground, because he was away from our stepmother. He came home every week and he'd be polishing his buttons and his boots. I still remember the oxblood polish for the boots.[‡] I think he was in Portobello Barracks. He was a private at first, and I don't think he rose much higher than that. He was in the Commandos, a wireless operator. He was in the Army right through the War, and it was only afterwards that I

★ Ita: 'You had to pay a fee – you paid the shop a fee and you served your time.'

† Val Mulkerns: born 1925 in Dublin; books include *A Peacock's Cry* (1954); *A Friend of Don Juan* (1979); *The Summerhouse* (1984); *Very Like a Whale* (1986).

‡ Ita: 'He took after my father in the boot-polishing. Boot-polishing was the only domestic chore that my father ever did.'

heard about some of the hardships. There was one story; they were camped somewhere, and the camp was flooded out and they slept on sodden mattresses, which can't have helped his arthritis in later years – but he'd have been the last man to blame the War for anything. He was quite happy. When he left, after the War, he got a commendation. I still have it, and it ends, "Bolger was always clean and neat in his habits." I thought it was the funniest thing. It's there, typed out: "Bolger was always clean and neat in his habits."

'Máire left school before me. She was going to do a commercial course; I think she might even have started, but she'd sat the Civil Service examination, and she was called. There was keen competition for jobs in the Civil Service; they used to print the names of the successful candidates in the papers, the first hundred out of, literally, thousands. So, she was delighted. She worked in Dublin Castle, for the Department of Industry and Commerce. The offices were pretty miserable, badly heated. But you had a job, you had your money at the end of the week; she seemed to be very happy. And that was where she met her husband.

'He was Eunan James Peoples and he came from what his mother used to call "the cathedral town of Letterkenny".* When he arrived up to Dublin first, people used to called him Onion or Union, and everything else except Eunan, so he just said, "Call me Jimmy." So, from that on, he was known as Jimmy. He was a lovely man, very good company, very witty, and very talented. He knew Greek and Latin. If you asked him about flowers, he knew all the Latin names, the ones in brackets.

---

* In County Donegal.

He was really a very bright man. He played the guitar, and sang all the songs of the day. And he acted. He was in a drama group with the Civil Service; we used to go to see him. He was very good.

'Máire was only twenty-two★ when she got married, and Jimmy was about sixteen years older. He already had a house in Harold's Cross,† which I know he bought for £600. The wedding was very early in the morning, in St Joseph's church, in Terenure. I was the bridesmaid. White weddings were rare, particularly during the War when material was scarce. Máire had a green-coloured frock; it was lovely. Some of the girls in the office where she worked gave her some of their clothes coupons, and various other friends gave her some too. I had a kind of a pink dress, off the hanger. I was quite plump at that time – a thing I hadn't been before or since – but, I suppose it was my age. I thought the dress was beautiful but I think it exaggerated my size. It was very early in the morning because there was only one train a day to Galway, where they were to spend their honeymoon. So the reception was held in a hotel opposite Westland Row Station, so they could dash across and get the train; I think it was called the Grosvenor Hotel. It was a nice reception but it finished very early; the whole thing was over by ten o'clock in the morning.'

After leaving school, she went to a commercial college. 'I can't remember whether it was spelt "Skerry's" or

★ Ita: 'If a woman worked a certain amount of years in the Civil Service, she got a lump sum when she left. Because there was a marriage bar; a woman had to leave the Service when she married. But Máire wasn't there long enough; she got no lump sum.'
† Suburb of Dublin, about three miles south of the city centre.

"Skerries", but it was on Stephen's Green, a few doors down from the Department of External Affairs, where my father worked. The building has since been knocked down. I don't know why that particular college was chosen, but my father had decided that I should do a commercial course, and I was quite happy to do it; it never crossed my mind to look for anything else. And I was to sit the Civil Service exams. That was always the aim in our house, the Civil Service – permanent and pensionable was very acceptable. But I never did sit the exams. At the college, we did shorthand, typing, book-keeping, English and maths. I remember, there was a Miss Warren in the office; she was a very distant person. And there was a Mr Hammill in charge – he was very nice – and various teachers for the different subjects. I took to it straight away, although the maths was always a mystery to me. But I was very quick with the short-hand, and I took to the typing and got the speed up very quickly. I quite enjoyed it, and I liked the place itself. We had to do an essay every week, and I was happy doing them and always got good marks. I tried to make them humorous and they were often read out in class. I was exactly a year there.

'Jobs were very scarce then; this was in 1944. But there was a phone call to the college from the Pathology Department in UCD★ which was just around the corner, on Earlsfort Terrace. They asked if the college had someone who had the Leaving Cert and was good at English. I was sent around, and I was interviewed by Professor O'Kelly and Professor O'Farrell. I did a little test – shorthand and typing; there was a Miss O'Toole

---

★ University College Dublin.

in charge, a very efficient woman. I got the job. I was to start at twenty-five shillings a week, which was good, because lot of girls started at fifteen shillings a week. I was over the moon.

'I remember going in the first day, and I was first there; nobody else had arrived. I sat there, waiting, and the first to come in was a girl called Chris Lynch; she was from Cavan. We became great friends. It was Chris who showed me what to do. I thought, because they'd asked for someone who was good at English, that I'd be doing some writing. And I also thought that I'd be doing lots of shorthand. But, from the first day, my ability at English didn't seem to be that important and I never did one stroke of shorthand. But I did do the books – I kept the day-book, and I also did a fair bit of typing.

'The Pathology Department was run by Professor O'Farrell and Professor O'Kelly; T.T. O'Farrell – I think it was Thomas Theodore – and W.D. O'Kelly. I got on with both of them. T.T. was a pure gentleman, although I never called him T.T. – he was Professor O'Farrell. But he was a thorough gentleman. He was a big man and he shuffled along; someone told me he had gout. The other man I also liked very much, but some people weren't all that keen on him. He was a bit sharper in his attitude. I remember, one day, a woman said to him, "Excuse me, Professor, have you got the time?" and he said, "Yes, but I haven't got the inclination."

'I bought lavender soap with my first week's pay. The money was in an envelope; the tax was stopped. I think it was called lavender oatmeal soap; you could see the little pieces of oatmeal in it. It was supposed to be good for the complexion; I can't say it helped with the lines, but it did its best. But it had this beautiful lavender perfume; it was really lovely.

'There were so many different types of soap. The lowest form was a black soap known as "dirt shifter". It was used for scrubbing doorsteps – people really did scrub doorsteps in those days. A lot of the doorsteps were made of granite, including ours, and they really benefited from a good scrubbing because the mica in the granite really shone. Then there was Sunlight. You got a box with two big hunks of Sunlight, stuck together; you needed a knife to cut them apart. Sunlight was used for washing clothes, and everything else; it was a yellow colour. There'd be one of the Sunlight blocks in the bathroom. Then, a step up from Sunlight was toilet soap, Lifebuoy or Palmolive, but it wouldn't have been used on a regular basis. Palmolive was gorgeous; it was a green soap, and it was wrapped in a green crinkly paper – I can still see it – with a gold and black band.

'The second thing I bought was a navy-blue blouse, with white spots. It was linen, and I bought it in Bergin's drapery shop, in Terenure. I think it was five shillings. And I bought a new bike, on the never-never. I got it in a shop in Rathmines; I can't remember the name. I paid for it every Friday. I'd cycle back from work, and pay them whatever I owed. I was always prompt with the payments; I never missed. It was a smashing bike. I'd been using Máire's old bike, but I'd wanted one of my own. I was earning my own money and I wanted something I'd bought myself. I wanted a better bike. It was state-of-the-art, with three speeds – this was really high-tech. It was maroon-coloured and it glided along; it was marvellous. It had a basket at the front and a carrier at the back. I used to cycle to work and home for dinner, and cycle back in; the bus fares and lunches would have eaten away at the twenty-five shillings. I went everywhere on it.

'I remember when I heard about the end of the War. I was standing, waiting for a bus on Harcourt Street – I mustn't have cycled that day – and I heard someone say the War was over. There was great excitement, but nothing like in England. I remember having the radio on that night, the BBC, and hearing the cheers. I was nearly sorry we hadn't suffered bombing the way they had, so we could rejoice in the same way. And then, after, there were the newsreels and those awful scenes of the prison camps. I couldn't look at them. I used to close my eyes. In a way, it was cowardly, but I used to say, "At this stage there's nothing I can do about it, so why have nightmares?" But it was dreadful. It was shocking – nobody could believe it, what had been happening.

'My friend Noeleen was a few years younger than me but she'd left school after the Inter, when she was sixteen, so she was working and we both had our few bob. We used to go to the pictures. We went in for the romances; I can't remember any one specific film, we went to so many of them. And then we started going to various hops – dances. And there was a girl working in UCD; I've forgotten her name, but we were quite friendly. She was a member of the Dublin Musical Society, and she asked me if I'd like to join. I thought it was a good idea, because it was a way of meeting people; it's a kind of crossroads in life when you leave school and you're on your own. So I joined. I was able to sing a bit; I was fine for the chorus. We performed *Rose Marie* in the Gaiety. I had three or four chorus parts. It was great fun.

'I remember, this one time, myself and Noeleen went to the pictures in the Carlton. There was a restaurant upstairs, and we often went to have tea and a cake after the pictures, so up we went and ordered our tea and cakes. They usually put a plate of cakes in front of you and you took your pick, and they knew by the number left on the plate how many you'd had. But we were sitting there, chatting, and this man came in, and he was French. He spoke little bits of French in between his English, and we had our schoolgirls' French, so we knew what it was. He ordered coffee, or tea, and cakes. So he had his cake on his plate and, to our huge amazement, he asked the waitress for a fork, and he sat eating his cake with a fork. At that time it was unheard-of. We thought we'd never get out, to fall around laughing at the idea of a man eating cake with a fork.

Chapter Ten – Rory

'When I got to the stage where I could save some of my earnings – that would have been towards the end of my apprenticeship – I began to feel that I wanted to buy clothes for myself. Because my mother bought clothes for everybody, for herself, my father, brothers and sisters. I wanted my own independence. So I looked around at the kind of clothes I liked, and I saw some people wearing Donegal tweed. I liked the look of it, so I went to Kevin and Howlin's, on Nassau Street, and I paid £10 for a handmade suit in Donegal tweed; that was cash money, almost two weeks' wages. I felt great in it, and my mother was delighted with it. It hung on me OK. People who didn't know me may have thought

I was somebody important or eccentric, or one of those Gaelic League people who went around talking Irish out loud. I wasn't talking Irish out loud but I was going around in this lovely suit, and enjoying myself. Then I wanted a hat with a wide brim. That, I suppose, was the artistic look; artists wore wide-brimmed hats, and that was what I was looking for. I never found out where Seán O'Sullivan* or Seán Keating† got their wide-brimmed black hats. But I knew I could get a lovely green velour hat in Kingston's,‡ and I paid £3 for it. I was caught out in a dreadful rain shower and the green dye from the hat ran down my face. So I went back to Kingston's to complain, and the fellow said, "Actually, with that hat, one should carry an umbrella to protect it from the rain." I told him I'd bought the hat to protect my head from the rain, and so I succeeded in having the hat changed for another one.

'When I started the apprenticeship, I went to the school of printing, at Bolton Street College of Technology, a half-day, every day, for two years. And the following two years I went to night classes, twice a week. The third year was book work, how to design and assemble books, and then, in the fourth year, general display and jobbing.§ I was always interested in the display aspect of print, and thought I'd like to develop my knowledge and skills. So I went, first of all, to Rathmines, the technical college there, and found that it was more geared towards advertising agency work. And I discovered, after general conversations with other students,

* Seán O'Sullivan (1906–64): born in Dublin; portrait-painter and illustrator; examples of work: Ulster Museum, Belfast; Abbey Theatre, Dublin; National Gallery of Ireland, Dublin; British Museum, London.
† Seán Keating (1889–1977): born in Limerick; portrait- and figure-painter; examples of work: Musée Moderne, Brussels; Hugh Lane Municipal Gallery of Modern Art, Dublin; National Gallery of Ireland, Dublin.
‡ Men's clothing shop, on O'Connell Street. Ita: 'There was an ad, a man in top hat and shirt, only, and the slogan: "A Kingston Shirt Makes All the Difference."'
§ Rory: 'Raffle tickets, dance tickets, legal forms, anything that you can imagine in the way of printing that wasn't book work. "Jobbing" was the generic term given to this kind of work.'

that the advertising agencies offered a whole lot of jobs; nice jobs to go to, you were honoured to work for them, but they didn't pay you much. Unless you owned the place, you got paid buttons, but you felt good. So I said to myself, "That's no good for me," as I was earning a good wage as a compositor, and I decided that I might learn more in the National College of Art. So I went there the following year. I originally went to learn design – that's what I signed up for – but there was this Dutch professor who had a habit of imposing his ideas on the students. Everybody ended up with the same-looking poster, or that sort of thing. That wasn't what I really wanted, so I changed my mind and decided to go to drawing school.

'I discovered that I liked the pure art aspect, and I forgot about commercial design. I could do design work but I became much more interested in the aesthetics of art. You couldn't make a living; it seemed that most of the best contemporary artists had to teach to survive. But it was much more attractive to me. And, of course, there was the wonderful world of the galleries. At that time, the drawings and etchings of the masters, Rembrandt and Orpen and O'Sullivan, were on display in the National Gallery, and I loved them. I learned about perspective, and then went and did a lot of drawing in what was known as "the antique", that is, drawings of plaster casts of classical figures and heads. Then I was promoted, to go to life class. It was a great achievement, the idea of drawing real naked women. When I told people, they got quite excited. In fact, it was an artistic thing; one never thought of it in terms of being sexual. It was just the art. But I think my friends thought I was just a dirty old man, in a privileged position.' He doesn't remember any of the models. 'They came and they went. But there's one man I remember, a German, a fighter pilot who'd been a prisoner of war in the Curragh camp. I think his name was Heinz Grau – that's the name in my memory. He attended the College but, now and again, he sat as a model. He was a rather arrogant man. We didn't know much about Nazis or their attitudes because we'd been sheltered from it, but it was only after the War ended, and in the years after, when I was looking at films, I began to see him as the quintessential Nazi. He had it in his very expression, manners and behaviour. He'd go about taking up your space in the drawing room, as if it was his, and, once or twice I had to remind him to take a walk or to move aside, because he was standing in the way. He's the only one of the models I can really remember, because I still have a pencil drawing of him.

'I went to the College of Art in the evenings. I started going twice a week during the first year, and I ended up going five times a week. I had a ball. I got involved in the students' society as well, and actually got to editing a students' magazine called the *Garret*. It was short-lived; everybody read it, but few bought it. We also spent weekends sketching, in places like Powerscourt and the zoo. And we went to all sorts of peculiar places, for parties. There were many places around Leeson Street; some of the students had digs there. I went to one party, and I brought along something in a brown paper bag. The room was three flights up, and we thought we'd open a window; there was a terrible smell in there. One of my friends opened the window, and the next thing we saw was a drop of three storeys – it was a door that opened to a drop. It may originally have been some kind of warehouse. But it was only the grace of God that stopped one of us from falling out. After all that, the parties and the dances, I'd get my bicycle and go home, find my dinner that my mother had left in the oven, eat the dinner, go to bed, and be up to go to work in the morning. It was a great life.

'I had my first bottle of stout in McDaid's. It didn't taste good but everybody else looked like they'd been drinking it all their lives, and I wasn't going to be any different. So I stuck it out; it took me about an hour and a half. After three bottles of stout you'd be ready to sing, fight, or have a deep philosophical conversation  with neither beginning nor end. I'd gone with Dick McGuirk and Jack Gleeson, from the College of Art, and a couple of other characters. We decided we'd get adventurous and we went down to McDaid's, which was frequented by many artistic types. There were four of us at the College of Art who, generally, worked and partied together, or went to dances. I'd already known Dick McGuirk from secondary school; he was an accomplished water-colourist. There was Des O'Sullivan, a laconic type who, somehow, was always up to speed with the news and gossip of the art world. Kevin Borbridge was the fourth man; he was always in need of fixing up with a girl for the dances.

'We drank bottles of stout. There were very clear distinctions about what was drunk. There was stout, which was in bottles. It was Guinness, but every pub had its own labels; it was bottled down in the cellars. When you were in the pub, you called for a bottle of stout. You could also call for a pint, but that was porter. Working-class men drank pints. The porter was also Guinness, but was a brownish colour, more brown than the black Guinness stout. So, a "pint" was a pint of porter. I never drank one. I drank bottles of stout. Occasionally, you'd go wild and ask for "a small one", a small whiskey; that was when you were feeling good. A lot of regular drinkers would call for a bottle of stout and a chaser – a small whiskey. Pints were rarely drunk. There were, however, a few clients who asked for a "half and half", a mixture of stout and porter.

'About the time of the polio epidemic – it must have been in the early 50s – the iron lung was introduced, to save people's lives. This apparatus helped to control muscular movement and breathing. It was, literally, a miracle machine. At that time, Guinness introduced the big aluminium pressure kegs, to replace the traditional barrels. The drinking fraternity discovered that there was a consistency to the drink from the new barrel, so they'd say they wanted a pint "from the lung". That's when the universal drinking of pints of stout started.

'One particular night we went into McDaid's and we were into our second bottle, and someone said, "There's Behan coming in the door," and we all just left our drinks and went out the other door. When Brendan Behan walked into a pub, contrary to what everybody is writing now, as many people as possible drifted out, because he could be the most obnoxious individual – a dreadful personality. He'd insult everyone in sight, and demand that you buy him drink – and then pass remarks about your sisters and mother. I find it very amusing, and difficult to take seriously, all these famous people talking about the Brendan Behan they loved. He had no friends in my young days. I think he only got friends when he'd earned a lot of money. Naturally, he got friends then, but he was a dreadful nuisance and a bowsie.'

'I started my apprenticeship at eight o'clock on the 8th of July, 1940, and it ended seven years later, 1947. I was now on full pay; I'd a pocket full of money. I got slightly silly drunk with a lot of my friends, celebrating. I came back down to earth the following week when I discovered that a lot of people had been hanging around, waiting for me after my seven years in Purgatory, and their hands out in all directions. The Revenue Commissioners took a greater interest in the few bob. My mother thought I was earning a fortune now, and demanded that I make a bigger contribution, because she had a house full of younger ones who had to be looked after. I thought they were already well-looked-after but, however, I increased my contribution. At one stage, after two or three weeks as a journeyman, I was contemplating going to Australia.★ However, I settled down to life as it was.

'I stayed on at Juverna Press for a year or so. But I was beginning to get restless because I'd been there seven

---

★ Rory: 'A journeyman was free to move, after being bound for seven years as an apprentice. The term "journeyman" was used across many other trades. It meant that, when you finished your apprenticeship, you were let go and you then roamed from one place to another, picking up jobs and experience. Eventually, with all that experience, you might return to your home town and get a job back home. A lot of Irish journeyman headed for Dublin, where there was a better chance of a job.'

years and, as well as that, I'd been regularly promised that I was going to be flung out when I'd finished my apprenticeship; there was no doubt that I was going to get the boot. That was the usual fate of apprentices; you got your walking papers and became a journeyman, and there were seldom jobs to be had in Dublin. It was a bit of a worry, there in the back of my mind. But here I was in 1947, and into 1948, and there was a scarcity of craftsmen, business was beginning to pick up, and there was no sign of anyone wanting to deprive me of a livelihood. So I started looking around. I discovered that the best-paid jobs were in the newspapers. But you had to get into a newspaper first, and that wasn't easy. You had to take the chance of applying for summer work. The papers had such huge staffs that, during the holiday season, there were always vacancies which were filled by casual labour. You took a chance of being appointed to a permanent job. So I took the great gamble and applied to the *Irish Independent*. I was interviewed by the works manager, an Englishman called Bell. To my surprise, I got a job almost straight away; I got a telephone call, at Juverna Press. Then I gave in my notice and all hell broke loose.

'Jacko, my uncle, was out sick,* and the manager, Hennebery, went wild when I gave in my notice. He didn't want to lose me; I'm not boasting, but I was a good, skilled worker and good men were now scarce. Hennebery pointed out how good the firm had been to me. All I could think of was the hardship and tormenting I'd endured all that time; I didn't hold it against them but I wasn't going to gratify them either. He then said

---

* Rory: 'It turned out to be the end of his career.'

that I'd get an additional half-a-crown over the rate, if I stayed. I gently reminded him that he'd promised to fire me at least a dozen times, when I had completed my apprenticeship. The poor man, a fundamentally decent sort, couldn't understand how and why I could be so ungrateful. He danced around the place and was nearly crying at the idea that I was going to leave them in the lurch. But I did.

'So I went to work for the *Independent*, to a totally different world. There was no yesterday, no tomorrow, only today – now. When you commenced in the paper each day, there was hardly a sound. The odd metallic sound, if somebody dropped something, but everything was quiet. But then, very gradually, the tempo began to rise. People would arrive, editors, journalists, advertising clerks. They'd whisper something to the stone man,⋆ who was busy assembling the pages. And then the bits of paper began to fly out from the overseer's little office; each story was cut up into small takes.† The linotype operators, when available, would walk up to the overseer; they were handed a piece of the story, and the noise would increase, especially after 9 pm. The linotype hall was an absolute bedlam of clanking machine parts. And the stink of metals, all beautiful – you were part of it. Then everybody would be shouting at everyone, as you came near to printing time; an enormous

---

⋆ Rory: 'The stone was a flat steel table where the type pages were assembled. The name derives from the fact that, originally, they were slate or stone. The stone man was the page assembler.'

† Rory: 'A take was the name for a linotype operator's share of the story. Essentially, a story was cut into small pieces of copy that would produce about two inches of type matter; a long story would be assembled from a number of operators.'

amount of din that kept increasing. Certain pages were sent away to be processed by the stereotypers, into big metal plates that were fitted on to the printing press. But the main, important pages, like the news and the sports, were held back until the very last minute. Journalists dashed hither and yon. In the clamour, men exchanged the vilest of insults and forgot about them until the next time they'd had a few jars. And then the editor, in all his majesty, would appear and he would make a pronouncement about closing the edition. The din and the shouting and the roaring gradually ceased, but it happened every day. And you never discussed yesterday's paper, unless you'd made an awful mistake and there was an inquiry. And tomorrow's paper – that was non-existent.

'In terms of mistakes, the only things that were absolutely sacrosanct were the births, deaths and marriage columns. These were so important that there was a standing rule of the house that, if you made a mistake or passed a mistake, you were sacked on the spot. And the union concurred with that.

'I worked with Mick Molloy, the man who set the type for the Proclamation of Independence in 1916, and Charlie Bevin, another 1916 man, who was interned in Lewes Jail, and Paddy McKee, brother of Dick McKee, who was murdered by the British in Dublin Castle on Bloody Sunday.* There were also British Army veterans who'd fought in the Boer War and the Great War, and veterans of the Civil War. But these matters never

---

* 21st of November, 1920: the IRA killed eleven British intelligence officers; later that day, the Black and Tans fired into a crowd of football spectators, at Croke Park, killing twelve.

intruded into the workplace, and were never referred to. There was a strange civility among the men; there was never any unpleasantness and I wasn't aware of any undercurrent and, actually, I was only made aware of the situation later, by an older friend of mine. There was an unwritten rule that you didn't draw on certain subjects; religion was never discussed. You'd be told that somebody was a Protestant, but just for your information, so you wouldn't say anything derogatory about another religion and cause offence. Politics wasn't discussed, as it was a subject that was likely to cause rows. Football was discussed, a lot, especially English soccer, and sex.* But the overriding moral force was the strength of the companionship – the chapel.† No outside influence was allowed to intrude.

'I made a couple of close friends, Nick McGrath and Stephen Judge, and we'd have a different kind of conversation; we'd talk about how we'd change the world. Nick was particularly interested in socialist politics, with the result that he was labelled a Communist. But I liked him. He was older than me. Stephen was an older man too; he had eight or nine kids. He had a great store of information, because he'd been all around Dublin in lots of different jobs. He was very good-humoured. We were quite good friends. It wasn't fighting politics we

---

* Rory: 'In all its explicit glory. But, in school, sexual matters were never discussed or mentioned, except in very vague terms. At Christian Doctrine class, the good brothers warned of the dangers to one's health of participating in certain sinful practices. Nothing specific was mentioned, but it was hinted that one's eyesight could suffer. My classmates must have heeded the advice, because I was the only boy in the class who needed spectacles.'

† Rory: 'The chapel was the union branch, or brotherhood. The father of the chapel was the head of the local union.'

talked, more union matters, because of the fact that we lived and worked in that atmosphere all day or night. We were immersed in printing and with printing people – the functions of the job, whether they were being overstepped – young, over-enthusiastic journalists lifting linotype slugs, doing what they shouldn't have been doing – or being restricted; all of these matters were given deep consideration. I also made a lot of money, very good wages. After about six months, when the summer season was coming to an end, I was formally told by Tom Hopper, the overseer, "Mister D, you have been appointed to the staff." So I asked Nick what exactly being appointed to the staff meant, and he said, "You get a fortnight's fuckin' notice, the same as the rest of us."'

'I became involved in Fianna Fáil because I was born into Fianna Fáil. I never joined; I was born into it. I never joined, and I never left.★ My father was one of the Republicans who followed de Valera when he founded Fianna Fáil in 1926. I remember Fianna Fáil as a very small child; I remember working in that famous election when we made the McEntee paste for the posters. Then the *Irish Press* arrived, and that reinforced it. A marvellous paper it was; it was a good literary paper as well as displaying a republican side of politics. And it made balanced papers of the *Irish Independent* and the *Irish Times*, who'd never given any reporting of republican matters before

★ Rory: 'I have never been a card-carrying member. People talk about "card-carrying", but any genuine Fianna Fáil person is not a card-carrying member. Now and again, they introduce cards and send them around. But anyone who belongs to Fianna Fáil, just look at them; they don't need a card – they are who they are.'

the founding of the *Irish Press*.★ Then de Valera came to power and said, "Don't give the British any land annuities." And this was great; this was really fighting talk. He did things like that – a land war, which made us feel that we were big enough and gave us a sense of national pride. It cost money but we really didn't have much to lose, and it gave us that sense of pride that sustained us. That is his great legacy. There was no great material gain but, then, nobody had anything – the whole world was in recession. The 30s were bad years for most people. So all you had was your pride. And Fianna Fáil was a socialist party, in the real sense; the aim was to help the poorest in the country.

'After that famous election, when we made the paste, I had very little hand or act or part in any elections, until the election held during the War.† I became involved in canvassing and putting up posters, and suchlike. We were nearly always at the wrong end of election results in County Dublin. You could nearly write down on the register who was going to be voting for whom, and get it right to within the two or three people who might have been telling lies. There were a lot of Unionist-types and old Blueshirts in our area. We were fighting a losing battle, but we kept going. And one of our greatest antagonists, Liam Cosgrave,‡ came along and swept up most of the votes. He caused us great annoyance, he was so popular.

★ In a poll on the *Irish Times* website, in December 1999, readers were asked to choose the worst event of the twentieth century. The foundation of Fianna Fáil came second, after the Holocaust.
† June 1943.
‡ Son of William Cosgrave (b.1920); TD, 1943–81 for Fine Gael; Taoiseach, 1973–7.

'During 1948, I was secretary of the Tallaght cumann★ of Fianna Fáil. I went to the Árd Fheis,† I represented the cumann at constituency meetings, and, as secretary, I organised everything. I carried out all that, and went to the College of Art, and worked, and did all sorts of other things. It's amazing what one could do in those days. I actually attended several Árd Fheiseanna in the Mansion House, presided over by Eamon de Valera. My abiding memory is of the large numbers of tough-looking country men, wearing big rough overcoats, smelling of damp and farm life. They invariably had their breakfasts, dinners and teas in their overcoat pockets. I remember one particular Sunday, when de Valera was winding up the proceedings. These thousands of country men listened with rapt attention as Dev described for them, in great detail, a method for sewing a *fáinne*‡ on the lapels of their coats. Said he, "Let ye get an indelible pencil and put the cap of your fountain pen on the lapel of your coat and draw a circle. Now get the little woman, with a needle and darning wool, to sew a circle over the pencil mark. Everybody will then know that you have an interest in the Irish language and you won't have the expense of buying the silver *fáinne*." Poor old Dev, he was an innocent. He'd be astonished to discover what his "little women" get up to these days. And so would most of his Mansion House audience.'

The College of Art friends decided that they needed a studio, 'for our artistic advancement. But, finally, Kevin

---

★ Branch.
† Annual Conference.
‡ A ring, silver, worn on the lapel; the mark of someone who was prepared to speak Irish.

and myself decided to take the plunge and we went in search of a suitable place. We were told that a room was available in a house at the end of Nassau Street, just at the beginning of Clare Street. The house front was set back from the street, and it had a peculiar overhanging balcony-type window. We arrived at the door and knocked, and knocked. Kevin decided to look up, to see if there was any life in the house. There was. As he stepped back from the door to look up, the window above opened and the contents of a bucket were poured over poor old Kevin. He was very annoyed, and didn't smell too good. So, we got on our bikes and went home. We then heard of a place on Marlborough Street, and we eventually rented a room up four flights of stairs, in a very rickety building. We paid the first week's rent and, before we'd even installed our studio equipment, we had a constant stream of visitors of the female persuasion; they'd heard that a couple of fellows were setting up a peculiar establishment, and they wanted in on the act. In spite of our best efforts, we couldn't persuade them of our artistic bona fides and, after a week, we packed it in. We never did have a studio.

'There was a College of Art fancy-dress hop, at the Bolero, a café-restaurant near the Stephen's Green end of Grafton Street; there was a small ballroom at the rear of the restaurant. I persuaded Des Sharkey and Michael Kennedy to come to the hop, and when they didn't appear, I was slightly worried. However, at the midnight hour, Mick appeared in the doorway, dressed in a sailor's gear, and he told me that Des had had an accident. He'd been dressed up in a doctor's white coat; he'd a large pocket watch, a stethoscope, and a black tall hat. Cycling down the South Circular Road, his wheel got caught in the tram track and he was catapulted over the handlebars. He split his forehead and an ambulance was sent for. As the stretcher was being lifted into the ambulance, some kind soul placed the tall hat on his chest, and away he went to the Meath Hospital. He was alive and well and bandaged the next morning when we were allowed in to visit him.

'Terence Douglas and Eddie McMahon were two other fellows I knew in Tallaght. Eddie was one of the barmen in the Fox's Covert; he was from Monaghan, I think. Terence was one of the lads I went to school with; a good-looking fellow, and he worked in Urney's factory. We were outside the chapel gates after eleven o'clock Mass, and Terence said to me, "Why don't we go down to Templeogue Tennis Club? There's a dance down there on a Sunday."' This was 1947, New Year's Eve. 'I said we wouldn't be let in, but we said we'd chance our arms. So, we went on our bicycles. First of all, we went to the Morgue.* At that time I had acquired a taste for Jamaica rum, so I had three or four glasses of that. I was feeling in great form. We got into the dance and, looking around, I spotted this lassie. I thought it was two of her at first, until I got my eyes focused. I liked the look of her, so I headed in that direction and, eventually, ended up beside her. I asked her up to dance.'

---

* A pub in Templeogue.

Chapter Eleven – Ita

'The earth did not move. He wasn't quite footless, but he was on his way there. I didn't like him one bit. I thought, "There's nothing here, and I won't be dancing with this fellow again." I just didn't like him.'

'There were forms that we had to fill in, with the results; they'd have to be done in the afternoon. Each form had the patient's name and doctor's name. There was a section for the results of the tests. I often thought of the people getting these results, some positive, some negative. But, really, they were all just pieces of paper to us; it's only years later that you begin to think of the stories that could have been behind them.

'At that time, a lot of hospitals didn't have their own pathology departments, with the result that swabs used to arrive into us, for examination for TB, which was rampant then, and diphtheria. Even pieces of limbs, for examination for cancer. These came from every county hospital, and from hospitals in Dublin. My job was to enter a description of each item into the day-book, for fee purposes, and to send out results as soon as they were available. I knew the various charges for each item. I remember a man coming in with a parcel one day. The parcel was tied up with string and was the shape of a leg. I wasn't very long in the place at the time, and I said to Chris Lynch, "What is it?" And she said, "It's what it looks like. It's a leg." Some poor devil had had his leg amputated and it was to be tested for cancer, or whatever – I knew nothing about the medical side of things. Most of the limbs arrived very discreetly wrapped, but this one was obvious. The messenger had a little handle on it, made of string, to carry it. Mind you, it wasn't his own leg. He had two.

'Another time, I happened to be in the laboratory, and the pathologists were all sitting around at their microscopes. They were examining prostate glands, for cancer. And Professor O'Kelly – I don't remember how many he'd examined that morning – said, "Do you know what? There won't be a prostate left in the country." In my youthfulness, I scurried out; we were a sheltered generation.

'But I loved it there. There was myself and Chris Lynch, and our boss, Miss O'Toole. When I was there a few years, extra staff were needed, and Muriel Long came in. We hit it off very well. She was very gentle. I often went cycling with her on Saturdays, and the odd time, we went to a dance together. I was the youngest of the office staff, before Muriel arrived, and every morning it was my job to make the coffee and tea. I was quite happy to do it; I didn't feel in any way servile. And it gave me the chance to get out for a few minutes, because I had to go across the road, to Leeson Street, to get a bottle of milk. The doctors, but not the two professors, used to come into our office and have tea and coffee with us. It was great. It was nearly like *Upstairs Downstairs* because – they were in no way rude to us – but, as far as their conversations were concerned, we just didn't exist. We sat there with our ears flapping and we got more information, about their romances, and about people who shouldn't have been with other people. And we took it all in. We never blackmailed any of them but we could have. I remember, one of them was going on a great date one night; she was a lovely girl – he was all excited. Stephen Breen was his name, from Waterford, a very funny man. And the next day, he was asked all about it. And he said, "A dead loss. You might as well have been dancing with a lamppost. She was that well corseted, you couldn't get near her." And we were sitting there; we weren't supposed to hear. Then, they were discussing another doctor. He was very well-known. He was doing a line with a lady who was also a doctor, who had a sister who was yet another doctor. But the steady line was with the older sister. He had one of the earliest soft-top cars; you could roll the top down. And he was driving somewhere with the younger sister, and he spotted the older sister. He pretended not to see her but, because of his distinctive car, she'd have known who it was. So he got the younger one by the head and pushed her in under the seat, until he was well past the older sister. The doctors were standing there, drinking coffee and laughing; we knew the doctor mentioned in the story – he came in and out of the laboratory on occasion, a really nice man. We also knew the two sisters, who came in occasionally. We could have caused awful trouble, but we didn't. Anyway, he married the older one.

'The room where we worked was beside one of the lecture theatres. A lot of the students going in and out of the lectures would stick their heads in and say, "Hello." That made life very exciting for us, all those handsome and not-so-handsome men. I remember one day, there was great screaming and roaring along the corridor, really mad screaming. We didn't venture out, but we were told afterwards that it was this Polish student; it was immediately after the War. He was studying medicine, but he drank absolute alcohol; he found the bottle and drank it and went completely out of his head, screaming up and down the corridor. I don't know how they tackled him, but he went off in an ambulance. I remember seeing him coming and going before that, a harmless-looking guy.

'I loved it there. It was my first job and it was great to have a few bob in my pocket. I liked the whole atmosphere and the place; it was kind of alive.

'Miss O'Toole was a highly organised, highly intelligent woman; she ran the office very, very well. She dressed beautifully and she had a lovely figure; she was rather plain because she had rather big teeth, but she dressed so well and held herself so well and she was so slim that she still looked kind of attractive. She was, I always thought, a very lonely lady. The only relations she seemed to have were a sister and brother-in-law; I don't know if there were nieces or nephews. She used to come in after the weekends, and she'd tell us about various romantic assignations she'd been on, and I remember hearing about one man who had a car with an open-top roof. They drove up to Killiney Hill and they sat looking at the moon, and it was so beautiful – much to the titters of the laddoes who wouldn't have dreamt of wasting time looking at the moon. Then she met a man, and he was a farmer; she really thought that this was the one. This farmer came and showered her with gifts; she came in with jewellery, and I remember a little white fur jacket. In fact, she lent it to me once, when I was going to a dance. But she discovered that he was married. She seemed to have no problem attracting men but they just didn't last. She had a flat on her own, on Waterloo Road, and she had a romance with a son of the owner of the house. But that filtered out, and she moved to a very nice bedsit on Orwell Road, in Rathgar; I used to cycle over and call in to see her. She was always very sincere about these men, and hugely romantic, but she never did marry.'*

'I can remember girls who'd go out on Saturday morning; they'd buy material, and be wearing dresses made from that material that night.† And I remember being in a shop one time, and two girls were standing at the counter and they bought two lots of material each. And one said to the other, "Which one will I wear tonight?" But it was just material on the counter at that stage.

'I made most of my own dresses, and jackets as well. It was a way of making the money stretch and, the thing is, you didn't want to appear in the same dress all the time. We all made our dresses. Noeleen was lucky; her mother was a great dressmaker. She used to turn out the most beautiful dresses and skirts. But I made my own. It was easily done. I was young and fairly slim, so it was easy enough to cut out a round neck and no sleeves, and suchlike; a little tuck at the waist and you were away with it. Making them was an everyday affair; it was nothing unusual. I did make some with sleeves as well, but I've no memory of ever having a pattern – but I must have had. There was a Singer sewing machine at

* Ita: 'I saw her death in the paper, some years ago, and she was deeply regretted by her brother-in-law, and I thought that was very sad.'
† Ita: 'Although the dances were more usually on a Sunday night.'

home, which had belonged to my mother, and I used it all the time. I'd buy material during the week and I'd be able to wear the dress on Sunday. In summer we'd deck ourselves out in three or four dresses, and we'd wear them turn, turn-about. You could make them very cheaply. You could make a dress for half-a-crown, even less. I remember making a corduroy jacket. It was wine-coloured, and had a belt and pockets. And I bought what was all the rage then, a Goray skirt, which was quite expensive – Goray was a brand-name – and I had to save for a few weeks to afford it. It had the same wine colour as the jacket, and it toned very well. If I bought in a shop, I was inclined to buy things that were really more expensive than I could afford. So I saved for them, if I wanted a suit or something like that. I always liked quality. Máire said once, "You can't afford that." And I just said, "Well, I have it."

'We usually went to the dances together, myself and Noeleen; I don't remember going with anyone else, except an odd time with Muriel Long. But we'd meet a crowd there; there was always a crowd. After going a few times, we got to know a few other people. Some of them we never knew by name; we just got friendly with them, sat and chatted, or just knew them by their first names.

'The hops were held all over the place; they were marvellous. The halls were quite small, but we all fitted in. It was band music, but very small bands, maybe three or four. You danced around the sides of the hall – one group going on the outside and another on the inside. The dances at that time were like that – you kept moving. There was the waltz – but that took up a lot of space. There was the quick-step, and the slow foxtrot – very romantic, so they'd have quite a few of those. Now and again, they'd throw in an Irish dance – the "Walls of Limerick", the "Bridge of Athlone". That could be hair-raising; you could be kicked in your shins. We cycled everywhere; there was no other way of going. But we'd walk to Templeogue. We were well able to walk home; it wasn't far. Or, if you were lucky, you'd get a crossbar home. This was a great method of travel, except when there was a "three-gear" on the crossbar; that was a rather bruising experience.'

She didn't often suffer the indignity of being a wall-flower. 'I got most of the dances. One time, however, myself and Noeleen went on a holiday to Arklow,★ and we were sitting around waiting to be asked. I mustn't have looked my best because I was sitting there for the best part of the night, and Noeleen was up for every dance. I couldn't understand it, but then one fellow asked me up to dance and, after that, I was away. And another time – they used to have *céilís* in the Mansion House on St Patrick's night and, often, on Sundays throughout the year. One of the girls living beside me, Marie Sullivan, asked me to go with her. I wasn't that keen, but I decided to go. So, off we set. We paid our way in, and sat there – and there we sat for the whole night. It turned out they all knew each other; they were really a clique and

★ County Wicklow.

not one of them asked us to dance the whole night. We ended up dancing with each other and more or less jeering and sneering at the Irish zealots around us. We could speak Irish too, but no one spoke to us. We were disgusted with them. We never went again.

'But the dances were great. They were mostly in the tennis clubs around the area. And the rugby clubs. There was one in Kenilworth Square; there was a tennis club there. There was one in Lansdowne Rugby Club. There was one in Templeogue Tennis Club. Templeogue always ended up with "Goodnight Sweetheart"; we knew it was all over then. There was only the piano and drums, but it filled the whole hall. The people who played the music were Thelma and Jack Kent. Thelma played the piano, Jack played the drums. Thelma had actually been to Eccles Street when I was there, and I knew her. I remember, she used to do cartwheels in the corridors. Needless to say, the nuns weren't around when it happened, or they'd have been horrified. But Thelma was great fun. They did a good job, just the piano and drums; it was quite sufficient. We had great fun. Alcohol wasn't served at the dances; there was never any drink, except it came in somebody's stomach.

'I was never in a pub; it was unheard-of to go into a pub. I wouldn't have known what the inside of a Dublin pub looked like. I do remember going into one in Wexford; there'd been a hurling match and I was there with my father – I was a teenager. The man who owned the pub had been in St Peter's College with Daddy. We went in, and I was immediately whipped away and taken out to the kitchen. It wasn't fit that I stand in a pub, so I had nice tea and cakes out in the kitchen, which suited me fine. On another occasion, I went with my Uncle Mike when he was a pig buyer, and we stopped in a village where he was buying pigs for Buttles. I sat in the car while he did that part of the job. Then we went into the pub, where Mike and the dealer shook hands on the deal and exchanged drinks. Again, I was immediately taken into the kitchen. I think that any women in those days who went into pubs were looked on as fallen women. I know from reading that there were pubs in Dublin where they had a snug for the women, a little private place. They had a little hatch to the counter where women were able to ask for drink, but they didn't mix with the men.'

She still went to Wexford every year. 'I always looked on it as my place to go on holidays, even when I started to work and could afford to go to other places around Ireland. I went down each summer, sometimes maybe only for a week, and a week then somewhere different, but I always went. I stayed with Aunt Bessie, in Kilmuckridge.

'Card games, like twenty-five, were arranged in houses around, followed by supper. Aunt Bessie always started the ball rolling with a card night. We travelled to Carberry's, a farm down the road, and to Miss Redmond, a teacher who lived in a thatched house opposite the church, and to others too, but the names I can't recall. We were an all-female group and the cards were secondary to the chat and the supper. To me, those nights were magic. Sometimes, Mary Carberry's holidays coincided with mine, and we cycled hither and yon. Once, we visited an elderly cousin of Mary's, a Miss Parker, who lived with an elderly brother, near Blackwater. Mary's sister, Maggie, lived with them. Miss

Parker was a really old-style martinet and she ruled the house with a rod of iron. Her list of things a young girl should not do included dressing with bare legs and bare arms. Fortunately, she was quite blind and quite immobile. Mary and myself arrived and put on our cardigans. When I was introduced, I stood well back, and reached my hand out to shake hers. The old bat ran her hand up and down my arm, and then shook hands with me. That was it – I was fit to eat in her house. After that, we took our cardigans off and had a pleasant afternoon.

'I'd cycle over to Coolnaboy. The children were small but growing fast. There was Joan, then Johnny; Jim, I think, was next; then Paddy, Matt, Liam and Breda, and then Eilish was the youngest. It was a big family. Nobody could bake apple and rhubarb tarts like Aunt Katie. They were packed with fruit. The juice used to blend with the sugar and, in places, it seeped out and a lovely toffee formed on the sides. If there'd been an Oscar for tart-making, Katie would have won it. I can still taste them. One day, I remember I cycled back to Kilmuckridge from Coolnaboy, full to the gills with apple tart. When I was telling Bessie about the events of my day – I'd left Kilmuckridge early, to cycle the fourteen or so miles to Coolnaboy – I told her about the wonderful apple tart, the juice, and the toffee on the sides. Silence for a minute, then, "She mustn't seal her tarts properly. Juice should not leak out of tarts if they are properly sealed." That remark has gone down in family history. Ever the diplomat, I heaped praise on Bessie's tarts and scones from then on.

'My Uncle John lived in a place called Pouldearg, in the townland of Balnaslaney, not far from Oilgate. The farm had belonged to my grandmother's family, the

Whittys. The lease was dated 1660.* The farm was beautifully situated; the River Slaney ran at the end of the orchard. John was a bachelor, and quite shy with us, but, I believe, he took umbrage easily. I can remember, when I was a young child, visiting John. He had tea set out on a big mahogany table with a white cloth and lovely china. We had bread and jam, brack and shop-bought cake. I thought it was great. John fussed around, telling us to eat up – which we did. I loved the jam. I had never tasted jam like it before.† That day, I remember, John had a boat in the water. Joe got into it and pushed off, and was floating down the river when he was spotted. There was consternation but, with the help of a hook, he was hauled in. Joe was quite unperturbed, but my father was in a state of collapse. I gather John was not much of a farmer. I never did hear the exact details but, anyway, the house burned down and the land was taken over by the Land Commission. John went to live with Katie and Watt until he died.

'I remember Bessie telling me that when she was a little girl, her mother had told her that when she, the mother – Johanna – was a little girl, living on the farm in Pouldearg, a horse had died. The men dug a hole to bury the horse, and the ground caved in. She saw a set of steps leading down into the ground. The men were frightened; they just filled the hole again, and buried the horse elsewhere.‡

---

* Ita: 'My Uncle Watt gave Rory this piece of information.'

† Ita: 'Years later – I was married – I bought a pot of jam in my local shop. It was marked "Mixed Fruit"; it was nice and cheap. The minute I tasted it, I remembered my tea with Uncle John. It was the same-flavoured jam. Cheap or not cheap, I still thought it was lovely.'

‡ Ita: 'Some years ago, my cousin, Johnny Bolger, brought Rory, Máire and myself for a drive, and we visited Pouldearg. You would have thought that there'd never been a house there. Everything was gone. It was sad.'

'Now and again, Bessie mentioned the time she spent in school. Aunt Una* went to secondary school, but Bessie finished after national school. She was an avid reader and had beautiful handwriting. One day, she said, they had a lesson on the Ten Commandments. She

was walking home later with two friends.† They were discussing the commandment "Thou shalt not commit adultery." They just couldn't understand what adultery was and, if they didn't know what it was, how could they avoid committing it? Suddenly, said Bessie, she saw the light and told her friends: "I know what adultery is. It's watering the milk." She also added that it was quite some years before she knew that that particular sin was not about watering milk.'

'I wasn't really going to go at all, but Noeleen was very keen to go because, the week before, she'd met this handsome man who'd danced with her for the night. She was really keen to meet him again but she wouldn't go on her own, so I said I'd go. So, off we set. We went in, and the dancing started. Noeleen's handsome fellow was there, and he never came near her for the night. He

---

* Una married Robert Brennan.
† Ita: 'One of them I knew later as Mrs Ryan, and the other as Mrs Mernagh.'

ignored her, and she was very upset. She was very nice looking, and tall, and she got plenty of dances, but she was terribly upset that this fellow didn't dance with her.

'About halfway through the dance, this tall man came over and asked me to dance. He was the worse for wear. I didn't like him one bit. I thought, "There's nothing here, and I won't be dancing with this fellow again." I just didn't like him. I decided that that was it; I'd have no more to do with him. I remember telling Noeleen about this awful fellow and she commiserated with me and I commiserated with her, about the fact that her handsome fellow had ignored her. She'd had a disappointing night and, as far as I was concerned, I'd drawn a blank. We straightened our backs and decided we'd "start from scratch".

'One of the girls we were friendly with in Templeogue was Joan Flynn. One night, a man she fancied, called Tom O'Reilly, danced with her quite a lot, and then asked her would she like some fresh air. Off she went, smiling. She was back again in about ten minutes. We asked the usual question, "How did you get on?" "The dirty-looking eejit." she said. "Instead of just going ahead and kissing me, he asked me could he kiss me. Then, of course, I had to say No." Joan would have been delighted to be kissed but, at that time, well-brought-up girls had to make a pretence of being badly shocked at such a suggestion.

'Anyway, the following Sunday myself and Noeleen went along again, and Rory appeared bright and early, stone-cold sober, a completely different man. He asked me to dance straight away. He was very nice and we got on very well. We danced a lot that night.* I can't remember if another week went by, or if it was that time, when he asked me out. That was the usual thing; if a man liked a girl, he asked her to meet him in town. Men always did the asking. We met at the Metropole† the first night. And afterwards, on other dates, we'd meet at either the Metropole or the Pillar‡ – they were very popular places to meet. There'd be lots of boys and girls waiting. Another waiting place was under Clery's clock,§ or outside the Savoy.¶

'I remember once, meeting this guy in Templeogue, a very handsome fellow altogether, and making a date with him. This was before Rory. I thought this was great but, while he was very good-looking, I was a bit dubious about him. I told Chris Lynch, my friend from work, about him and the date; we were to meet at the Metropole at eight o'clock. Chris said, "I'll be over at the Pillar and I'll be watching, and if he's not there – we'll give him about a quarter of an hour – then I'll meet you and we'll go off somewhere." So, he didn't turn up – well, not by a quarter past, anyway – and I was beginning to

---

* Ita: 'Noeleen and Jim Algar had met some weeks before our New Year's Eve let-down. They had danced quite a lot together, had had one date, but had seemed uncertain about each other. However, the following Sunday, the same night I met Rory again, Jim danced the night away with Noeleen and, shortly after that, they were an item.'
† Cinema, ballroom and restaurant, on O'Connell Street.
‡ Nelson's Pillar, O'Connell Street.
§ Department store, also on O'Connell Street.
¶ Cinema and restaurant, also on O'Connell Street.

feel a bit of a fool, but Chris came over and we went off to the pictures, and I wasn't a bit upset. I never saw him again afterwards; he didn't come back to Templeogue. So, that was it. But Rory was never late. And he always had a box of chocolates.'

Chapter Twelve – Rory

'I had enough sense, even though I was half-sozzled, to realise that a different approach was necessary. Something told me that there was something I liked about this lassie. I thought about it all week, and I came back the following Sunday stone-cold sober, to see if she'd be around – and she was.

'We danced, after a fashion. And we talked. I probably told a whole lot of lies. The music was just drums and a piano. "Whispering while I cuddle you". "Red Sails in the Sunset". "The Isle of Capri". I liked the way she spoke. I liked the way she looked, her face and her shape.

'I don't think I was nervous when I asked her out for a date; I was prepared to chance my arm. But I *was* nervous that she wouldn't turn up. I hadn't really asked many other girls out. I'd had a few "brief encounters" between about 1944 and 47, when I had a few pounds in my pocket but no intention of hanging around. They were brief, mutually enjoyable – or, at least, I enjoyed them – singing and dancing, but none of "that". A brief kiss and cuddle and happy memories. And I'd met a red-haired girl in Juverna Press. She was delivering copy and proofs for a magazine. She turned up at a dance in Tallaght, and myself and Des Sharkey walked herself and her friend home, to Annamoe Road; it's quite a con-siderable distance.* But we enjoyed ourselves and got

---

* Annamoe Road is in Cabra, seven or eight miles from Tallaght.

home at dawn. Myself and this girl made a date, and I booked two tickets for the revival of Handel's *Messiah*; I thought it would impress her. I think it nearly killed her. It wasn't a bright idea. I suspect that she was frozen with boredom. I never saw her again. Two telephone calls were unproductive, and I got the message. After that, I went on my own. I remember going to the Gate Theatre, to Lord Longford's productions. The one I remember best is Molière's *The School for Wives*. The acting and the crystal-clear accents of the actors were very attractive. About this time, I also rediscovered Rathmines Library; I hadn't been there since I was in school. I borrowed and read Dickens, Galsworthy, Conrad and a host of other writers. I also read an auto-biographical work by Clemençeau, the French politi-cian. It was called, I think, *In the Evening of My Thoughts*. At the end of his days, he had nothing to offer or to look forward to. The book was so devoid of any hope or feeling for the future, or any sense of belonging to human fraternity, that it quite cured me of a budding agnosticism.

'I was there first, outside the Metropole. I don't really remember the day, only the season. I was wearing an overcoat, and the light was fading; I watched people appearing through the street lighting. I remember being enormously relieved and delighted when she arrived. And elated. I know that we went to the pic-tures' – he doesn't remember the film – 'and that we went to the Savoy for tea and she ate a whole plateful of cakes.'★

★   ★   ★

★ Ita: 'He said I broke him eating cakes. I always had a sweet tooth.'

'Independent Newspapers was founded by William Martin Murphy, ★ of 1913 General Strike fame, and when I worked for the firm, the Chairman of the Board was T.V. Murphy, son of William Martin. Now, the Murphys took a lofty view of the ethics of newspaper publishing, and an occasional ukase would come down from on high, from the Great Presence. He was particularly vigilant that the editorial content was very respectful of the clergy of any denominaton; no critical reporting of any nature was ever tolerated. On one dreadful occasion, the report on the death of a much-respected Presbyterian minister included the line: "He is survived by three sisters and two brothels." And occasional howlers occurred, generally in the Sports section. In a report on a jockey's wedding, it said that "he hoped to get his first ride in France in the New Year".

'Now, the editorial board decided that the cartoon, *Curly Wee*, was old hat, and they promptly dropped it from the paper. All hell broke loose among the general readership.† Many of the complaints went directly to T.V. Murphy, who was perturbed that some of his eminent friends were discommoded. He issued an ukase, and *Curly Wee* was reinstated.

'Early one night, it was discovered that the *Curly Wee* plates hadn't been delivered from Liverpool. There was consternation among the powers-that-be and some amusement among the lower orders. Urgent telephone calls were made and a special plane was hired to transport

---

★ William Martin Murphy(1844–1919): born in County Cork; Home Rule MP, 1885–92; founded the *Irish Independent*, 1904; refused a knighthood, 1907; leader of Dublin Employers' Federation up to and throughout the Lockout of 1913; spoke on British recruiting platforms, 1914; opposed Partition.
† Rory: 'Among the fans of *Curly Wee* was Ita's father.'

the plates to Dublin in time for the edition. Meanwhile, people held their breath or crossed their fingers, or maybe prayed. And, in the general lull, temptation entered my head. I got a large sheet of paper and drew a likeness of Count Curly Wee, and a reward of a considerable amount for the return of the lost hero, who, of course, was a pig, a famous pig. I slipped upstairs to the stone room during "cut time"★ and fixed it to the wall. When it was discovered, there was pandemonium, and managers, editorial staff and overseers were ordered to find the culprit. My immediate overseer, Harry Stephenson, vehemently denied any knowledge of the outrage. He had a fair idea, but he wasn't going to talk. He probably guessed that he'd be included in the sanctions that were awaiting the culprit. As a matter of great urgency, news of the outrage was conveyed to T.V. Murphy, who had to be disturbed from whatever it was that gentlemen of that status did at that time of day. He arrived in full dinner regalia and assumed overall charge of the situation. It sounds funny now, but it had all the trappings of a constitutional crisis. It was even rumoured that T.V. had actually spoken to his good friend, the Garda Commissioner. Whether he did or not was never verified, for, in the midst of all the hullabaloo, the plates arrived by taxi from Baldonnell Aerodrome and all was suddenly right on the night. While there was a continuation of the search for the perpetrator of the poster outrage, it gradually subsided – to my relief. All the best fun and games happened on the night shift.

★ Rory: 'Cut time was the term used to describe a short break for a meal in the early hours of the edition. Everybody headed for the canteen, lights were covered and an almost eerie silence descended.'

'Among the matters to engage the attention of T.V. was the quality of the illustrations for the advertisement for Madame Nora, who sold corsets and sundry other articles of feminine underwear. Discreet alterations to the illustrations were requested or demanded from time to time, to comply with T.V.'s sense of decency. He also conducted a long running argument with Clery's advertising department about the description of boys' short trousers as "Boys' Knickers". T.V. didn't like it, but Clery's full-page advertisement was big business and their old-fashioned drapery description prevailed. Money talked, as always.

'The editor of the Woman's Page was Ita Mallon, a very competent North of Ireland journalist whom I'd previously met at Juverna Press when she edited the retail grocer's paper, the *RGDATA Review*. There was an article written for the page by a teacher in the National College of Art, Mary Frances Keating, who specialised in embroidery and needlework. This particular article was concerned with the transferring of the design to the cloth, for embroidering. Jack Spain, the stone man, received the typematter, and duly inserted it in the place planned for on the page. Next, the heading arrived. The wording caused Jack some anxiety – after proofreaders, sub-editors and others had processed stories, it was very often the stone man who copped the overlooked howler. The wording read: "Tracing By Prick and Pounce". You can imagine what the ignorant and uncouth would do with that heading. Jack held his fire until O'Connor, the assistant editor, a tall, laconic North of Ireland man, strolled down to see how the paper was progressing. I should say here that the editorial staff either strolled to the stone room or rushed excitedly. Jack casually pointed out that the Woman's Page was almost complete. O'Connor took one look at the heading, said he had urgent business in the Prince's Bar, and promptly disappeared. He could smell potential trouble; he wasn't assistant editor by chance. Later, the other assistant editor, Michael Rooney, another North of Ireland man, but peppery, bounced down to the stone room, to survey progress. Jack Spain casually waved his hand over the page of type, and remarked that the paper was almost complete. Rooney glanced at the page, saw the heading, and hit the roof. He demanded that the word "Prick" be changed to "Pricker". Jack duly complied with the order, and Rooney went back to his office. Shortly afterwards, Ita Mallon strolled in, to oversee the completion of the page. She got extremely vexed and off she went to the night overseer, Paddy Masterson, and demanded that the original wording be reinstated. The journalist, of course, had the absolute right to decide the word-content, and Paddy Masterson bustled down to the stone room and ordered Jack Spain to alter the heading. He said, "If Miss Mallon wants 'Prick', she'll have to get 'Prick'." Jack changed the wording. Shortly afterwards, Rooney bounced back to the stone room and casually remarked, "That was a close thing." And then he caught sight of the offending word again and he went incandescent with rage. He said the bloody woman would have to be told the facts of life, and Jack said, sorry, but he wasn't going to be the person to do it. Eventually, the wording was changed again, the edition went to press, and Miss Mallon, who was a lady, wasn't seen in the stone room for several weeks.'

★　　★　　★

'We went to the pictures a lot; it was the thing to do. I actually liked the films, except for those musicals with Ginger Rogers and Fred Astaire, with their interminable lines of dancing girls, and Gene Kelly dancing up the walls. No plot, no story and, to me, utter boredom. But there's one I remember, with Betty Hutton – *Incendiary Blonde* – the life of Texas Guinan, a famous torch singer, and quite a girl. It was a particularly good film.★ And Greer Garson, in *Mrs Miniver*,† she made quite an impression on me. And I particularly liked Dorothy Dandridge in *Carmen Jones*,‡ I liked the way she spit the sunflower seeds.

'In the summer we'd go out cycling with Ita's friend, Noeleen, and her boyfriend, Jim Algar. We went out to Lucan, to the Sarsfield Demesne.§ We'd bring sandwiches and have tea. Or we'd go to the sea; it could be Blackrock or it could be Portmarnock. We had our bikes, and distance was no bother at all. We'd generally talk and cycle out there.

★ Released 1945: the life of 20s night-club queen Texas Quinan; 'It runs its noisy but high-minded course through steamy emotion, painful misunderstanding and dramatic self-sacrifice, winding up in the snow among the blood of dead gangsters' (*Halliwell's Film Guide*).

† Released 1942: an English housewife survives WWII; 'That almost impossible feat, a war picture that photographs the inner meaning, instead of the outward realism of World War II' (*Halliwell's Film Guide*).

‡ Released 1954: 'a factory girl marries a soldier, and is strangled by him for infidelity. Black American updating of Bizet's opera, not really satisfactory but given full marks for trying, though the main singing is dubbed and the effect remains doggedly theatrical' (*Halliwell's Film Guide*).

§ Patrick Sarsfield (d. 1693): commanded James II's Irish forces in England, 1688; returned to Ireland; expelled the Williamites from Connaught; defended Limerick; fought and defeated at the Boyne, 1690; created Earl of Lucan; sailed for France, with Irish Brigade, 1691; died at the battle of Landen. His home was the Demesne, Lucan, County Dublin.

'The bicycle was central to civilisation. If you hadn't got a bicycle, you were like a cowboy out in Arizona walking along the dusty road. The bicycle got you anywhere and everywhere. It was sixpence into Dublin from Tallaght on the bus; people didn't have that kind of money. And you weren't confined to any particular road. I remember Tom Lee; he cycled eight or nine miles to work every morning, with his shovel tied to the crossbar – he worked for builders. He got to his work every day, hail, rain or snow. He couldn't have done it without his bicycle. I did the same. I cycled seven miles into Abbey Street, from Tallaght, and seven miles back, against the wind and the hill. My memory is that it was raining, nearly always. I had one of those slicker things on me, like a cape, to keep the rain off, and it caught the wind as well, and it was like a sail. And leggings, to cover the trousers. And then, of course, I was wet inside from the sweat, as well as outside from the rain. A rather unpleasant experience, when I come to think of it, but it was everyday life. There was a great scarcity of bikes, generally, during the War, and just after, and your bicycle could be put out of commission by a badly burst tyre. A new tyre wasn't easily bought. You had to talk to people who knew people who knew a shop that might give you a tyre. In the meantime, my three sisters were reduced to one bike. So they worked out a strategy. They went off, and one would ride the bike for a mile and then get down, and the next one had a go; they more or less piggy-backed the bicycle all the way. Then, when Breda and Nancy started going down to Templeogue Tennis Club on Sunday nights, Aileen wouldn't have any of that nonsense; she'd take two or three magazines and a bag of sweets to bed, and she looked at her sisters as if they were right half-eejits going out in the terrible weather – but there was still only one bicycle, so they went off to Templeogue, in their high heels and all, half-riding the bicycle and half-trotting beside it.

'It was a fortnight after we met that we first kissed, outside Ita's front door, or maybe it was three weeks. It was probably about three weeks – you couldn't go rushing into these things. I just liked Ita more and more. Not long after I'd met her, actually, I made up my mind that I'd like to make it a permanent arrangement. I was standing at her door, saying goodnight to her, and I decided that I wanted to make my intentions clear. I think I said something or other, but, for the life of me, I can't remember.'

Chapter Thirteen – Ita

'He was extremely thin and he had a very thin face, but he'd lovely hair. Black curly hair, very, very nice. I rather liked his face. He was a very pleasant man, very easy to get on with. He was grand. We used to talk from the time we'd meet to the time we left. He was always very witty and funny, and he got on very well with people. And another very important thing was, my father took to him very quickly.

'The first time I brought him home to be introduced, he was invited for tea. That was the usual thing. Most people had their dinner in the middle of the day and then their tea in the evening. He was invited for tea one Sunday, and I'm sure he was feeling a bit awkward in himself and my father was actually a very shy man. But when Rory arrived my father was doing a crossword – he was a great man for crosswords – and there were a few clues he couldn't work out. He handed the paper to Rory, I suppose as a way of covering his shyness, and Rory managed the clues and, I think, from that day he was elected. They got on very well and there was also the fact that Rory worked in the *Independent*. Printing establishments of any description held a great attraction for my father; having started his career at the *Echo* in Enniscorthy, I think some printing ink got into his veins. But I think the two combined – the job and crossword – meant that they got on very well after that.

'"Going steady" was the phrase. We used to meet every week. The following summer, I went to Kilkee with Noeleen and Rory went off on a walking holiday around Cork, and I think it was after that that we decided we were what you'd call a steady couple. But I don't remember the first time he kissed me; I've no recollection in the world. Terrible – I'm a dead loss really. He did ask me to marry him, I think he did, but I can't remember that occasion either. I should; it should be hugely romantic but, I must admit, I don't remember.

'My stepmother took to him very well. Pearl was a very smart lady and anyone my father took to, Pearl automatically took to. And anyone my father disliked, Pearl automatically disliked, very often without any reason. But, I must say, my father didn't dislike many people. He was a very easy-going kind of man. She took to Rory very well and she was very pleased that he drank whiskey, an important part of her life. I can remember one Christmas Eve – we were engaged by then – and she kept giving him hot whiskeys. It was a very cold night, and every time he'd take one, she'd say, "A bird never flew on one wing." The words came out very slurred, and it became a family joke between myself and Máire. But Rory missed the last bus to Tallaght, so myself and Joe took my bicycle out. The traffic was very light, and I put Rory up on the bike and away he went, down the hill and off to Tallaght. It was a good three miles away but he lived to tell the tale. He fell into a ditch and woke up sometime on Christmas morning, and managed to get home; nobody ever knew. He told me a man bent over him as he lay in the ditch, and said, "Are you alright, son?"

'I remember being very nervous before meeting his

family and, really, I had no need to be. They welcomed me immediately. Rory was the eldest, so it was quite an occasion, for the first one to bring somebody home. He had five sisters and two brothers and they were all living at home at the time, and I discovered that I had actually been in commercial college – Skerries – with one of his sisters, Aileen, although, naturally, I didn't know who she was at the time. They all gave me a great welcome and, after that, there was no problem. I was asked out regularly, to a groaning table. It was always food, piles of food on a groaning table.

'His father was a very gentle man, and a small man. Rory's mother ran the whole shooting gallery; he was just a quiet man in the background, but she had great respect for him. He was a very gentle, quiet man and he seemed to be delighted with everything in life. Rory's mother was a marvellous woman for organising everything. She was a tall, big woman, a very stately woman, with a straight back, and she used to dress very well. She was like royalty coming down the street, with her straight back and, what was very much in vogue then, an edge-to-edge coat.* She used to wear picture hats, wide-brimmed hats which only the likes of her could wear. And she looked terrific in high heels; if they were to cripple her, she'd still wear the high heels. A very strong woman too. She had a lovely face, very soft and very generous – a very generous woman. Nothing seemed to be too much trouble for her.

'And Aunt Lil was great. She was a little stout lady;

---

* Ita: 'It was, literally, an edge-to-edge coat. The front of the coat met edge to edge, no lap-over, no buttons. It was very popular, but it wouldn't have been too useful because, the first gust of wind, it blew open. So you had to grab it and hold it. But part of the effect was the way you held it.'

she always seemed to be in good humour. From the day I arrived she treated me like one of the family.★ I didn't see much of the Uncle Bob. He was a bit shy of me. He was very polite and he used to call me "Mam". He was a man who admired big ladies. He admired Jackie Doyle's wife, Delores, because she was lovely and tall. In trying to relate to her his admiration, he really upset her when he said, "Be gob, you weren't behind the door when they were handin' out the size."

'There was an awful lot of walking. We went to the pictures alright, mostly in the Classic, in Terenure, but we used to go for walks, all over, around the Dublin Mountains; out to Rathfarnham, passing St Enda's, and way up – it's all built on now – and there was a place called the Bottle Tower in Rathfarnham – it's still there but it's completely surrounded by houses – and there were fields and fields there, and we used to just keep walking. Sometimes we'd get the bus to Bohernabreena and walk on further. I'd have a bag of sweets and he'd have his pipe. That was it; we'd walk and talk. There was no such thing as going out to dinner. The nearest to that would have been an odd time we'd have tea out. I used to love rashers and eggs. That was the kind of tea you could have, or cold ham and salad – lettuce, tomato, hard-boiled egg and salad cream, that kind of thing. Rory's favourite was eggs, beans and chips. The waitress would kind of look at him, because beans didn't normally

---

★ Ita: 'We were always told that the 15th of August was Lil's birthday and every year, up until she died, we'd give her a present. We only discovered when she died, the 15th of August wasn't her birthday at all. I suppose they just picked on that date; people didn't really bother with birthdays then.'

go with egg and chips. But he always looked for the beans – he was ahead of his time.'

'We both had our own Post Office accounts. I can't remember how much a week I put by. I was being paid £4.10s a week, and I handed up ten shillings at home; Daddy said that was enough. I'd started work on twenty-five shillings, which wasn't a bad salary then. And then I was put up to thirty shillings; I was on that for a few years. While the professors were paying out the money, I think, strictly, they weren't really aware of how much each person got. My boss, Miss O'Toole, decided that we should all look for a rise, and her way of looking for a rise was to get me, the junior, to go into the professor, and ask him. So I went into Professor O'Kelly, not feeling too happy about it, because in those days you were very much in awe of your boss, no matter how well you got on with him. Nevertheless, I asked him for a rise. He was a smart man; he knew I'd been sent in. He said he'd consider it. So, out I came and I told the others that he'd consider it. We were paid every Friday, cash in a little envelope. The following Friday, my pay had been doubled, to £3. Now, the others didn't get a rise at all, and there was a little bit of a to-do about it. Professor O'Kelly said, "Nobody else asked for a rise," and raised his little red eyebrows and walked out. I was absolutely thrilled, and I guessed it was because he knew I'd been sent in. The next week, everybody got a rise. And then, later, it rose to £4.10s. I managed to save £100, towards a deposit on a house. And Rory saved £100. From the time we got engaged. I had put a little bit by, and so had he.'

★   ★   ★

'I remember Rory called for me, and he was dressed as Sir Walter Ralegh. We were going to the Arts Ball. He had silk stockings and a velvet thing to his knees, and a velvet coat. He'd actually cycled in from Tallaght in his Walter Ralegh outfit.★ I can't quite remember, we  may have got a taxi the rest of the way but, certainly, he cycled in from Tallaght. I made my own outfit. I made a long dress in black taffeta. I made an old-style bonnet to match, and went as an old-fashioned lady. I was able to wear the dress afterwards, so it served a dual purpose. The College of Art dances were great. There were so few things like that in those days. The affair began with a formal dinner, and then dancing to the music of a big band. I always wanted to dance every dance. You could talk if you wanted to; the band didn't drown out conversation. It was great fun. I remember once, going to a dress-dance with a fellow – this would have been before I met Rory – a small fellow, not much taller than myself. Normally, I wouldn't have looked crooked at him, but his friend had asked a girl I knew then to go with him – I can't recall her name – and then this fellow asked me, and I can't remember his

---

★ Rory: 'In the case of Sir Walter Ralegh, I didn't cycle from Tallaght. I dressed in Juverna Press, and walked down O'Connell Street, to the usual remarks; it was daylight. And then I got a taxi. I'm sure I did cycle from Tallaght in fancy dress, but I can't remember the costume. And it wasn't Sir Walter Ralegh; it was Sir Francis Drake.'

name either. It goes to show how impressed I was, but the chance of going to a dress-dance didn't come so often that you could turn your nose up at it.' So, she

went. 'Mrs Fry made my dress, blue taffeta with blue net over it. And I thought I was the belle of the ball. I had a very good night. He was quite pleasant and mannerly; we had a great night, but that was it, as far as I was concerned.'*

'I had done work for Cyril Fry.† He worked as an engineer at Jacob's biscuit factory, but he was also an agent for Meccano and I used to work for him at night. I just typed a few

letters for him but, again, I nearly became one of the family. They were very nice to me, and there'd always be a dish of sweets beside the typewriter. Cyril and his wife, Nancy, brought me for a lovely picnic on my

---

* Rory: 'The Urney factory had a dinner dance every year, in the Metropole or Savoy. And one of the lads brought this lady along. Thomas Stynes was his name; I went to school with him. He had a slight stammer. Anyway, Tom said to her, "What would you like to drink?" and she said, "A Tom Collins." So, he said to the waiter, "We'll have two Tom Collinses." So, the waiter brought the two Tom Collinses and said, "That'll be three-and-six-pence.""What!" said Tom. "F-f-fuck you and the T-t-tom Collinses." Three-and-six was an enormous amount for two drinks, when you could buy a bottle of stout for sevenpence.'

† The original owner, and creator, of the Fry Model Railway, at Malahide Castle, County Dublin.

twenty-first birthday; they picked me up after work. And I used to go to them every Christmas. I'd eat at home and then I'd cycle over to them; they lived in Church-town. Mrs Fry was a great cook, and had great taste about everything. They lived in a bungalow, which I loved. I thought that, whenever I got married, I'd buy a bungalow. An odd night, if we went out anywhere, I'd stay overnight. They had a young daughter, Patricia, and I used to stay in Patricia's room with her.'

'It was Christmas Eve,* and Rory gave me the ring in the sitting-room, our sitting-room at home. It was just the two of us and it was freezing cold but that didn't dampen our enthusiasm. Then we told everyone. My father knew already; he was well-pleased – he was very fond of Rory.

'We'd bought the ring in McDowell's,† about a week before Christmas.‡ We bought it together, but he was paying. It had three diamonds, at kind of an angle, and two arms with little diamond specks in them. I was keen to have one with five stones across, but I have very small hands and they looked ridiculous. But this one suited me better. It didn't take very long to choose. There were a fair number of rings but the prices were on them, and I knew what we could afford. It cost £17.10s.§ We could have had a cheaper one, but it was

---

* 1950.

† On O'Connell Street – 'The Happy Ring House'.

‡ Rory: 'There was an initial difficulty, because I thought this ring was a total waste of money. It wasn't so much a row as Ita being a bit discon-certed and upset, and I didn't realise I was doing that. I just wasn't thinking, that this ring was essential. So off we went and bought the ring in McDowell's; we bought the ring that Ita wanted.'

§ Rory: 'It was £27 – a slight difference.'

what we could afford.★ The most important thing was to save the money for the house. The engagement ring was to be worn, but it wasn't going to rob us in the process.

'So, on Christmas Eve, we'd been out, just walking around, buying things, up and down Henry Street; you could hardly fit, it was so crowded. And then we went back to the house, and the ring was put on my finger, and I went flashing it all around.'

★ Ita: 'It was £17.10s, but we told everyone it was £27.'

Chapter Fourteen – Rory

'We were dancing and Ita asked me would I mind her keys for her. So I put them in my pocket and, the next thing – we'd said goodnight and I'll see you again – I found the keys in my pocket. So, the next morning, I had to turn around and bring them down to Terenure. I knocked at the door, rang the bell, and this very unprepossessing woman came out. I said to myself, "Oh-oh." I'd always heard the good advice that before you get involved with any woman you should always look at her mother, and, working on that principle, I was a little bit shook – until I'd made a date with Ita, and she told me that she was actually a stepmother. Well, that kind of solved that matter; she couldn't be held responsible for her stepmother – otherwise, I was on my way for the hills and over.

'Then I was persuaded to go to tea, and I went. I liked her father; he was kind of quiet, and had a country accent. The first thing he did when I walked in was, he pushed the *Sunday Times* crossword in front of me. I suggested a few answers, and he said I was right. The main thing was, I'd solved two clues for him and, such was the make of the man that, after that, if I'd molested his daughter, he'd have said it was her fault, not mine. And I must have been regarded as respectable because they insisted that I come to tea more often.★

'I fell into the art of poker when I was on night work in the *Irish Independent*. Instead of going home at three in the morning, in bad weather, I'd wait for the first bus and, invariably, there was a poker school going on in the canteen. And, eventually, I joined in. I joined in far too much, as it happened. But it's like asking, why do you drink or smoke too much. Poker is an invasive kind of demand and, once you get it, you start to believe it – it's like betting on horses. I'd be losing steadily, and then I'd get a good hand. Everybody else would throw their hands in and I'd pick up the winnings, but they'd be small because nobody was betting against me. It's one of those things you go through. The trouble is, I lost a fair amount of money,† over £4 or £5 a week. Not enough to be broke, but a lot of money; I was paid about £13 a week. I should have been taking it home and saving it. But I lost it. Then I started day work, and that broke the spell.

'Independent Newspapers published, and still does, morning and evening papers. There was a requirement for two staffs. Each paper had a corps of permanent overseers and key men, and the rest of each staff was drawn from a large pool of compositors and linotype operators who alternated on day shift and night shift. But it wasn't week-about, as in general industry. There

---

★ Ita: 'One night, Rory arrived to collect me for a party, at Billy Farrell's, who worked with Rory and was newly wed. Rory was wearing a new sports jacket, blue hound's-tooth tweed, and grey flannels. My father looked him up and down, turned to Joe, and said: "Get that man a glass of sherry." Joe was delighted; he had a caustic wit.'

† Ita: 'He told me years later that if he hadn't been playing poker in the *Independent*, we could have had our house and been married sooner.'

were two lists posted up in the composing department, the day and night lists. Each month, the two people at the top of each list transferred to either night or day shift. The lists were closely scrutinised in order to assess one's chances of being on day work, because there were two circumstances that affected the scheme. One was the factor that no movement occurred during the months of May, June and July, the holiday period. The second very important factor was that a person could elect to stay on the night shift. There was no such choice on the day shift, and so, it was like an annual lottery. There was always intense speculation as to whether somebody or other would pass up their turn for day work. Every once in a while somebody broke the habit of a lifetime, opted for day work, and that set the cat among the pigeons. Expectations of remaining on the day shift for a longer period were shattered because the new names went to the bottom of the day list and the hopeful ones were moved higher up the list, into the danger zone. Now, when I was made permanent my name was put on the top of the list for night work and my turn came in September of that year, 1949. That night shift lasted into early 1950. The result was, my turn to go back on day work came along in time for my marriage the following year. It worked out perfectly for me, and I never had another bout of night work.

'One of the benefits of day work was that the Sunday newspaper was crewed by a list of volunteer staff. The pay was overtime, at double time for a minimum of four hours, and an additional twelve-and-sixpence for "call money", an old agreed method of paying workers for being disturbed when producing a "stop press" edition of the paper. Nobody was discommoded by being asked to work on Saturday night. You could almost be killed in the rush.

'Every now and again, a world crisis would call for the staff of the Sunday edition to be held in extra time, as the news unfolded. It produced a very welcome extra two or three hours of double overtime. On one famous occasion somebody important was on the point of death. As he lingered on, the staff waited for the news, to produce a late Sunday-morning paper. I got eight extra hours, a small fortune, and the gentleman held on into Monday, missed the morning paper, died in the early afternoon, and the news was stale by the time the evening paper was on the streets. It may have been George Bernard Shaw, but I can't remember.★ All of the work of assembling the obituary went into the metal re-melting pots.

'One of the staff of the quasi-permanent night shift was an old gent of about eighty years of age. His name was Ned Sykes and he came from Maryboro, now called Port Laoise. He put together the bits and pieces that feature in every newspaper, the cartoons and the newspaper permanent notices, weather reports and, at that time, shipping lists. We all thought he had a soft job and we used to joke with him about it – until Ned went off on his holidays and I was given his work. I never toiled so hard in all my life, collecting all the bits and pieces, and I couldn't believe that this old man could be so casual and get the work done, without the slightest fuss.

'Printers, generally, weren't inclined to divulge to their wives the exact amount of wages they earned. The printing industry had been awarded a pay increase by

★ Shaw died on the 2nd of November, 1950.

the Labour Court, and all the details were printed in
the papers. The next night, a few of us were playing
poker in the staff club, in Henry Street. During a lull
in the game, Tommy Doyle, a stereotyper – no relation
– said, "Jaysis, lads, the wife nearly caught me out badly
over the rise. When I got home this morning she met
me with a big smile and 'Isn't the rise great?' 'What
rise?' says I. 'It was in the paper this morning, with the
new hourly rates,' says she, 'and me and me ma went
down to Woolworth's and bought one of their ready-
reckoners, and you should be getting so much an hour
now.' I nearly died," said Tommy. "She was within sixpence of the rate. 'Show me that ready-reckoner,' says
I, and she handed it over. I looked at the cover and
noticed that it was printed in 1939.★ And I said to her,
'Will you look at that? The ready-reckoner is out of
date.' 'Ah, Tommy,' says she, 'I knew it was too good to
be true.' But, I'm telling you, lads, I'm still not the better
of it."

'One of the consequences of working at night was
that I could not now enrol for the National College of
Art. I considered myself to be as good as I'd ever be,
but that wasn't uppermost in my mind; it just happened.
Another casualty was my political activity. We'd lost the
1948 election and there was little to do, and we didn't
believe in just going to meetings, looking miserable, and
making each other more depressed than we were. We
could only endure the next five years and hope the
Coalition Government wouldn't ruin the country. My
outlook was devoid of any partiality towards the

★ Rory: 'Woolworth's had bought up a pre-war publisher's stock, and had
an almost endless supply of cheap dictionaries and ready-reckoners.'

Coalition or its adherents. But by the time we got rid of them I was married and in a different world.'

'I had no time frame at all. There was nothing in my mind saying we'd be getting married in a year's time or two years' time. I mean, I didn't know how you went about it. And, as for where we were going to live, well, I was prepared to live in a tent. At that point, Ita said, "Well, I'm not." We were out walking, just past St Enda's, in Rathfarnham. So, we decided that if we were going to get serious, we'd better start saving some money, and we decided we'd look somewhere for a house. Ita said she'd like a bungalow. Well, as far as I was concerned, if she'd said she wanted Áras An Uachtaráin,* good, I'd go after it.

'So I heard about bungalows out in Stillorgan, a place called Linden Lee, and we went out and had a look at one. The show-house was quite nice, a semi-detached bungalow;† it had a nice little kitchen and it had a fridge – a fridge in the kitchen.‡ It was small, about the size of a microwave, not much bigger. It was an Electrolux; I thought it was the most unusual thing. Nobody had fridges; any kind of perishable goods were kept in what was known as a meat safe, made of metal gauze and hung outside the back door. Anyway, there were none of these houses available but there were more being built, so we said we'd put our name down for one. And then,

---

* The President's residence, Phoenix Park, Dublin.
† Ita: 'We looked at houses on the southside and a lot of them looked lovely, because our house at home was so old and all these new houses looked fresh and new and bright.'
‡ Ita: 'There was a kind of square hall and all the rooms led off that and, wonder of wonders, there was a small fridge fitted in the kitchen.'

shortly after that, we discovered that there were no more houses being built; the County Council wouldn't allow it because the water supply was inadequate for the sewerage. But they told us that there was one last house available; some doctor had passed it up. But I hadn't enough money; it was far too soon, so we had to let it go.★

'I saw this advertisement for bungalows out in Kilbarrack.† Nobody had ever heard of Kilbarrack, so I looked it up in an old map of Dublin and I discovered where it was.‡ The ad gave the name of the estate agent, in Dawson Street. So I went in to the agent, but I wasn't satisfied with the details, and I came away. I actually had the £200 deposit in my pocket. £100 was mine and £100 was Ita's. But a few days later, I saw an advertisement in the paper, giving the builder's name and address. So, the next chance I had, I went out to Kilbarrack and I called on Jim Kenny, the builder. He told me that his solicitor was a Mr Bergin. So I went to Bergin and Company and I paid the deposit to him. And that was it.'

★ Ita: 'We were told that, when they got the sewerage and suchlike sorted, the other houses would be built, but, strangely, they never were built.'
† A suburb, about six miles north of Dublin's centre.
‡ Ita: 'Rory was on night work, and he was cycling home and he saw an advertisement, I think it was in Grafton Street, in an estate agent's window, for bungalows in Kilbarrack. I'd no idea where Kilbarrack was.'

Chapter Fifteen – Ita

'We had to get two buses, and it was one dreary, horrible day. It was either January or February, 1951. We got off at Kilbarrack Road – it was called Kilbarrack Lane then. There were two-storey houses on the right-hand side, a small number of them, and there were bungalows on the left, further along. Mr Kenny's was the first one built, on the left. Rory went in to Mr Kenny; I don't think I went into the house – I can't remember. Most of the houses hadn't been built yet. We were sent to an existing road, to the top of St Margaret's Avenue; we were given the key to one of the houses which hadn't been occupied yet, and we thought it was lovely. I thought it was terrific, and we decided to take it. First of all, it was so new, and fresh and clean. And the roof was bright red. The red roof and the red-brick front seemed to brighten up the day, and the two bay windows, just everything about it, I liked. The kitchen was fitted, and I don't think I'd seen a fitted kitchen before. It was absolutely super, and beautifully fresh. And it was a bungalow, which I had particularly wanted.'

But that house had already been sold. 'We were shown a map of the layout of the estate, as it would look. Our house was to be built on Kilbarrack Lane. At that time it was a green field; there were no foundations, no markings. Never having bought a house before, we never asked about whether the back garden would get the sun, or where this was or that was. So we were lucky that we got a house with the sun in the back. Our name went on the map, and I think we got that particular house because somebody had reneged on a deposit.

'We applied for a loan from the Corporation,* a small dwellings loan, which we got. I think the house was £2,150. There was a grant for £250, or something like that. It came to less than £2,000. Rory made all the financial arrangements, as was expected of the male partner back then, and the house was in his sole name.'

'Máire came over and stayed with me, and I slept very well. Máire said, "I didn't sleep a wink and you slept the whole night." But I was very excited, really. And, of course, I went to the church in a car, with Daddy. And the neighbours came out; we had a mixture of people, Catholics, Protestants, Jews, and they all came to the church. It was a dry day, but it was bitterly cold. And, of course, the weddings were very early in the morning then; I think it was around eight or half-eight – but it was cold.'

Rory's sister Breda made the dress. 'She used to come over once or twice a week; all of Rory's sisters were great for making dresses. I had my mother's sewing machine, and I brought it upstairs to the bedroom. It was a mauve material; I remember buying it. Breda came with me, which was fair enough, as she was going to make the dress. We bought it in Cassidy's, in O'Connell Street. It would never have crossed my mind to have a white wedding. All my contemporaries would have done the same as I did. Breda cut it out, and it had a plain

---

* City Council.

top with what is called a mandarin collar, a stand-up collar. She was a much better seamstress than I was. Each dressmaking session became a social occasion; I brought tea and sandwiches and cake upstairs, and we talked for hours. And the pleats – I think they were called concertina pleats – they were done professionally; Breda had them done. But she made the dress. She did it in a few months; it could have been done quicker, only there was no hurry on it. But there was a kind of feeling of excitement for the months leading up to the wedding. If I began to get any way calm about the whole thing, I'd meet some of Rory's sisters, and that would be it; there'd be great excitement again. A lady up the road, Eileen O'Reilly – she was from Thurles★ – she made the hat to match; it was mauve too. It was like straw, but stronger than straw. It was beautiful; she made it perfectly. In the front, it had a double layer of straw and, in between the two layers, Eileen had inserted tiny flowers, around the rim; the flowers were pastel colours. Máire was my bridesmaid, and she had a stone-coloured dress; she made her own – she was very good at it. And Eileen made Máire's hat too; I think it was a very pale yellow, but the same style as mine. And I had a small bouquet, just a few flowers I made up myself, with a bit of silver ribbon. And, of course, you always brought your prayer book, so I covered mine with a piece of the mauve material, to match the dress.

'I had to go and book the hotel for the wedding; the arranging was done some months before. I tried a few hotels and ended up with Jury's, off Dame Street.† I've

---

★ County Tipperary.
† Bloom's Hotel, on Anglesea Street, is built on the site of Jury's.

forgotten how much it was per head,* it was soup and main course and dessert, and tea or coffee. My father paid, and he paid for wine with the meal, and other drinks. And I bought the wedding cake, in Penelope's Cake Shop,† in Orwell Road, Rathgar. Three tiers, and they made it beautifully. I had to do everything; there

---

* Rory: 'I think it was twenty-seven shillings and sixpence, but I'm not sure.'
† Ita: 'It only closed down about a year ago.'

was no one else to do it – that was my responsibility.

'It was just close family, and all the aunts and uncles were asked. I asked Katie and Watt but they had a young family, so they couldn't come. But I had Bessie and Mike, and my Uncle Bob and Aunt Una. And Rory had some aunts. He arranged and paid for cars to pick them up. I had Chris Lynch and Muriel Long, from work – the two of them had to go back in the afternoon. And, of course, Noeleen, with Jim – they weren't married at that time. But we didn't have a huge array of friends there; they were mostly relations. Rory had a big family, and they all came. There was great excitement with them.

'I didn't mind leaving work at all. I loved work, but I didn't mind leaving, because it was the thing to do in those days. You just accepted that you had to leave work. The marriage bar was up, and you were out on your ear. In some places, I suppose, you could stay on but not where I worked, in UCD. I've a vague memory of getting double money the last week, which we used to get at Christmas too. And I got a little bowl of flowers, Royal Doulton, from Professor O'Farrell; I still have it. I can't remember what Professor O'Kelly gave me, but he certainly gave me something. And the cleaner, Lily – I can't remember her surname – brought me a white table cloth with napkins. And the men who worked there, the technicians, they put in a few bob each – none of them were well-paid; in fact, they were pretty poorly paid – and they got me a glass bowl, with glass dishes to match. My neighbour, Mrs Carmichael, brought me over a tiny little teapot, with a pound of tea stuck in it. And Mrs Hingerty opposite brought me a set of glasses, with a jug to match. I can still remember the glasses, the red and white spots. Mr and Mrs Wilkinson next door gave me a glass cake dish, still intact, and their daughter, Ruth, who worked in the China Showrooms in Abbey Street, gave me a cheese dish in the shape of a little cottage; I still have it. Then there was the usual collection of statues of the Blessed Virgin and a few Children of Prague and a few other holy pictures as well, and the Sacred Heart. And we got three irons. Nobody gave us blankets. We had to buy our own and, because of the war in Korea, the price of wool shot through the roof. The blankets cost five pounds; £1 per pound weight. We bought the cheapest we could get. Rory's Aunt Mag gave us an eiderdown, and this saved our lives.'

She doesn't remember much about the wedding ceremony. 'I can still remember arriving at the church with my father, and going in.* Early in the morning and very chilly; it had never crossed my mind that it would be cold, but it didn't worry me. Rory's brother Jackie was the best man. I can't remember the ceremony; I just can't pin it down. I can't remember saying, "I do." I must have said it, but I can't remember. My wedding ring had a little design etched into it; the design has long since worn off. I don't remember it going on my finger. I remember coming down the aisle and, of course, there was confetti; Rory's sisters had the confetti. And all the neighbours outside, and all the relations. I remember all the talk and chat outside, and all the neighbours wishing us well, and a few distant cousins. There was one in particular, a nice woman, a cousin of Rory's, and she came to see the wedding; she had a tweed coat and a beret on her head and a pair of solid shoes on

---

* Ita: 'The bride was on time in those days, by the way.'

her feet and she just plonked herself there in the middle of the photograph – with all our palaver. Nobody would have been rude enough to tell her to buzz off, so she's there in that picture for ever more. And, of course, Aunt Bessie always stood out; she always stood with the heels together and the toes parted; it was part of an affection I had for her – that was the way she was. She's there in the foreground, with her feet apart. Everyone was very happy.

'The wedding meal was a great success. Daddy had a few old friends there: Pádraig O'Keefe,[*] and his wife, Peg; and James Carty,[†] another Wexford man, who was also Máire's godfather. My going-away suit was made of fine grey wool, a plain tailored jacket and an accordion-pleated skirt. I bought it in Macey's, in George's Street.[‡] My blouse was mauve silk, and my small, plain felt hat was also mauve. With black court shoes, black leather handbag and black kid gloves, I decided I was fit to go anywhere. And we both had new cases. Mine was grey. Suitcases were all made of cardboard then, except you decided to have a leather one, which would have been hugely expensive – and ridiculous, because we never foresaw the day when we'd be travelling.' It was the 17th of September, 1951. 'It also happened to be the day that the *Irish Times* burnt down – two historical events in the one day. And the problem was getting the taxi from the hotel to the railway station; we thought we were going to miss the train. The traffic was held up along O'Connell Street because of the fire. The taxi man was

---

[*] He was the General Secretary of the GAA at that time. The GAA stadium in Cork is named after him.

[†] The author of *Carty's History of Ireland*.

[‡] Ita: 'Now long gone, but a wonderful shop for suits and coats at that time.'

taking it very easy, until Rory had a go at him and explained to him, in a not too polite fashion, that there were other routes available. It must have been Amiens Street Station we were going to. We were quite sure we were going to miss the train.'

Chapter Sixteen – Rory

'The taxi turned down, into Westmoreland Street,★ and there were fire brigades all over the place. The *Irish Times* had gone on fire. And the taxi man just rested his hands and arms on the steering wheel and said, "We won't be getting through here for a while." So I said, "I don't care if all of Dublin goes on fire, we've got to catch the train for Cork." Then I said to him, "Turn around,† and go down Anglesea Street and on to the quays and you'll get clear of this jam." I was peremptory, and annoyed, and I felt like taking his life. He knew it: he looked at me in amazement, and said, "OK." And off we went and made the train just on time. I firmly believe he was going to stay where we were and wait for the street to be cleared. I don't know if I gave him a tip; probably not.'‡

'The house was red-bricked, with a kind of paler colour, a yellow ochre pointing, between the bricks. That appealed to us; it had a warm, friendly look. And the

---

★ Rory: 'We had to catch a train from Amiens Street (now Connolly) to Cork; the train ran from Belfast to Cork, and it stopped at Amiens Street. I think it went through a tunnel under the Phoenix Park in those days, under the Wellington Monument.'

† Rory: 'Westmoreland Street wasn't a one-way street; there was no such thing.'

‡ Ita: 'The train started to "puff puff" when we threw ourselves and our cases on to it.'

inside was fabulous, because it was a bungalow; there was space – loads of space, as you'd expect in an empty bungalow, and we were both used to relatively small houses. Mine was particularly crowded. We were both in agreement about what we wanted, we both liked the look of it, and we decided that it was the one we'd go for. It was more expensive than we'd thought; the general price of a three-bedroom house was about £1,600 and ours was going to cost about £2,000. But it didn't make any difference; we had our minds made up.

'We paid the deposit, and I got a mortgage from Dublin Corporation. The Small Dwellings Act provided mortgages to people who had incomes between a minimum and maximum amount. It was pitched for a certain class of buyer; if you earned over the maximum, you weren't eligible – you didn't need it; if you earned below the minimum, it was considered that you wouldn't be able to pay. There was always much manoeuvring to get employers to give you a favourable account of what you were earning, to get through. I had no problem in that regard, since my wages met the required criteria. The full price for the house was £2,154, to be exact, minus the grant which came from the Government because it was a new house, and the deposit, £200. I was granted a thirty-five-year mortgage, £1,700, at 4 per cent. I was rather aggrieved because, if I'd applied for it a month earlier, I'd have got it at 3.75 per cent.★ We

---

★ Rory: 'Years after, people were looking at me as if I was living off their tax. Because mortgages went way up, after we got married, but our rate was fixed. I paid back almost twice the amount, over the whole thirty-five years. One of my amusements was working out how much it would all work out at. Towards the end of the thirty-five years I could have cleared it off, without any great difficulty. But the earlier years had been heavy,

were saving money then, and the house was being built. We had to buy furniture – I didn't even know that we had to buy our own light bulbs – and we got various presents; we had three statues of Our Lady of Lourdes and a couple of the Child of Prague. We had two magnificent kettles. But it was mainly a matter of saving. We had barely enough to get married, and make arrangements, taxis to the church and on to the hotel for the guests, particularly aunts and family.

'At home, there was much cutting-up of yards of material, sewing, making, deciding what hats to wear and, to tell you the truth, I skedaddled. I just had my meals and left, because I couldn't understand what half of the fuss was about. I was getting married, and that was that. But there was a considerable amount of activity. My sisters were expert dressmakers – it came naturally – and they took these things very seriously. I bought a grey suit in Clery's, and a white shirt, a covert cloth overcoat, a corduroy jacket and a grey flannel trousers, and a green velour broad-rimmed hat. I must have been the best-dressed pauper in Ireland. My brother Jackie was the best man; his suit was a lighter colour.

'Ita and I went to see the parish priest of Terenure, to make the wedding arrangements, such as the date and the time of the ceremony. His reverence suggested that the matter of the expenses be settled as soon as possible in order to avoid unnecessary distraction on the day itself. He was naturally anxious to get his fee, which, I suspect,

---

interest-laden amounts, so I decided I wouldn't gratify them, and I paid it off at £7.11s a week. The last payment was £7.60, about €10 in today's terms. We had lunch in the Glenview Hotel, in Wicklow, to celebrate.'

often went unpaid. He then mentioned the matter of the reading of the banns. At that time, people of a certain social status paid a fee of about £5, in order not to have the banns of matrimony read, as prescribed by the laws of the Church.* The Christian outlook in Ireland at the time was that the reading of the banns was the hallmark of the dregs of society. However, Ita and myself didn't subscribe to that view, and we told his reverence that we'd be delighted to have the banns read. When I went home and casually mentioned the matter, my mother went ballistic. She described, in terms that would now be called politically incorrect, the type of people who had the banns read. Almost simultaneously, Ita was getting the same message from her stepmother. We were both definitely in the doghouse and decided, for the sake of family harmony, to return to his reverence and reverse our decision. He smiled quietly and held out his hand for the five-pound note.†

'I had six aunts at the wedding, no uncles. My family was a country family, and the men weren't involved in things like that, unless it was their own children. But the women were. So, that was six aunts and all my sisters and brothers, and the rest. There was a considerable amount. We had cars for them.

'I slept alright the night before, but I'd caught a cold,

---

* Ita: 'He told us that the money was to cover clerical expenses, writing to parishes, to confirm that neither of us had been married already.'
† Rory: 'We got our revenge when our first child was born, and certain people raised the subject of churching for Ita. It was looked upon as a kind of purification ceremony. It was really meant to be a form of thanksgiving for the baby, but the original idea had been given a warped meaning by the usual zealots who infest every religion. So, we disagreed and refused to play ball.'

making the final arrangements, booking taxis and informing my aunts about the times.* The cold didn't manifest itself until later in the day – I was sneezing a bit, but it wasn't bad. The wedding ceremony itself, in my memory, tends to go by like a dream – nothing substantially memorable. But there was quite a crowd outside, Ita's neighbours and some of my innumerable relations. A photographer turned up – we hadn't thought to engage one – and various groups were photographed, in one of which an elderly lady from Balrothery, Mag Carthy, insinuated herself conspicuously in the front of the grouping. Mag had a particular *grá*† for me, possibly because I was polite and civil to her when we met around Tallaght. She wasn't used to such behaviour and so she travelled down for my wedding, uninvited. My friend Dick McGuirk and Gwen were there as well, to wish us luck; they'd been married a fortnight earlier.‡ And the wedding breakfast was quite pleasant; it was very, very good – a decent meal; everybody was quite happy about it – but, of course, it was very early. There was a short speech from Jackie, and I made a speech, thanking the bridesmaid and all who were at the wedding. That ended the speechifying.§ I don't recall any telegrams; they weren't a feature of weddings at the time,

---

* Ita: 'There were no phones.'

† Liking.

‡ Rory: 'Dick had met Gwen when we'd walked, along with Des Sullivan and Kevin Borbridge, from Cork City to Bantry in 1947. Dick was smitten and, luckily, he worked for CIE [train and bus company], and his travelling to Kinsale cost him very little. Around the same time, Des and Betty Casey married, and went off to Canada. Kevin went to South Africa, and then to California, but never found a suitable mate.'

§ Ita: 'My father smiled amiably but made no speech. It wasn't expected of him. He'd paid for everything, so that was his job done for the day.'

but my father spotted the piano and started a bit of a sing-song. My father, incidentally, could knock a tune out of a zinc bucket. We left them to it. We had a train to catch.'

Chapter Seventeen – Ita

'We got the train back from Cork to Amiens Street, and from Amiens Street to Howth Junction.⋆ We'd no money left, and taxis were a great luxury, so we lugged our cases up the road. He didn't carry me over the threshold. He was romantic enough in his own way, but he had enough to do with lugging the cases without humping me up on his back as well.

'When we arrived at the house, Rory's sister Breda was here. She had a fire lit, and she had the cupboards full of food donated by Rory's mother; everything you could think of, tea, sugar, bread, meat, sausages, rashers – she kept us fed for a week. We'd hardly any money and, of course, Rory had to work a week before he'd get any money.†

'The house was pretty sparse, but I suppose we had as much as most people. We had the bedroom suite which Rory had bought, and the floor in the bedroom was stained. I'd made a rug, and that ran beside the bed, and I'd made net curtains for the front windows; they were flimsy but they were OK. I'd made heavier curtains, also for the front windows. We had no problem with street lights, because we had no street. We had no

---

⋆ Train station, on Kilbarrack Road.

† Rory: 'We'd all this spare food but no money – until I found a pound, in one of my flannel trousers. I took it out of the case, to hang it up, and the pound note fell out.'

curtains on the back windows; we were surrounded by fields. In the sitting-room, we had the chesterfield suite which Rory's three oldest sisters had bought us between them, and his father and mother had given us money and we'd bought a carpet square for the sitting-room and lino for the dining-room. We called it the dining-room but it was actually the living-room, and used more than any other room. And we had the dining-room suite, which I'd bought. It was a nice light oak; I was very pleased with it. We got it in Roche's Stores; it was actually their Spring Show display piece that year. The other two bedrooms were empty, not a thing in them. And the hall had bare boards. That was it really, and the little ornaments we got for wedding presents.* The kitchen was bare, except that the cupboards were fitted. We'd no kitchen table, not for a few months. And I'd no ironing board; I spread a blanket on the floor and ironed on the floor. All those things were kind of extras; we got them as we went along. We had a cooker – we had to have a cooker; we got that on the never-never, from the ESB. We didn't have a fridge, and not for years afterwards.

'It was very exciting. The house had been empty; no one had lived in it. We used to come out and look at it, before we got married, but to arrive and to fix up your things in your own house and to know it was yours – and the weather was fine for quite a while, and

---

* Rory: 'Before the wedding I had to transport my belongings out to Kilbarrack. First on the list was my studio easel. It had to be carried across the city, two buses, and it wasn't a lightweight object. My next trip was to carry my collection of Walter Scott's Waverley novels, all of them, in a brown suitcase, a substantial weight, and I was physically exhausted at the end of the trip. However, I read and re-read those books over the years. They now reside in the attic. Like many old classics and favourites, they're virtually unreadable.'

everything seemed to be falling into place. It was wildly exciting.★

'The house actually went up in a field, built in a row of bungalows, and there was no road. There was a driveway and a front wall, but no road. I remember, Rory's sisters called, and they walked along the tops of the walls, to avoid walking in all the mud. It never cost them a thought – they laughed at it; they were delighted that we were fixed up. In fact, I was well pregnant before they started the road. It was very muddy at one stage, and there was a foreman who went up and down on a motorbike, and he instructed the men to put boards, planks, across the mud, so I wouldn't slip.† It never bothered me.‡ The whole thing was so exciting. Everything was new, and I got to know the neighbours.

'We all met down in the grocer's, Peter Butler's shop.§ That was the meeting place. Peter served at the counter. He was a very friendly, big Mayo man, and everybody liked going into the shop. I got to know a lot of people that way. I remember, the first woman who spoke to me was Aileen Turley. She had her eldest son with her, in his pram. She had been an Aer Lingus hostess. At that time there were a lot of ex-Aer Lingus hostesses living here; they were all very pretty women. And I met a Mrs Thompson that first day – I've forgotten her first name. She was a beautiful woman. Again, she'd been an air hostess; her husband was a pilot. Then Drugan's, the

---

★ Rory: 'We used to walk out and look back at it.'
† Ita: 'I saw that man again years later, and he remembered me and said, "How's that baby?" and I think the baby was nearly a teenager by then.'
‡ Rory: 'Eventually, we got a brand-new road, and two cars a day passed by.'
§ Today the Hamburger Bar, on Kilbarrack Road.

chemist, opened. I was their first customer. And, again, it became a meeting place.★

'And I got to know Maura Coghlan, two doors down, very quickly. And there was Sheila Mulvaney, and Leo. And then there were the Mays, Ena and Barney. We were walking past one day and we saw a man standing in their doorway, and Rory recognised him as a man he'd known in the College of Art, Harry Burton. He was a very nice, quiet type of a man and he introduced us to the Mays. They were lovable characters. Barney was by way of being a Walter Mitty; he read an awful lot of detective stories, and he lived in a little world of his own.† He was also an alcoholic. I remember coming home one day – I think it was a Sunday morning – walking past the Mays'. They had a rockery in the middle of the front garden, and Barney's car was up on top of it – like a decoration, a cherry on a cake.

'Mr and Mrs Winks, Dave and Eva, were our next-door neighbours. They were from Scotland. Dave was quite a prim and proper man, a gentlemanly man. Eva told us she was from the Gorbals, in Glasgow, and she was Jewish. She was a terrible gambler – she told me herself she was, and that her father had been a profes-sional gambler. I wasn't quite able for her. She'd borrow money from me, money I couldn't afford, and I was nearly afraid to ask for it back. She was tougher than

---

★ Ita: 'We never had to go further than Desmond Drugan's. He had cures for everything – cures for bee stings, cures for worms, which nearly all the kids got; he had a cure for them. I remember once, I got fierce chilblains – I think I was expecting – and the itch was an absolute torment. I went down to Desmond Drugan, and he made up this ointment, which I used, and I never got them since. He was a real chemist, an old-style chemist.'
† Rory: 'Reading Peter Cheyney and smoking Woodbines.'

I was – put it that way. I didn't dislike her at all, but I was a bit wary of her. Her mother-in-law used to come from time to time, from Scotland; she used to bake cakes to beat the band and they'd often end up on our table.

'I settled in very quickly. At first, I was feeling around and getting to know people, but I can't say I ever felt lonely. I went off walking and moseying around the place. I didn't miss work. I kept myself busy. I was wrapped up in my own affairs and my own life, and my own house. When we told people where we were going to live, they'd say, "Why are you going so far away?" And my answer was always, "Away from what?" I loved Terenure, as a place, but I was happy enough to leave the atmosphere, and everything else at home, and to get away on my own.★ On Wednesday, I'd go over to Terenure and have my dinner with my father and step-mother. I cycled over, at first, and cycled back, to cook Rory's dinner when he came home.

'I wasn't very long before realising I was pregnant. I just began to feel sick; I didn't know what it was all about, and it was actually Mrs Winks who told me. I said, one day, in all my innocence, "I don't feel well. I felt awful sick this morning." And she said, in her best Scottish accent, "Ach, you must be pregnant." So, she was right.

'It had its ups and downs – same as they all had. It stopped me doing a lot of what I'd normally have done,

---

★ Rory: 'I was an enormous distance from home, but that didn't worry me at all; I had no regrets, no lingering thoughts of wanting to go back to Tallaght. I just transferred my home allegiance to where I was. I never knew the meaning of Northside or Southside; it was a Dublin City thing. I was from County Dublin.'

but – I was a funny kind of person – I accepted whatever hit me and just got on with it. Every morning, for about three months, I was sick – dreadful vomiting – and an hour later I felt fine for the day. I remember, we had our Christmas dinner and, within twenty minutes, I got rid of the lot. I just thought, what a waste. But I was excited, especially when I began to show and started to feel well. I made all the baby clothes. Money was really scarce, so you had to make as many clothes as you could. At that time, babies wore long flannelette night dresses, little belts around them, and a shawl. You dressed the baby in nightdresses for two or three months after it was born; you'd tuck the flannelette, it went down over the feet and toes. I made five or six nightdresses.

'I was at home one morning, on my own, and the waters burst. I didn't know what to do at first. I went down to Sheila Mulvaney, and I stayed with Sheila nearly all day. Until Rory came home – it probably seems strange now, but you didn't take people out of work; you couldn't phone up and tell them to come home. Sheila was awfully kind to me and so was Leo. Leo had a car, and it was they who brought me into the nursing home that evening. Aideen was born that night.★

The nursing home was over in Phibsborough; a Nurse Borrowman owned it. I stayed there for nearly two weeks; that was the thing then. They were very nice, but I was dying to come home. I can remember being as proud as punch. And she was the first

★ Rory: 'I was at work, at the *Independent* – it was a Saturday night – when I got a phone call from the nursing home. There was great rejoicing around the place. But, otherwise, I was working; it was the next morning before I saw Ita and the baby.'

grandchild, on Rory's side, so there was huge excitement. They all arrived with presents galore, all kinds of things; Breda made beautiful little dresses, beautiful work altogether, smocking all across the bodice. I was in there for my birthday and they all arrived with birthday presents.

'Aideen was christened while I was still in the nursing home, in Christ the King church, in Cabra. But we had a tea when we came home from the nursing home. I still had the top tier of the wedding cake; that was her christening cake. We had the grandparents out, and Rory's Aunt Bridge, Aunt Mag, and Aunt Lil, and Máire and her husband, Jimmy. There was a bottle of sherry, the height of luxury. I've forgotten who was pouring the sherry – it could have been me – and Rory's mother said, "You can give a glass to Bridge and Mag but don't give much to Rory; he's not used to it." She really believed he'd never had a drink.

'We had a new pram. I think it was about £14. It was dear enough, but it was lovely. People would stop to look at Aideen; they'd seen me pregnant, and they'd stop, and I got to know everyone that way. It was mostly young couples, starting off; we were nearly all newlyweds. We went walking miles with those prams. Saved heat in the winter; got us out in the summer. I brought her out every afternoon, no matter what the weather was like, up to Sutton Cross or, sometimes, up Baldoyle Road – three or four miles sometimes.

'We had to borrow the cot. She slept in the pram for three weeks, maybe a month. Then somebody who worked with Rory in the *Independent* lent us a little cot; it was big enough for her – it was grand. Then, there was another man who worked there – I've an idea his name was Bob Peffers★ – and he made us a lovely cot. He charged very little for it. All our children slept in that cot.

'Being a mother was a question of trial and error. But what could I do, only take to it; I had the baby and I had to take care of her. I tried breast-feeding for the first few weeks, but I obviously couldn't; she screamed and screamed and screamed. And it was my doctor, Dr Chapman, who said it would be better to put her on the bottle. I must be quite honest and say that I wasn't upset at having to give up. It was a relief: I was very sore and uncomfortable, and Aideen wasn't happy. I put her on the bottle and she stopped crying; she was the quietest baby after that. And if I went out and left her with Rory, which was seldom, he could give her a bottle – he couldn't breast-feed her.

'But I loved the whole idea of being a mother. I managed it fine. She was the first grandchild in the Doyle family and, as far as her Grandad Doyle was concerned, she was absolutely perfect. She was late walking, and he'd say, "All the better. When they walk too early their legs get bandy. Much better." She was late having teeth: "All the better, much better; she'll have them longer." There were sleepless nights – there are always sleepless nights. You'd be livid when you had to get up, but it didn't seem to matter the next day. Loss of sleep never really affected me; I seemed to get by great on what I had.

'I was delighted when Rory changed jobs; it was what

★ Ita: 'Rory came home one day and he told me that some man in work had passed wind in a noisy fashion, and Bob Peffers turned around and said, "Don't tear it. I'll take the piece."'

he wanted. And he'd worked very hard in the *Independent*. He used to work on Saturday nights, for extra money. He'd cycle in, and work until two in the morning, and cycle home. It was heavy going, but it was the money that enabled us to pay the mortgage and everything else. But, now that he was teaching, he had set hours. He had long summer holidays. I was delighted that he was at home more, although he was never what you'd call a great man for hoovering or dusting; he wouldn't have known how to put the hoover together.* He cycled to work at first, and then he started getting the train into work. The same group of people used to run up the road to the station every day. There was one woman, Teenie Moloney, who was living in her bungalow with her sister, Belle, before she got married; she was a civil servant. They used to go haring up the road, and they'd cut through a field, a short cut. It was the usual Irish thing, of *bóthar*. The word for a road in Irish is *bóthar*, and it really means a cow track, the way cows cut through the shortest way possible. *Bó* is "cow". And they really made a *bóthar* through the field to the station. But I remember, one day, they were running up and there was a young priest with them; he was a cousin of Teenie's. He tripped in the field, and he was delaying the others. And Belle, at the top of her voice, shouted, "Get up, you dirty-looking eejit, or we'll all miss our train." It was an unusual way to address a priest, even if he was your cousin.

'I had one miscarriage, between the first two children. It was in the third month. I was taken into Holles Street.† I went in at about six in the morning; our neighbour

---

* Ita: 'He still doesn't.'
† Dublin maternity hospital.

Kiernan Coghlan ran me in. He was very kind; he was one of the few men on the road with a car. I was put on a trolley – I had the miscarriage; the baby came in the hospital – and I was still on the trolley at six o'clock that evening. And not only that, but nobody asked me if I had a mouth on me; I didn't even get a cup of tea. I'm not blaming the hospital either: the nurses were busy and I just lay there. That was the kind of sucker I was; I took whatever was coming.* At about six o'clock a matron came around, and she went through a few of the nurses, and I was put into a lovely, comfortable bed; I thought I'd gone to heaven. I was very weak when I got home. I remember my legs being weak, and feeling groggy. I don't know how distressed I was; I can't remember. It was just before Christmas. Rory had changed jobs by then. He had time off and he was able to mind the baby.

'I was happy when I was pregnant again. It was still a shock – it's always a shock when you realise you're pregnant. There was no such thing as a planned pregnancy; it just happened, and that was it – you took whatever was coming. Some women had babies year after year. I did well; I had two years between mine – I got a good break. I went to the same nursing home, Nurse Borrowman's. I don't remember going in. I was well cared for. I remember one particular night – it was an oldish house – there was a storm. Those windows rattled like hell all night. And I could have sworn I heard a mouse scratching too. I thought I'd never get home.

'And now I was juggling two babies, two girls, Aideen and Pamela. And, of course, the grandparents were

---

* Ita: 'I can see the difference between then and now; people are maybe right to be more demanding.'

delighted. In the Doyle household, there was no such thing as, "Oh, it's a pity it wasn't a boy." Rory's father always seemed to pray for girls. Pamela was a very quiet baby, placid and healthy; she hardly ever cried. I fed her on the bottle from the word go; I wasn't going to have her crying with hunger. I fed Pamela on Sister Laura's Food, the same as I had fed to Aideen. But nappy-washing was the bane of my existence. It was a terrible time of the year, and that November was an awful month. You had to soak the nappies in a bucket, and then you washed them by hand in the sink. You hung them out, and you hoped that God gave you a dry day. And you looked along the road – there were no walls or hedges yet; it was just wires between the gardens – and there were nappies flying to the left of you and nappies flying to the right of you. And maybe, "Hello, how are you?" and "How are *you*?" and the nappies going out. It didn't matter what day it was. We broke the Sabbath, and out went the nappies.

'The only social life consisted of meeting people and chatting, or visiting each other. There was a picture house in Sutton but we seldom got to it. The first time we went out was for our first wedding anniversary. We went to the pictures and had our tea out. That was a great treat. I can't remember the film.* But I never felt isolated from the world. As far as I was concerned, this was the world. I always got a newspaper, the *Independent*, and the radio was a godsend. There were sponsored programmes. I loved the music. I used to join in; I had a bit of a voice then. "What'll I do – when you – are all

---

* Rory: 'A few years ago, we went to *Lawrence of Arabia*, when it was re-released, and it had been so long since I'd been to the pictures that I was totally unfamiliar with the size of the screen and the volume. When the camels started bawling I leaned forward and looked for the volume button.'

alone . . ." "Are You Lonesome Tonight?" And the songs from the shows. "Whispering While You Cuddle Near Me". There was the Hospital Sweepstakes programme; I liked the mix of music they played. And there was Frankie Byrne – she was Jacob's biscuits – an agony aunt. And, of course, there was the Walton's programme – "If you feel like singing, do sing an Irish song." We bought a second-hand piano in Walton's, when the girls were bigger, and I can still see old Mr Walton, a grey-haired, good-looking man, with a kind of a beard. There was *Living with Lynch*, with Joe Lynch; lots of Irish music, and the conversation was witty and easy. And then there was Din Joe's programme. Din Joe became famous for having Irish dancers on the radio; it was the one thing he'd be remembered for. He was a big, heavy man, and he lived in Tallaght. And I believe – it may or may not be true – that when some of the kids said, "Hello, Din Joe," he'd get annoyed with them, because it was only his stage name. He was actually a motor dealer.'* And I was really keen on *Mrs Dale's Diary*; I looked forward to it every morning – it was the time I had my coffee. Looking back on it, she was such a smug lady, but it was great.

'We went to Mass in Baldoyle, which was our parish at that time. And very awkward it was; it was like a country parish. There was a bus, but we couldn't go together because of the babies. One of us went first, and then there'd be a second bus for the second Mass. I'd go to the first Mass, and it was a Father Dillon who said that Mass. He was a brother of that Fine Gael TD, James Dillon. He'd start off, and that was fine. But then he'd

---

* Rory: 'He wasn't a native of Tallaght. He was a runner-in.'

get up to make his sermon. He'd take out his handker-chief, a big white handkerchief,★ and he'd wipe his fore-head and blow his nose, quite a loud blow of the nose. And then he'd begin talking. If the TD was good at talking, he wasn't a patch on his brother. He went on and on, and on and on, and all I'd be thinking about was getting home and seeing if the girls were alright and getting the meat into the oven for the dinner. When that particular priest got older, he became very forgetful. One Christmas morning, I decided to go to Mass in Raheny instead – fortunately, because Father Dillon forgot it was Christmas Day and somebody had to go and wake him up. But he was getting on in years, so I suppose he can be forgiven.'

'He was born in the same place where I had the girls. But I never saw him. Rory saw him. He was blue – his lips were blue – but Rory said he was a fine-looking baby, with black hair, and he was big. He was over the eight pounds, or even bigger. But they knew, from the time he was born, that there was something wrong with him. So he was taken to Temple Street Hospital straight away, and I never saw him. He lived just a day and a night. They asked Rory could they do a post-mortem, and they discovered that his whole insides seemed to be wrong – the valves of the heart weren't properly attached, there was something wrong with his stomach, the bowels were all twisted. So, it was just a day and a night.† We called him Roderick Anthony. He had to be christened straight away and I said, "Call him Roderick Anthony."

★ Rory: 'It was red.'

† Ita: 'They can do marvellous things these days, that they might have been able to do something, but, at that time, they couldn't.'

"Roderick" because that was Rory's name. And "Anthony" for the simple reason that I was told that Saint Anthony was great; if I prayed to Saint Anthony, the baby would be grand. I gave somebody half-a-crown to put into Saint Anthony's box in the church, and to light a candle. I thought, well, call the child after him and give him half-a-crown, the least he can do is take care of the baby. But he didn't; he let me down. I don't pray to Saint Anthony any more. I decided he was a dead loss.

'He's buried in the Angels' Plot, in Glasnevin. Rory and my sister, Máire, went with him. I'm not certain what happened. But, even in death, there was something to laugh about. My stepmother had given Rory an umbrella for Christmas; you pressed a button and it shot open. Well, it was a wet, miserable morning and Rory had the umbrella with him. And himself and Máire were running for the bus after the funeral, and Rory hit the handle of the umbrella in some way, and it broke. The handle was full of some kind of white powder, like chalk, and it flew all over the place, on to him, on to Máire, on to the road and everyone in sight. The two of them held each other up, laughing.

'I was kept in the nursing home the same length of time as if the baby had lived; I think it was ten days. It was very distressing, but Rory's mother, I remember, sent me in wool. I had some patterns and I began to knit for the two girls. I was very upset, but I took everything and got on with it. You couldn't be lamenting in front of the two little girls; they might have thought that he was more important than they were.

'The strange thing is, three other babies died in the locality, at that time. All women around my own age, all within a few months. I often thought about it but, in my usual procrastination, I never did anything. I always felt, well, these things were meant to happen; they happened, and that was it. It did seem very peculiar but, as it was, everybody accepted things that came along. They'd probably query the whole thing now.'★

'When all the payments had been made on the cooker, I had my choice of a fridge or a washing machine. Strangely, I went for the fridge. So, when that was paid for, I got the washing machine. I can't remember the make, but you had to fill it from the tap with a hose, and the hose went out the back door, to empty it. But it was a miracle, in its way. And the mangle. Of course, there was no dryer, so I still had the problem of drying. But it was great. I was very busy, with the kids' – she had three by now† – 'and getting them to and from school, but I always managed to go for a walk in the afternoons. I enjoyed life. I used to meet Maura Coghlan, two doors down, and Aileen O'Connor, from around the back, and the three of us would go off, pushing the prams. We had great chats. And, in a way, life was easier than it is now. The kids had great freedom; they could play tennis and football on the road. The world was their oyster. We didn't have to go rushing from this club to

---

★ Rory: 'In latter years, the thought crossed my mind that Windscale [nuclear power station, and plutonium production plant, in Cumbria, UK, on the Irish Sea; renamed 'Sellafield' in 1988] might have had something to do with it. But, at that time [1956], we hadn't heard of Windscale.'

† Ita: 'The only thing I remember is Dr Chapman saying, "It's a boy. That was what she was hoping for." I can still hear him saying it, but I'd never said that I wanted a boy. We called you Roderick, after your father and your brother. A lot of people said it was bad luck, so I said, "No, it's in memory of his brother. It keeps the name alive."'

that club and the other club, to keep them occupied. You could leave the doors open. They'd come home for their dinner, in the summer, and go off playing again; they were out from morning till night.

'We didn't get a television straight away. I remember the night that RTE started;* a couple down the road, the McCloskeys, had a television, and they invited us down to watch the opening programme. Down we went and, really, all we saw for the opening night was snow. You could see the odd little figure arriving through it, and you'd hear great laughing and joking, and then we'd get another fall of snow – but even to look at the snow was something. It was unbelievable, really. And when we got our own, sure, it was marvellous altogether. In the beginning, for about the first six months, I looked at anything; the whole thing was a wonder. I remember *Little Women*, and the cowboy ones, *McKenzie's Raiders*, and *The Virginian*, and *Have Gun Will Travel*.† I loved those westerns. Then RTE showed a lot of the old musical comedies. I'd seen them in the cinema and thought they were wonderful. I'm afraid, second time around, I lost interest; I couldn't really watch them at all. Nelson Eddy and Jeannette MacDonald. The music was still beautiful, but you could listen to that on a record. I couldn't take to all the dancing and swinging. Then there were the Laurel and Hardys, and all those silent films. I looked at everything at first, and just got a bit fussy after that.'

★ ★ ★

---

* RTE (Radio Telefís Eireann) first broadcast on the 31th of December, 1961.
† Rory: 'It was *The Restless Gun*.'

There was one more child. 'He arrived too soon. He was five or six weeks early.

'I began to bleed. We had the car by then, and I think Rory drove me in to the Rotunda. A doctor examined me and said I'd have to stay until the baby was born; otherwise I might lose it. That was kind of worrying, but it had to be done. I was only there a few hours – I remember being in the bed, and the labour pains started. I said to the nurse that I was getting labour pains, and she said, "Not at all; you couldn't be." But the pains persisted and began getting worse. I wasn't on my own; there were other women in the ward. And I told the nurse again, I was still getting the pains and they were getting worse. She said, "Nonsense"; she was quite offhand. So the lady in the bed opposite said, "Did *you* ever have labour pains?" And the nurse said, "No." "Well, this is this lady's fifth baby; she should know what labour pains are. If the woman says she's having labour pains, then she's having labour pains." I blessed her for it, because I wouldn't have shouted or roared in a million years. So a doctor came to examine me, and there was a mad rush.

'I remember, it was a coloured doctor who delivered him, an African man, I think. And I said to him, "Is she alright?" For some reason, I thought it was a girl. And he said, "It's not a she; it's a he." And he smiled. He was delighted with himself; he was really a happy, very nice man.

'I was brought up to the ward, but I was on my own. Shane had been left in an incubator. He was only four pounds. And we were told – one of the nurses told me not to hold out too much hope.

'When I came home, we had to leave Shane there.

We were told that he'd have to stay there, in the incubator, until he gained weight and, again, not to hold out much hope – the same nurse. He was a tiny little thing. And his poor little head used to wobble all over the place. But he was kind of spunky-looking; he'd look you straight in the eye.* We went in every day to see him, or every evening. There was a matron who came around, and she asked was this our baby. And I said, "Yes. Do you think he'll live?" And she said, "Of course he'll live." So I said, "The nurse told us not to hold out too much hope." The matron was absolutely livid; she wanted to know who the nurse was. He was perfectly healthy, just too small.

'And one morning, we got a card in the post: Please come and collect your son before such and such a time. A postcard – you see, we'd no phone. A plain postcard; it was actually handwritten, come and collect him – like he was a parcel in the post office. So we went in and got him. And I said to the matron, "When do I have to bring him back for a check-up?" She said, "You don't have to bring him back. He's perfect." '†

---

* Rory: 'I could only see him through glass; he was in an incubator. And the first time I saw him, I thought, "Mother of God . . ." But he looked at me, and I came away and said to myself, "He's going to make it." '
† Rory: 'He was so tiny, he had to be washed in a little pudding bowl; nothing else was small enough to take him. But he made it. I had that feeling, that look about him – he was going to make it.'

Chapter Eighteen – Rory

'We walked up the road and opened the door and Breda, my sister, was waiting for us. She'd been sent out by my mother, with a big bag of food, all sorts of groceries. And she had the fire lighting; it was very pleasant – that was our first image.

'We'd no curtains. There was nothing on the kitchen floor. The walls were bare. We were thinking about things, learning over the weeks, what we had to do. I knew nothing about how a household was run. At home, I'd just walked in and out, and saw nothing. I think I had a hammer, some kind of an old saw, and a shovel for the fireplace. Somebody had thought to put a couple of light bulbs into the bag from Tallaght; I'd never have thought of that. But we just felt excited – here we were.

'The next day, I got the saw and I cut down a young sally tree in the ditch at the edge of Kilbarrack Lane. I dug a hole in the back garden with the fire shovel, planted the sally tree and attached a rope between it and the downpipe of the house. I knew a house had to have a clothesline. Ita was in business; she now had a clothesline.

'We had a jungle out the back. It was just grass growing and growing, and bits of concrete and brick around the place. I bought a fork and a spade and I proceeded to dig the garden* and, in doing that, got to know the

---

* Ita: 'We did it, between us.'

240

next-door neighbours. How to dig, what to plant – all very important matters, and discussed over the garden fence. During that first week, I was taking my ease in the garden – I'd nothing else to do – when I noticed the clothes flapping on the line. I started laughing and couldn't stop. It was an hilarious moment in my life, when I realised that I'd never seen women's underwear on a clothesline at home.

'One of the first things we discovered, as autumn changed to winter, was that there were some awful draughts, as the house dried out, from under the skirting boards. So we spent the first winter in dressing gowns, in front of the fire. Then we discovered that packing wet newspaper under the skirting boards was very effective, and stopped the draughts. We also discovered draught excluders, for the doors, and other little domestic things like that. And we discovered that the easiest way to keep warm was to go to bed early, with the radio. On Sundays, we listened to Radio Luxemburg; it was very entertaining. The programmes were paid for by the various religious persuasions, in America, and a preacher would make a sermon – "You are saved!" and then they'd sing a hymn – *Old Pharaoh thought it was all a joke/And he went out without his cloak/And if he did he sure got soaked/My! Didn't it rain!* It was marvellous.* And, now and again, Helena or Harry Arnold from next door would drop a copy of the *News of the World* in the bedroom

---

* Ita: 'The preacher was saying, "You want to be saved? You all want to be saved. Sailor in the corner, put your hand up if you want to be saved." And the sailor obviously put his hand up, and the preacher goes, "Sailor, you are saved!" And I thought, "God, wouldn't that be handy." Do all the devilment you wanted to do, and then go to this thing and hold up your hand, and you're saved for ever more.'

window. Harry knew someone who worked on the boat to England, and one of the most exciting things was that you could get your hands on the *News of the World*. It was banned here. All the misdemeanours of the vicars and scoutmasters – it was bad enough then too.

'And then there was the wallpapering; that was a job. While I'd seen it happen, I'd never actually hung a sheet of wallpaper before. There was the measuring, cutting, pasting, folding, and then sticking it to the wall. The wet paper often ended up around my neck. We got an allowance for wallpaper, from the builder; if you wanted fancy stuff you paid the difference. We picked the best wallpaper for the sitting-room, the room we ended up using least of all. A kitchen table, a sweeping brush, and dozens of items we took for granted in other people's houses; we built up the home as we went along.

'On the day after we arrived, or the next day, we were going for a walk, and I met a man I knew from the School of Art, Harry Burton, a very good artist. He was living down the road, with the Mays, and he introduced us to Ena and Barney. Their next-door neighbours were Leo and Sheila Mulvaney. Then we discovered that we had Scottish people on the other side of us, the Winks, and they had a young boy and a little girl.'* Gradually, when children came along, we got to know who the other people along the road were, and in the houses behind us. And the Mays started to organise a few parties. Ena was a pretty, dark-haired woman and was very convivial. We were invited, and great fun was had by

---

* Rory: 'Unfortunately, that boy, Gerald, when he grew up, drowned in that dreadful Fastnet disaster [in 1979]. He got interested in sailing in Kilbarrack. They were things that happened that you could never have expected.'

everybody. And then others, including ourselves, threw a party – numerous bottles of stout, a bottle of whiskey, probably a bottle of gin, some tonic; that made a party in those days. Sandwiches and suchlike. You'd be broke for six months afterwards. There'd be singing and dancing. Harry Burton played his banjolele and also did a wonderful monologue on the piano. Ena and Barney knew quite a number of artistic, theatrical people. Her cousin was a well-known soprano, Louise Studley. We had Tom Round,★ the Welsh tenor, who was singing in concerts in Dublin; he came to one of the parties. And a few dancers; we had Des Domigan, who taught ballet. He put on a show – but half the people at the party didn't appreciate men carrying on like that. He was dressed up in tights, and all the rest. We were too innocent to realise that he was leaning towards the left wing, or however you want to describe it. We had Joe Lynch,† and Eamon Keane‡ – he was a highly talented man. He was inclined to get overcome with alcohol, and he'd be carted off and put behind the sofa, to sleep it off till the next morning. Listening to Harry playing the banjolele, I thought I'd like a banjo; I don't know why. I knew nothing about music, except that I could play musical instruments by ear, like my father and my brothers. So I bought a banjo in McNeal's, in Capel Street, and I took the banjo home and I fiddled around with it, got a book on how to play it, and got great enjoyment out

★ Tom Round: joined the D'Oyly Carte Opera Company, 1945; Sadler's Wells, 1952–8; best known for his rendition of 'Take a Pair of Sparkling Eyes'.
† Joe Lynch: actor and radio presenter; best known for the character Dinny, in the Irish soap *Glenroe*.
‡ Eamon Keane: actor, raconteur, broadcaster.

of it. My cousin, Vi, gave me a banjo that had belonged to her husband, Billy; he'd bought it many years before, in the 1920s, when the banjo bands broke out all over the musical world. I also bought a guitar afterwards. But I did like playing that banjo; I love banjo music.*

'The nearest pub was in Baldoyle, or away up in Raheny. So, to go out and get a drink, as I'd been accustomed to do in my single days, I'd have to go to a considerable amount of trouble. And I discovered that I couldn't just go in and ask for a bottle of stout; you'd be met with "What are you having?" and you were immediately into a round. So I came to a decision, and kept to it for the twenty-five years or more that I couldn't afford to go out drinking: I just stopped going to pubs. The money was needed at home. I never had a local. It was no inconvenience; I didn't want to go.

'Life was different; the whole thing was totally different. I was living in a house with a huge amount of space, with just one other person, having been used to hordes of people all around me. I had a bed that I knew was my own, the same bed every night — that was a change. Ita's sister, Máire, and her husband, Jimmy, gave us the wireless as a wedding present. It was the quality of the sound, and the programmes; I could never hear them properly at home, either because everybody was talking or it would get on my mother's nerves and she'd switch it off, just like that, in the middle of a programme. So, now we had uninterrupted radio; that was great, such a wide selection of song and music.

---

* Rory: 'After a number of moves, the Mays ended up in London, where they bought a boarding house. Barney was shot dead by one of his boarders, and Ena was badly injured.'

'I hadn't the slightest idea about the rhythms of women. But I was informed that there was a baby on the way. I didn't say, "How did that happen?" but I had only a vague idea; this was real life and not schoolyard theory. It didn't occur to me that this was an unusual occurrence; I just took it for granted. We just accepted: "That's that; here we are." We expected that something like this would happen. We didn't discuss it. We were going to have a baby – that was it. But it was good news. We went off to Dr Chapman, in Sutton, to ensure that Ita was medically alright. And then Aideen was born; that was the extraordinary part – there was no inter-mediate period. Suddenly, we had to buy a pram.'

'The house was in the City of Dublin but across the road was County Dublin. We went out the gate, and we were in a field that dropped down to the ditch, a great big ditch that flooded every time there was a shower of rain. And then the road was about forty or fifty yards from the house. Our houses were built in a straight line, anticipating the new road. And Kilbarrack Lane mean-dered. Jack Flood's farm was across the road. The field got muddier with use, for twelve months or more. But we didn't look on it as hardship. I got my bicycle out, past the mucky part, got up on it and went to work. I cycled in for the best part of the year. But when it came to the winter, I realised that, while the force of the wind coming down from the mountains above Tallaght would sometimes bring you to a standstill, it was nothing like the wind that came off the sea, when you were trying to cycle the seven miles into Dublin. So I took the train, and trotted up Talbot Street, into Middle Abbey Street, and that was fine. I was still on the day shift, and I did

Saturday night work, for the Sunday paper – at least four hours' double time, and call money. The whole lot made up a handsome sum.

'In 1952, we got into an industrial relationship problem – we went on strike, in other words. And we stayed out for about seven weeks. All we had was the £5 a week strike pay. In all that, the mortgage had to be paid, and we had to live. And again, my mother came to the rescue with a bag of groceries, every week, including two ounces of tobacco.* It helped us through. To give you an idea of what was at stake: we refused an offer of twelve-and-six a week rise and settled, after seven weeks, for fifteen shillings a week.† I was in favour of the strike, because I'd never been on strike before, and I never really knew anyone who had been. Everybody has a strike in them, or should. Because you learn a lot. I learned, shortly and very clearly, the difference between strong opinions and real principle, between what was desirable and what was available. A lot of the people who were shouting loudest for a strike all disappeared and got jobs – knew where to get jobs in England – and the rest of us were just busy looking at ourselves, because there was no picketing; it wasn't necessary. It cured me of my uncritical militancy, although I've always been a member of a trade union, and I helped organise one as well.

---

* Ita: 'Fish and meat, bread and tea, everything, even to the baby's food; and there'd always be some kind of sweet thing as well. She really kept us going. And the grocer, Peter Butler, let us run a book, because he knew we'd pay. I'd never owed money to anyone.'

† Ita: 'I was much relieved when the whole thing was over. I used to put money by each week, for rates and ground rent, and I'd stopped that. It took us months and months to catch up, even with the pay increase.'

'I saw an ad in the paper, just after the strike, for a temporary whole-time teacher in the School of Printing, in Bolton Street. I said, "I'd like that," and Ita was in agreement. The logical step from being a tradesman was to be a foreman. I didn't think I'd like that kind of job. But to be a teacher was something I wanted. I didn't see it in blue-collar, white-collar terms. It never crossed my mind. Those terms weren't used; they came across from America, I suppose, but we didn't have them then. You always went to work in Dublin with a collar and tie; you set out respectably dressed. But teaching was a step up, and something I felt I could do. It would, eventually, be a better job, and an advance on working as a compositor, although I had difficulty with the money. I got less at first; I went from about £13 a week, down to £10. But we decided to take the hit. It took me a few years to catch up. But it wasn't for the money I became a teacher; I just liked the job. I never regretted it.

'But it was hard-going, financially. If Ita managed to have the price of a threepenny bar of Cadbury's at the end of the week, she thought she was in absolute luxury. And there were bills that came along – the rates bill, which shook us; we'd never had to face that before. There was a particularly loud-mouthed rate collector, the lowest form of human being, a slob. He'd come to the door and abuse you if you were a bit late.* Because he was on commission. And ground rent† was £15 a

---

* Ita: 'I told him we were expecting a salary cheque within a few days, and then we'd pay the rates. He became very abusive, and bullying.'
† Rory: 'A perpetual payment on the lease of ground, in our case paid to the builder, at first; he sold it on. Eventually, we bought it out – a move facilitated by a Fianna Fáil government.'

year; that was nearly two weeks' wages. I paid it and begrudged it. And the income tax never went away.

'I was the only man in Ireland qualified for the job, so I got it by default. There was no one else. Most of my fellow apprentices never bothered to do the technical examination. I did. So I started as a temporary whole-time teacher, not permanent, not pensionable, but I took my chances. And then, I was caught up in a bit of difficulty. I had to do an Irish test. And the man who was examining me was Dr P. Ó'Súilleabháin, from the Department of Education. He was known as *An Dochtúir*.* He was a dreadful bloody bully. When it came to the oral test, I wasn't doing too well, and he said, "What is this at all? Sure, any of the labouring men down in Connemara can speak Irish." So I said, "Why don't you get them to teach printing?" At that, he hit the table a belt of his fist, nearly broke it, and I was thrown out. And I got a notification that I wasn't being re-appointed. So I went in the next day anyway, I just took it upon myself to go in, and I met Donal O'Dwyer, the Head of the College and a gentleman, and he said, "Mr Doyle, I thought you might have got some bad news." So I said, "The only really bad news would be if I couldn't get another job, and I'd have no difficulty there. I just want to see about this teaching post." I was fairly certain that if I went back to the *Independent* they'd give me the job again; I wasn't too worried about that, but I preferred being a teacher. So he asked me into his office, and the head of the printing school, Bill Fitzpatrick, was there, very annoyed at the idea that I wasn't being re-appointed. He was also annoyed about the difficulty he'd have in

---

* The Doctor.

getting a new teacher. The school was specialist, unique, and there was no pool of teachers. So, they got on to the CEO, the Chief Executive Officer, at the headquarters of the Dublin Vocational Education Committee, the VEC, and he said I wouldn't be re-appointed. So, I said, "OK," and went down to the union headquarters, the Dublin Typographical Society, where the Secretary was Billy Whelan, who also happened to be a member of the Dublin Vocational Education Committee. So, Billy says, "I'll see to that." And he phoned the CEO. He said, "Martin, we have a problem here. One of my men is being flung out." So the CEO, said that these were the rules and regulations. And Billy said, "The way it is, Martin, if you don't like my man who is going to do the teaching, you're not going to have any apprentices." So, the CEO said, "What do you mean?" And Billy said, "The apprentices are sent to the school by their employers to learn printing, not fuckin' Irish. My man is fully qualified to teach printing, and if that man isn't reinstated, you won't have any apprentices next Monday. So, make your mind up, Martin." So, the CEO said, "Leave it to me," and he came back in about half an hour and said that the Department of Education had decided that I should be temporarily re-appointed for another year. So, I was back again and, in the meantime, *An Dochtúir* retired and a decent man named O'Flanagan became the chief inspector. He came to the school, and I had done some translation of the printing terms into Irish, and he asked me a few questions in Irish, and I answered him in Irish. And then I was required to give a small demonstration of teaching in front of the class. And before O'Flanagan came in, I told the class that this was a demonstration on how the Irish language could be used for teaching printing: "So, when I ask you a question in Irish, just answer it in Irish." One of the lads said, "Suppose if I answer with another question?" And I said, "If you do, I'll break your fuckin' neck"; it shocked both myself and the class. So, he didn't ask a question, and O'Flanagan said, "*Tá go maith;*★ very good," and gave me *An Ceird Teastais,*† permission to teach in the vocational services, guaranteeing that I could teach through the medium of Irish. So, I was then made permanent and pensionable. I'd already been teaching for three years.'

'I took fatherhood in my stride. I never considered it as a philosophical thing to look into. I just went about my business. The children came along as a result of this miraculous thing that happened. I enjoyed it, of course. But Ita did all the making and mending. I might have changed a nappy, once or twice. But under extreme provocation – absolute necessity. That wasn't part of the curriculum at all. The children came along, and you made room for them; they became part of your life. But I didn't think about it in any special way. Don't forget, I was one out of nine children. I was surrounded by the whole idea of procreation as something natural in life – and family planning was in its infancy.

'I enjoyed the teaching. I met some very peculiar and very funny characters.‡ One of them was Butch Moore.

★ 'That's fine.'
† The Trade Certificate.
‡ Rory: 'I was down in the Dollymount Inn one day, having lunch, and this little oul' fellow came up to me and said, "Hello, Mr Doyle. Do you remember me?" I didn't remember him at all, and then my mind flashed back nearly half a century to this little fellow, who was still a little fellow. He was one of my pupils, all those years ago. "I've just retired," he told me. "I'm a grandfather as well."'

Butch was a nice young fellow, always a smile on his face; you could hear him warbling in the back of the class. I went down to him one day, and said, "Whatever chance you have of earning a living as a typesetter, you've none as a singer."★ I got on well with the students, with only one or two exceptions. The vocational teaching service didn't allow corporal punishment, so I'd take the fellow to one side and tell him that if he didn't behave himself I'd put him out of the class, and then report the matter to his employer. This could have serious consequences for the apprentice. Every second year, we'd get a new batch of students who suddenly realised that, unlike the Christian Brothers, we couldn't use a stick, and they thought they could do what they liked on us. So, a couple of times, if someone did something that was over the top, I'd give him a gentle nudge in the ribs. It was risky but the fact is, I got two years of absolute peace and a reputation – "Don't mess with Doyle or he'll do for you."

'My trade was compositor, which was setting and arranging type for printing. So, I was teaching the craft of composing, and its associated crafts, which included readers' marks, how to correct, how to do proofing, how to design print. In my later years as a teacher, I taught typographic design, how to design books, how to lay out magazines, and all that sort of business. It was quite an extensive curriculum. I worked about a thousand hours a year.† I went in at nine every morning, to half-twelve, and then two o'clock till half-five. I taught night

---

★ A showband star, Butch Moore sang Ireland's first Eurovision Song Contest entry, 'I'm Walking the Streets in the Rain', a good song, in 1965. It came sixth. He died in 2001.

† Rory: 'Eventually the TUI (Teachers' Union of Ireland) was formed, and

classes as well, for my troubles. I got an afternoon or a morning off if I had a night class. The night-class students were studying for the Senior Certificate examinations. Some of them did the higher levels of the City and Guilds of London examinations. I preferred lecturing to the senior fellows, because I could go on rambles of imagination, and bring them with me. And the holidays were marvellous. End of June, classes finished, and that was it till September. Now you couldn't just take off at the end of June. There were roll books to be filled up, and other curricular activities. Eventually, the principal would say, "Off you go." And then it was heaven. I didn't realise until much later that a huge part of the attraction was the holidays. I didn't work at all. I'd be sitting in the garden, listening to cricket. I saw the great test matches, between England and Australia – on the wireless. Very pleasurable.

'My nickname was Doyler. I was also called Rip Kirby, after the comic-strip detective in the *Evening Mail*. He had curly black hair and horn-rimmed glasses. They thought I looked like him.'

'I remember, Ita went into the nursing home, and the little boy was born. And the high delight, and then Dr Chapman phoned me up and told me that the baby was being moved to Temple Street. We didn't have a phone; it was our neighbours, the Coghlans, he phoned – I think: the baby was being moved to Temple Street to have him checked up. So, he was brought to Temple

---

I became one of the organisers of that. We had Charlie McCarthy as the general secretary and he was first-class, really very good. We got the teaching hours down to a maximum of nine hundred and sixty a year. We enjoyed the luxury.'

Street and, after a day or so, he died. He was a beautiful baby, a lovely child. I still remember him. Dr Chapman asked me if I minded if they had a post-mortem, that it might help someone else. I said, "Have the post-mortem." And then he told me, the baby would never have lived outside the womb, that his organs were all mixed up inside – some congenital thing.

'I had to buy a little white coffin. Kiernan Coghlan drove me, with the little coffin, up to Glasnevin. And I had the little fellow buried. I just think of it in terms of carrying the little white coffin. A profoundly sad experience. I don't know where I got it – some undertaker I was told about; somebody else had had the same problem. And because of the cost of the nursing home, the undertaker said that we could also have the baby buried in the Angels' Plot, for ten shillings. And that is where he is.

'After the funeral, myself and Máire went to visit Ita in the nursing home. I had an umbrella that Ita's step-mother had given me for Christmas. And when we came out to get the bus, we saw it was on the point of leaving, so we both started running. I let the umbrella fall, and what I picked up was the bottom of the umbrella, and a heap of chalk – the handle was filled with chalk or some kind of plaster. I was left holding this thing in my hand – comedy on a day of tragedy.

'It was a distressing time. It was traumatic. But we both took it. Certainly, Ita did. She just looked sad but she didn't – she is not that way, the kind that kicks up a fuss. She just took it. We had to live with it. And we did. In those days, short of dying, you went to work – no such thing as taking time off. I think Aunt Lil looked after Aideen and Pamela while Ita was in the nursing home. I think it was Lil – my memory isn't too clear on that, forty-five years ago.'

'We bought Tintawn* for the floors; it was marvellous. It was made in Ireland, in Youghal, from tough grass, sisal, grown out in Africa, and they could weave it into a tough floor covering. It was quite popular. So, we had red Tintawn in the hall, and an oatmeal one in the sitting-room. It was everlasting, and it caught all the dirt and dust, underneath, where it couldn't be seen. The kids' legs must have been made out of steel, because they sat and played on it, and it was really tough stuff. But that was a big thing; we no longer had to go around with a knife and wet newspaper, renewing the newspaper under the skirting boards, to keep out the drafts, because the Tintawn was fitted right up to the boards. We still had lino in the dining-room.

'And the washing machine came to stay – no more of the old handwashing. And then we rented a television after RTE began to broadcast. I was absolutely gobsmacked by the whole thing. The wireless wasn't a common thing in most people's homes for most of my youth. And now, not alone the wireless, but a television. It was a marvellous window on the world. I thought at the time that it would have a tremendous educational effect on people, and on our children. It had a profound effect on everybody. Visual news had a very great impact. Discussion programmes were humanised – the people were literally in your room. I also enjoyed the sports. For the first time I enjoyed watching a hurling match, because I could now see the ball. We also got a

---

* *Tinteán*: fireplace, hearth; home.

phone but it's important to remember that, in my working days, when you went to work, you went to work and you left your family behind. No woman would have dreamt of phoning her husband to come and settle problems; whatever they were, you heard about them when you got home. Things happened at home during my time at work that I didn't see or experience, but heard about later. That's a difference from today, when it's an all-enveloping thing: you go to work but you're looking over your shoulder or someone is talking in your ear. The universal usage of the phone hadn't been thought of. So, the phone in the house did make a difference but, then, it was still only a phone.

'We had a bungalow with a garage. The garage looked very nice, but it never crossed our mind that we'd ever own a car. We could put the pram in it, and other things, like bikes – it was a handy thing to have. However, after I'd become a full-time vocational teacher – permanent and pensionable – I decided that we might be able to afford a car. For a few years, after a couple of rises in salary and a couple of increments, we'd had £4 or £5 left at the end of the month, so I'd opened a bank account – that was a big thing – in the Provincial Bank, in Capel Street. And I knew we could get a very good second-hand car for around £200, so I went down to the bank and I asked to see the manager. I went into his office and he sat me down, and asked, "What can I do for you?" So I explained that I wanted a loan, and the bank manager, a little, fat, pompous shit with a moustache like Ronald Colman's, told me in no uncertain terms that I wasn't getting a loan, that there was no way that the bank would even consider giving the likes of me a loan. And so, I left the bank, humiliated, shaken, and I never went back.★ When I got over the shock, I went up to Raheny and opened an account in the Bank of Ireland, and transferred any money I had from the Provincial Bank, shook the dust off it.

'Later, I decided that getting a second-hand car, no matter how good, wasn't an option. I didn't know anything about motor cars so, if anything went wrong with it, I hadn't the skills that a lot of other fellows had, to be able to raise the bonnet and talk about the innards and fiddle with them. So, I decided I'd go the bold step and buy a new one. One day, while mulling this over, I saw an ad in the paper – a dealer on Usher's Island had Ford cars for sale. A new Ford Anglia; it was £500-odd – £10 a month, for God knew how long. And I decided I'd have it.

'In the meantime, my sister Nancy's husband, Brendan Walsh, gave me about half an hour's driving lesson in his Volkswagen, up and down the coast road, the James Larkin Road. Half an hour – that was my training. I never did a driving test. I got my licence and insurance, no bother whatsoever.† Eventually, the car was delivered to Usher's Island, and I went along to collect it. I asked the dealer would he drive me across the city. He did, and stopped the car outside the Cat and Cage pub, in Drumcondra. I got in and hit the accelerator and took off up the road without killing anyone or myself.‡

★ Ita: 'He came home livid. As soon as he could manage it, he took our huge wealth away from the Provincial Bank and put it into the Bank of Ireland.'

† Ita: 'I never drove. At one stage I was going to learn, and I lost my nerve and I didn't bother. I often regretted it. In later life, I regretted it.'

‡ Ita: 'I didn't know he was driving it home, but he arrived at the gate with the new Anglia, and I'll never forget the gorgeous leather smell inside it. It was beautiful, it was wonderful; we were made for life.'

'The following Sunday, we all set off, a carload of kids and all, to visit Ita's father in Terenure. And the car kept jumping, every time I changed the gears; it was ferocious.★ The next day, our neighbour, Leo Mulvaney, who had originally been a mechanic, took a look at it and discovered about two inches of white twine stuck in the carburettor. It was a miracle the car went at all. But afterwards, the kids would say, "Make the car jump, Daddy." But I could never make it jump the same way again.'

★ Ita: 'It stalled on Portobello Bridge; it wouldn't start. And then it hopped, before it started again. We were at the stage where we felt like throwing it back at the dealer because, every time we stopped and Rory tried to start it again, it would hop along. I remember, the kids in the back enjoyed it thoroughly.'

Chapter Nineteen – Ita

'I'd knitted Aran sweaters for the children, and I must point out that they weren't knitted especially for Kennedy's visit.* But I think it was an NBC crew came over to us. They were very keen to put the four kids on camera. They filmed them waving at thin air, but they were going to make it appear as if they were waving at President Kennedy. They told us it would be on American television that night but, naturally, we didn't get to see it. But when he came out of Áras An Uachtaráin† in the car, we had our cine-camera ready – there weren't many other people there – and he waved out at us. I was amazed; it was very easy to see him, while he'd been crowded out everywhere else. But all we got on the cine-camera was his hand. The rest is darkness, but the hand is still there.

'The camera came from my brother, Joe. He was over here on holiday.‡ He slept in Terenure, but had most of his meals with us and we went around a lot with him. And when he went home to Washington, he sent us this cine-camera. It was a great thing, a Kodak Brownie. We got it the year Shane was born, and we have his christening, the First Communions and holidays on film, and

---

* John F. Kennedy visited Ireland in June 1963.
† The Irish President's residence. The President at the time was Eamon de Valera.
‡ Joe was Third Secretary at the Irish Embassy in Washington.

people like my father and stepmother, and aunts and uncles, in Coolnaboy and Kilmuckridge, and Rory's mother; they're all long dead now.

'Joe wasn't bad at that time. He was slow walking but he was able to drive. He was still working, over in the embassy in Washington, so he was able to care for himself, more or less. But he often said that the people he worked with over there were more than kind to him, and he probably couldn't have stayed that long, only for them. The one name he mentioned above all others was Noel Dorr.★ He said he was the kindest man that could have been. He'd often get Joe up in the mornings and bring him in to work. He was very slow, and I'm sure he was suffering. It was rheumatoid arthritis.'

Her father died in 1963. 'He wasn't ailing for long. I was in bed with the flu – I very seldom got sick. We still had no phone, but Mrs Rosney next door took the message and she came in and told me. He'd had an operation; we didn't know what for – we didn't ask. We didn't think he'd die; I thought he'd be alright. He'd stayed in good form while he was in the hospital. He was buried in Mount Jerome, with my mother. He had a fine big funeral, but

★ Permanent representative to the UN (1980); President of the UN Security Council (1981–2); Irish Ambassador to London (1983–7); Secretary of the Department of Foreign Affairs (1987–95).

I've very little memory of it. When my father retired he used to go walking in the park off Templeogue Road and he'd meet three or four other retired men, and the state of the universe would be discussed. We went in to see him in hospital nearly every night, and these men were often with him, chatting and talking. I think they got a bit of a shock too, when he died.

'He had a desk; it was one of these old-style, glass-fronted bookcases, with a desk underneath it. The front of the desk lifted out, and you could write on it. It had lots of little cubby-holes and, underneath, there were three drawers. After his death, I opened the desk and found this small black leather folder. Really, it was paper made to look like leather. And there were letters in it. They were from a John J. Beekman, in Hempstead, New York. And I remembered: there were little poetry books in the house when I was a child, with the name John J. Beekman on the covers. I read two of the letters, and I realised that the wife of this John was my mother's sister, and that her name was Mary. But I'd only barely started when my stepmother came in and told me that I'd no right to be reading them, because everything now belonged to Joe, and to put them away. Which I did. There was no use arguing. I just put them back and left them there. I knew they were there and I never forgot them.

'Pearl was in a very disturbed state after my father died. She'd go in and sit in the front room and just stare out the window for hours. She wasn't eating properly, and she got very, very ill. She spent some time in Linden Convalescent Home; she was there a few weeks. She really was very upset, and I was very sorry for her at that stage. We went to see her regularly. She'd gone fairly deaf and, as a result, she shouted everything. She'd point people out, put her hand beside her mouth, as if to muffle her voice, and remark on other ladies in the day-room: "Look at her! She's very nice but she drinks!" or "See her? She's nice but she's a Protestant!" We used to be mortified but, when we came out, we roared laughing. But she got alright after that, and she went back home again. And thanks be to God for television; she sat at it practically all day, and every night. She never turned it off. I'd swear if the Pope had come in, he'd have had to watch her favourite cowboy films. She had an elderly friend who lived near her, on Templeogue Road. This lady would cross the road nearly every night, to watch television with Pearl. She didn't have one of her own; she couldn't very well have had one, because she was drawing the blind pension. They spoke very formally to each other; she always addressed Pearl as "Mrs Bolger". They'd talk right through the film: "Is this a goodie, Mrs Bolger?" "No, they're all baddies." "Look at him, Mrs Bolger; he has awful eyes." "He's the goodie." And there was another one: "Who are they, Mrs Bolger? Are they the goodies or the baddies?" "No, they're the cattle." She had another neighbour, a widow, who dropped into her regularly. And this one time, she dropped in to show Pearl this new pair of shoes she'd just bought. When she went home, her lodger offered to make her a cup of tea. And when the lodger came back with the tea, Pearl's neighbour was dead in the armchair. The neighbours discussed how to break the news to Pearl, so as not to upset her too much. The next time I visited, Pearl told me about the neighbour's death, and she said: "They were worried about how to break the news to me. But why would it upset me? It wasn't me who died. She'd only bought new shoes. There's waste."'

'Jimmy Peoples, my sister Máire's husband, always said he was going to have a heart attack. He used to have his heart tested. His father had died suddenly; I think he was fifty-six. And Jimmy was the same age. He was actually going to Mass — it was during Lent — and he just dropped dead. And the next thing, a Garda arrived at the door to tell Máire that he was dead. That was an awful shock for her. She phoned here, and I phoned Rory, in the office,* and he went over to her.

'She hadn't worked since she was married and, at that time, civil servants' widows had no pension. She was fortunate in that she had been a civil servant, and she was allowed back in. She got a lump sum when Jimmy died, but she went back to work and, mentally, it was great for her. Their son, Jimmy Junior, was to be married a month afterwards, and Máire insisted that it go ahead. But going back into the Civil Service was her great saving.'

'You shopped every day, because there were no supermarkets. And Peter Butler's shop was great; it was nearly an outing — you met people out shopping. I'd have a roast on Sunday, and all the trimmings. And always dessert; every day, we had dessert. Then, on Monday, I'd make a shepherd's pie, which was a great way of stretching the meat — it was the remains of the roast. I had a mincer which had belonged to my mother. The shepherd's pie was lovely, actually. And then there'd be stew one day,

---

* Ita: 'He had changed jobs again.'

and there'd be maybe mashed potatoes and sausages another – things like that. It must have been acceptable. No one complained, and the plates were always cleaned. And Rory did the shopping, sometimes, in Moore Street; fruit and vegetables and fish. There'd be fish one day a week, on a Friday. The whole emphasis was on getting the best value. There wasn't much variety.★ I used to make burgers, our own burgers. They were nicer than the shop ones. They were softer, and I mixed in a bit of potato, and an egg and onion. And I'd make chips. And, of course, I used to bake every day. I had little glass bowls and I did fancy jelly, and banana chopped into it, and a dollop of cream on top. Or, sometimes, something soaked with custard – a sponge with a bit of jam and custard on top. All kinds of fancy little dishes. I wouldn't have dreamed of having dinner without a dessert.

'The Rosneys lived next door. First, there'd been another couple, the Arnolds, but they didn't stay very long, and the Rosneys came, Peter and Peg. Peter was a vet. We had an insurance man called Mr Durkin, a very nice man; he came every week to collect the insurance. He came in one day, and he said, "Mrs Doyle, could you give me an idea of what the man next door does for a living?" And I said, "That's Mr Rosney; he's a vet." "Good," said he: "That explains it. He's after coming out of the house with a little pig under his arm." And I remember, one of their sons had come in to play in the garden, and he kept saying, "Daddy's gone to kill a cow in Ballyboughal." They eventually moved, to outside

---

★ Ita: 'There still isn't. It hasn't taken off in this house. Rory is strictly a spud man.' Rory: 'That's an illusion. In my time, I've eaten yak, shark, kangaroo and ostrich. I even ate spaghetti once.'

Malahide, because it was nearer to his work. And then the Clearys came, Breda and Seán; they came up from Limerick.

'Kilbarrack changed an awful lot. The road changed from a country lane to a wide thoroughfare; it changed from a very quiet place, to traffic going up and down – it's a main road to the airport. A lot of things came into being that couldn't be held back. But it wasn't the same any more. It had been like a little village – you knew everybody, and the few little shops that were there – a little community. I'm not saying it's not still a good community, but it's a much wider, bigger community. But it changed at a good time. For example, we had no street lighting and we had very little in the way of transport, or anything like that, and, gradually, we got these things.

'I remember when the big sewage scheme was started, going down the centre of the road, the drilling of the road. Some of the windows at the front of the house were actually cracked, broken; the house used to rattle. They put down the big pipes and, of course, all the children in the neighbourhood had great fun running up and down those. They put a pumping station at the end of the road, at the sea. It was ugly, but it was only in later years that the ugliness began to annoy us. At the time, we thought it was great. We'd wait for the tide to come in – we'd look up the times in the paper – and there'd be an exodus down to the end of the road. We'd go in behind the pumping station; there was a platform and steps down to the sea. All the children would swim there, and their mothers met and had great chats and talks. So, it was a great place really.★

★ Ita: 'The pumping station has recently been demolished, to our great delight.'

'Flood's farm, opposite, was eventually sold, which was sad, because they were very nice; we'd been good friends with Jack and Cathy. Houses were built on their land, and the new estate was called Alden. Later, more houses were built, Verbena Estate. And Barnwall's farm up the road, their land opposite was sold. I remember when Bayside, further afield, towards Sutton, was being built, walking there one evening, a lovely summer evening; some of the houses were newly built, and we walked through them. It was extremely sandy, all along. And we met some man that Rory had known in the College of Art, and we stopped and Rory talked to him. I thought they'd never shut up.* I remember feeling midges biting my legs, but pushing them away and paying no heed to them, and coming home that night, and my two legs were swollen, like never before nor since. And I was shivering and shaking; I was in a terrible state. That was my introduction to Bayside.

'The Corporation bought land, Barnwall's, and the next farm, Loftus's. And the Corporation houses were all built. And one thing that brought us was a church, which was a great asset. And schools — although they were built too late for our children. It became a very lively place. Originally, you felt that you didn't want it getting so big, but you settled into it and accepted it.

'The Walshes were on the other side of us, after the Winks. I remember being pregnant when they moved in. Then they moved up to Sutton, and Mrs Eastwood came, with her two daughters, and she was a lovely woman. She had Joe's affliction, rheumatoid arthritis. I went in to her on a Monday, and kind of helped her

---

* Rory: 'I was enjoying myself.'

with the washing. And then, Tuesday was my official calling day; we made a joke about it. I can still remember her making apple tarts; her little hands were all twisted and she used her knuckles to press down the pastry – and lovely pastry it was too.

'Over the years, Joe deteriorated an awful lot. We were always very close and anything he ever wanted done, it was me he turned to. So, eventually – he was in his early forties, and he just couldn't manage; he was in a wheelchair. And he decided to come home from Washington. He wrote and asked, could we find a nursing home for him, near us. My stepmother was still alive but there was no chance in the world that he'd go and live with her. Anyway, she was getting on and she wouldn't have been capable of looking after a man in a wheelchair. So we didn't quite know what to do. Then our doctor at the end of the road, Dr O'Leary, found this nursing home, in Howth. It was just a kind of stop-gap, to see what we'd do when he came home.

'I remember him arriving, and I felt awfully sorry for him. There was some kind of a strike in America, and all his things were held up there, including his wheelchair. He was very upset about it. But, eventually, he arrived, on two sticks. He was barely able to walk. In fact, if there was silence, you could hear him creaking. His bones creaked.

'We brought him up to this nursing home in Howth. They were very kind there but, while he was pretty poor physically, mentally he was very bright. He'd read forever – he was like my father in that. We went up each day to him, but it wasn't right to see him sitting there. So we decided to ask him would he like to come and live with us. He was delighted.

'There wasn't much room, so we set up the sitting-room as a bedroom for him, until we decided what to do. We enquired about getting a bedsit built, a building in the form of a bedsit or motel room, out the back, and that was what we did; Rory designed it. It didn't take too long to build. And he settled into that.

'When he came home from America, he was allowed to bring as much furniture as he wanted to, and anything else; the Department paid for everything. The Customs people intervened, and all his stuff had to be put into our garage, and the garage sealed. And Joe had bottles of perfume here and bottles of liquor there, stuck to the legs of tables and chairs, and everything.★ Our boys were little lads at the time, and they were able to nip in and out – the seals weren't touched – and crawl between the legs of chairs and tables; the furnishings were full of the bottles. Between them, they took out quite a sizeable amount of the bottles.† But, even at that, when the Customs men arrived, they found what was left of it, and he still had quite a bill.

'I think Joe was as content as he could have been, under the circumstances. He had his bad days and he had good days.‡ He did his best to hide the pain; he

---

★ Rory: 'We got a letter, that the Customs would have to come and examine it. "Jesus," said Joe. He'd hidden away his store of duty-free liquor, perfumes, various cigars and cigarettes. Himself and one of the attendants in the embassy had parcelled up all his stuff; they were all attached to the legs of tables or chairs, and the Customs men were going to go through it.'

† Rory: 'I had the bright idea of using two small boys; put them in among the gaps, and they came out with a treasure trove. There was Cointreau, bottles of the finest brandy, whiskey, the original Redbreast – the one in the funny bottle.'

‡ Rory: 'He was quite badly crippled. He was also a bit difficult, in that he had a brand-new wheelchair but he wouldn't go out at all. Any idea of bringing him out into the open air was vetoed.'

was having piles of tablets. Then his hands went very bad, so much so that I had to feed him. It was Dr O'Leary who got him into Cappagh.* They were marvellous. I don't know what they did with his hands, but when he came back he was able to use his knife and fork, and even write again. But there was one episode while he was there. He smoked; he wasn't supposed to. But he used to sneak the smokes, and he smoked in bed one night. And the bed caught fire, while he was asleep. It burnt down one side, across the bottom, and up the other side. Somebody noticed, and put it out. And he was unscathed. We went in to visit him the day after it happened, and he was sitting in his wheelchair with a grin on his face. He told us about it. "D'you know what?" he said. "They're coming in to touch the hem of my garment." The nuns really were very impressed with it. He had no religion; he often said he wished he had. He was afraid of nuns. But the nuns in Cappagh he really liked. I think they recognised that he had a great brain and it was too good to waste. He used to go for physiotherapy. He was supposed to hold things in his hands, like soft rubber balls, and roll them around; I suppose, to try to keep his hands supple. But he just wouldn't do it.† So, one of the nuns – I can't remember her name now, but she came over here a few times when Joe was at home and she rode a motor bike; she had a helmet on. She was a great little woman. Joe had the greatest admiration for her. Anyway she decided that it would be a good idea to set up a little newspaper. She really did it for him, but he accepted that it was for the

---

* Orthopaedic hospital, in Finglas, north Dublin.
† Rory: 'He was always waiting for the miracle pill.'

good of the other patients in the wards, and it kept him busy for the months that he was there. He'd go around to various patients and get bits of news from them. I can't remember whether it was weekly or fortnightly or monthly, just a few pages, but he really got dug into it, and enjoyed doing it.

'Sunday afternoons, we'd all go out to visit Joe. And there was this unfortunate man – I always felt he was a very lonely man – but he had been a patient there. And he really haunted the house; he was forever there. He obviously thought that he was doing great good. First of all, he used to direct the traffic in the car park. He drove Rory mad and, once or twice, he threatened to run over him. However, he didn't. Then, he had this accordion, and he went up and down the wards with it. It drove Joe insane. I'd say, "Ah sure, the poor man; he's lonely, it's his big day." But Joe would say, "I wish he'd fuck off. He has a captive audience here."

'The nuns were so nice to him, and they never forced religion on him. They knew; he was what he was. There was, I think, a Sister Rachel; she was a tall nun. There were two particular nuns – I should never have forgotten their names but I'm afraid I have. But they decided that he should go to Lourdes.★ He was very loath to go, but he'd have done anything to please the nuns, and the nuns felt that he should go. So, off he went, to Lourdes. And he came back quite content, with all kinds of presents for us, the usual leather wallets and relics, medals and rosary beads, and delighted with life. That

---

★ Rory: 'He was very cautious, being a diplomat. He was a self-confessed heathen, but he didn't let that be known to the nuns. And he went to Lourdes.'

summer, we were down visiting Aunt Katie in Coolnaboy, and Katie was telling us about a man from Oilgate who went out every year, to help with the invalids in Lourdes. She'd asked how he'd got on, and he told her he'd met a small man, and "your own name, Bolger was his name. And we lifted him out of the wheelchair, to put him into the baths, and," he said, "the language out of him! I never heard it before." So, Katie said to me, "I knew it was Joe, but I never said a word." But the thing about it is: I remember the nuns telling me that Joe's spine was like the bones in a tin of salmon; move them in any way unusual, and they'd snap. If you even touched him – once or twice we tried to get him into the car – it was agony to him. So, I can just imagine what happened when they lifted him out of the wheel-chair.'

'Maeve Brennan wrote and said she was coming to Ireland. Now, I wasn't very close to Maeve. I'd seen very little of her, because she was that bit older than me and she'd gone to America when she was quite young. We were in the Brennan house in Cherryfield Avenue, in Ranelagh, when I was very young, and there were girls there, but it didn't register that they were cousins. I met Maeve when her father and mother came back to live here after the War. Bob was Director of Broadcasting, and they bought a house on Dodder Road. And, three or four times, Una invited me to dinner. I remember going over once, and Maeve answered the door, and I thought, "My God. Sophistication." She looked abso-lutely smashing. She was wearing a twin-set – but there are twin-sets and twin-sets; this was the finest of fine. And a beautiful pearl necklace. And her hair piled up on top. I thought she was gorgeous. She was smiling and friendly, and I liked her straight away. I met her twice there, before I was married. But, other than that, I didn't really know her.

'So, she wrote, and she came over; she was staying with her sister. Then she phoned me to know would I have room for her. I said I would. And she arrived. As always, she looked most elegant.* She had her type-writer with her, and she stayed a few months, if not longer. A lot of her time was spent reviewing books for the *New Yorker*. Large parcels of books used to arrive. Mostly books of Irish interest.† She used to go up to the shopping centre, which was quite new – Kilbarrack Shopping Centre. She'd walk up, buy *Ireland's Own*, go into the café there, buy apple tart and tea, and read *Ireland's Own* from cover to cover. I think she was ter-ribly sentimental about Ireland and Irish things. She was able to cocoon herself at her table, with her tea and her tart. She'd come home and she'd tell me about this one she'd seen, or that one; maybe some peculiar thing had happened, or some odd-looking person. But those trips to the shopping centre were for *Ireland's Own*.

'Another time, herself and my daughter Pamela went off, up to the Marine Hotel in Sutton, for a drink. When they came out again, it was raining. There was no sign of a bus, and they decided to walk home. So, they were walking along the seafront, and Pamela had an umbrella and she said to Maeve to get in under the umbrella. And

---

* Rory: 'A ring came to the door, and I saw this little pixie face, a beau-tiful face, and a wild crop of red hair and eyes as bright as buttons.'
† Rory: 'Now and again, I pick up a book and I ask, "What did I buy that for?" and then I realise it wasn't bought; it was left behind by Maeve Brennan.'

Maeve said, "No. I always said I loved walking in the rain, so now I'm going to test it." So, they got home and Maeve was like a drowned rat. And Pamela said, "Well, did you like walking in the rain?" And Maeve said, "No, I didn't. I'm drenched."

'I remember another time, we were all talking and, for some reason, there was mention of prawns. Prawn cocktails were a fashionable starter at the time. And Rory mentioned that prawns were lovely. Now, with Maeve, you dared not mention that you liked something because, the next day, you'd have it. I got very wary of it; she really was overgenerous. Anyway, she decided that myself and Shane – he was the only one at home that day – we were going to town and we were going to buy prawns. We went to Smith's On The Green.★ She bought a bottle of wine; at that time wine was strictly for special occasions. She bought a bottle of Tabasco sauce, and some kind of a sauce for making prawn cocktail – I think it was called Marie Rose. At that time there was a fish shop in Grafton Street, a very exclusive place; they had the best of smoked salmon, the best of prawns, and other fish, all beautifully laid out. She bought a pound of prawns, which was an enormous amount of prawns. And then, another thing: coffee was still a luxury in those days, and Maeve had mentioned this particular type of pot; you put the coffee in, screwed on the top, and put it on the stove. I realise now that it was an espresso pot, but at the time I didn't know what it was. So we went into Bewley's, and they had about ten different types of coffee pot there. And the ten different

★ Ita: 'It's long gone. It was a very exclusive grocery. There's a café there now.'

types of coffee pot were taken down, and put along the counter. And we were told how each of them worked, and Maeve listened intently – all different, filters, this make, that make – and thanked everyone politely, and sailed out. She then decided that we were going for lunch. We went to a hotel, in Wicklow Street – I can't remember the name. They had a very nice dining-room, and we were handed these huge menus. I've no recollection of what we ate; I do know I enjoyed it thoroughly, because it was a real treat. Maeve asked if she could keep one of the menus. And the waiter – slightly reluctantly, I thought – but, with her slight hint of an American accent, let her have it. Whether it was a souvenir or not, I don't know. Then we went back to Bewley's and we bought an almond ring – because I'd mentioned that I liked almond rings; I was lucky she didn't buy half a dozen almond rings. Then we got a cab home. And, when we came home, Maeve made the prawn cocktail, a great big bowl of prawn cocktail, and then decided that she wasn't that keen on prawns. But Rory liked them and that was all that mattered. So, we dined on prawns for days.★

'She ate like a bird. I often wondered what she lived on. Now and again, she'd eat a good Sunday dinner; she'd tuck in. But, other than that, she wouldn't eat with us. She'd pick at bits and pieces. I think she was afraid that she might be intruding. She had a separate place here – out where Joe lived; Joe was in Cappagh at that time. Sometimes, at night, you'd hear the typewriter

---

★ Rory: 'She said to me, "Do you like prawns?" I said, "I do, but seldom see them." So she went into town and came back with bags full of prawns and a bottle of Chivas Regal whiskey.'

hopping away. But she was always in good humour. I don't think I ever heard a cross word or a derogatory word, or a glum word from her. She visited Joe a few times. She was very close to him; they were great friends. They shared the same birthday, as did my father – the sixth of January.

'She smoked endlessly but, as Rory smoked the pipe, I was used to the smoke hovering around my head. Every now and again, she mentioned Mac; Mac said this, or myself and Mac went here or there. Out of the blue one day, Shane said, "Maeve, you're always talking about Mac. Who's Mac?" He was a very small fellow at this stage. And she said, "Mac was my husband. I was his third wife." And that was it.* Apparently, he was quite a well-known writer in America,† and he'd been over here once. I must have been in Wexford at the time, but Maeve and Mac visited Máire, and she thought he was a very nice man. Maeve did tell me that she often wondered why his family had welcomed her with open arms when it was announced that she was going to marry him, and she realised afterwards that it was because he was an alcoholic and she was going to take their troubles on her shoulders. But, other than that, she didn't slag him off in any way.

'She departed as suddenly as she came. I went up to Raheny for something, and when I came back she had

---

* Rory: 'She was very much aware of everybody and the kind of person they were. The kids absolutely loved her telling stories.'

† Mac was St Clair McKelway (1905–80); his books include *Gossip: The Life and Times of Walter Winchell*; *True Tales from the Annals of Crime and Rascality*; *The Edinburgh Caper*; *The Big Little Man from Brooklyn*; managing editor at the *New Yorker*, 1936–9. His *New Yorker* obituary states: '. . . he was married and divorced five times, and his former wives remained his friends.'

her coat on, and I said, "Are you going to town?" And she said, "No, I'm leaving. I've decided, I've stayed long enough. I don't want to outstay my welcome." And away she went. She was going to stay in the old Moira Hotel, at the back of Andrew's Street.★ I think she had sentimental feelings for that place, because she'd stayed there with her father when she was young.† I heard afterwards she'd rented a flat somewhere. But she only phoned me one more time after that. And we had a phone call from Store Street police station, to say that there was a lady there called Maeve and that she seemed to be somewhat upset; she'd given my number, as somebody they could contact – to check up on who she was. I said, "That's right; she's a cousin of mine." And the Garda asked would I speak to her, that she seemed to be upset about something. So Maeve came on the phone, and she sounded quite natural to me. But she said she was worried about her niece, worried that something was going to happen to her – some little thing had got into her mind and she was very upset about it. I spoke to her for a while. I said, "I'm sure she's alright," and not to be worrying about her. I asked her would she like to come out to us, and she said, No, she'd be fine. The Garda thanked me, and that was the last I heard.

'When Joe died, I got a very nice letter from Maeve; she was back in America. She told me how sad she was that Joe was dead, but also glad, because of the way he had suffered. And again, she thanked us for the time

---

★ Rory: 'It's now a car park, off Trinity Street.'
† Rory: 'I think she was somewhat nostalgic for old Dublin. She didn't take kindly to all the changes.'

she'd stayed, and how fond she'd been of us. That, really, was the last I heard from her. I read on the flyleaf of one of her books that she had died in poverty. That is only partially true. She may have haunted the offices of the *New Yorker* at one stage but she died quite comfortably. Her brother, Pat – his name was Robert but he was always called Pat – he told me that she died in a nursing home. She seemed to have lost her memory and could not remember any name that Pat mentioned to her.★

'I think it's an awful pity that the rediscovery of Maeve's work didn't happen when she was alive. But I think she'd have been thrilled with it. I'm delighted for her, that it's back. I love the stories; I can see bits of the life we all led in them – certainly in the ones about Dublin, even in the names. Mr and Mrs Baggot – there was a Baggot shop in Rathmines, near where she lived. All these names crop up. And the house where they live is nearly a replica of Cherryfield Avenue, where Maeve's family lived and, indeed, Brighton Gardens, where I lived. They were all red-bricked, three-bedroom houses.'

'Joe was in and out of Cappagh a lot. They were very good; they did their best to make him mobile, but he went kind of introverted. His friends in Foreign Affairs were excellent, all through the years; they'd call and visit him. Now and again, I'd go out to him and say, "So-and-so is here," and he'd say, "I don't want to see them." But we wouldn't allow that, and we'd bring them out. And once they'd arrived, he'd be grand; he'd be chatting and talking. I remember once, Brendan Quinn, who

★ Maeve died in 1993.

was actually a cousin of Rory's, came to visit Joe; he knew Joe.★ They were outside, in Joe's room, and, of course, there was a bottle of whiskey opened and Brendan began talking about the Dublin team; Brendan had trained the team. All the talk was about Gaelic football and the Dublin team and this team and that team. I can't remember the player's name, a Dublin player, but Joe said, "He was a very nice fellow." And Brendan said, "He was an impudent get."

'We had a buzzer, between Joe's place and our bedroom, and later that night, after Brendan had gone, we weren't long in bed when the buzzer went, and Rory went out, to find Joe on the floor. But the fall hadn't hurt him; he'd had a good night and hadn't felt it. We had to lift him back into bed.

'But he was getting more and more frustrated with his lot. He went into Cappagh again,† to get something else done; I can't remember whether it was his feet or his hands – he could never walk again, anyway. But he got pneumonia, and the nuns had always said that he'd have little hope if he ever got chest trouble, because his ribs were kind of digging into him. So he died there;

★ Rory: 'Brendan Quinn would come out to visit Joe, and another bottle of Redbreast would bite the dust.'

† Rory: 'He wasn't well at all. I sat beside him and I put my hand on his, and I spoke to him. He had been comatose, and he suddenly came alive. A similar thing had happened with Ita's Uncle Watt. He was very ill, and we were told that he didn't even recognise his own children. I went up and, as I came into the room, he looked over and said, "Rory, you came to see me." Not alone did he talk to me, he got up shortly afterwards and went into Enniscorthy and bought a new coat. Joe came out of the coma, but he didn't know where he was. He started talking away, like something that had been wound up – and *Finnegans Wake* poured out of him. It flowed out. I'd read it, and recognised it. He was calling the nun the "White Druidess".'

he died very peacefully, within a few days. He was fifty.*
And another most unusual thing: the nuns asked us if
they could use one of their habits to lay him out in. So,
he was buried in a blue Child of Mary habit which, I
think, would have tickled his sense of humour no end;
if he'd been alive to see himself he'd have broken his
heart laughing. And I must say, while there was a lot of
sadness, we were relieved for him. Because he was getting worse, but there wasn't a thing wrong with his mind.
So, really, it was a blessing.

   With all the drink he'd brought from America, he
kept saying that we'd have a big night. As a matter of
fact, the day he was buried, we had a bit of a meal here.
We took out the liquor and put it on the table and let
whoever liked dive into it. And there was a bit of a party
that night. A few weeks later, we went to a christening
and, on the way home, I asked Shane – he'd been very
upset about Joe's death – I asked him, "Did you have a
good time?" And he said, "Yes. It was great but it wasn't
as good as Uncle Joe's funeral."'

'The first time I went abroad it was to Rimini, in Italy,
in 1974. We hadn't managed to go on holiday while Joe
was with us. The flight was at night and I had never
been in a plane before; it was such an experience, I
wouldn't have dreamt of dozing or anything like that.
And I remember, we were told that we were over the
Alps. I kept looking down, and I thought I could see a
little house on top of a mountain; I could see the light.
Eventually I realised it was a light at the tip of the wing.
   'I remember being taken to our hotel, in the bus; it

---

* Rory: 'He was only a handful when he died.'

was about six in the morning, maybe a bit earlier. And all the shops were opening up, and people were coming to life. I couldn't take my eyes off this scene; it was so different to anything we ever had. I remember that day we had a pizza – our first ever pizza. We only stayed a week, but it was marvellous. We went to Florence and Venice and San Marino. I thought it was all wonderful. It was like the smell of the first car, that leathery smell – nothing could ever come up to it again. Then we went to Spain, to Benidorm and Torremolinos. And we went to Russia, and Greece and Crete.★ And Yugoslavia, twice, and back to Italy. And Budapest and Vienna, a week in each. And, of course, we went to Ballybunion.'†

'We were on holiday in Spain when my neighbour Jo Eastwood died. I was very upset over it; she died suddenly. But, fortunately, not long after that, I went back to work, and it was the making of me.

'My friend Gladys Williams, who used to live down the road here, had moved to Malahide, but we'd always kept in touch. She worked for a solicitor called Martin Kennedy, in Malahide. She phoned me up one day and said that Martin was looking for a bookkeeper, and hadn't I done books? I said I had, but I hadn't worked for twenty-five years, and I was sure that the bookkeeping I'd done was old-fashioned. So she said, would I try it; she'd love if it was someone she knew who got the job. So I said I would. At first, I was a bit dubious

---

★ Ita: 'I remember when I came home, after the solid sun from morning till night, I was going to work the next morning, and there was fine, light rain falling. I remember walking along to the train with my face up, and I thought it was gorgeous. Mind you, one day was enough of it.'
† County Kerry.

about it; Shane was still in school. But I felt it was such a great chance, and he was nearly due to leave school anyway; it was his last year.

'So, I set off the first day; I hardly knew where the place was. With Gladys's help, I soon settled in. The work wasn't very intricate. I made mistakes, but Martin Kennedy was completely patient. The original idea was I'd go there for a week, to bring the books up to date. Then I was to go in two days a week, to keep them up to date. But Gladys took ill, and had to go into hospital, so I was thrown in at the deep end. It was Dictaphone typing, which I hadn't done before. I was slow at first, but I managed. I used to come home exhausted, because answering phones, taking messages, typing whatever I could – it was all new to me. But, at the same time, it *was* all new, and it was grand. When Gladys eventually came back, Martin decided that he was busy enough for two of us, and he said he'd like me to stay permanently. And I did. I was twelve years there. And I enjoyed it; it was great. After twenty-five years of being at home – where I was perfectly content, but the kids were all growing up and moving out – it was absolutely mar-vellous. It was a whole new life opened up to me.

'My stepmother had problems with her legs; they were very, very swollen. She was hardly able to walk around; she was very bad. We put the bed in the living-room, downstairs, in her house. And we had to get a home help, a marvellous woman; she came in every morning, got her out of bed, gave her breakfast, put a meal on for dinner, and then she'd come back in the evening and put her to bed. That went on for quite a while. We con-tinued to go over, but there was little we could do to help her. And the neighbours were very good; they were in and out helping her. But when everybody went at night, she was there on her own; she wasn't able to get out of the bed. She was terribly helpless. So, her doctor said that, really, he couldn't be responsible for her any more, and it was then that we started looking for a home for her, and, eventually, we found one, in Rathcoole.

'But she was very discontented, always a bit contrary, always giving out about people; it was her nature to complain. She was there for quite a while. My cousin Joan* went to visit her. Joan also married a Doyle, Jimmy Doyle, and they brought her a bottle of sherry. Jimmy noticed that she was kind of licking her lips, and he said to her, "Are you thirsty?" And she said, "I am." So he said, "Will I get you some water?" And she said, "I'd like something stronger." She'd spotted the sherry; she was nearly ninety at this stage. So Jimmy poured her a glass and she looked down to the end of the bed, and she said, "Ho! Winter's Tale. Good."

'She died of old age; she was over ninety. It was a quiet enough funeral. She was buried with my father, in Mount Jerome, and I might as well be honest; I didn't grieve for her.'

'Rory, being semi-state, had to retire when he was sixty-five. I could have gone on; nobody was trying to get me out. But Rory was on his own. He never complained or suggested that I retire, but I felt, myself, that he was on his own all the time. So, I said to Martin Kennedy that I thought I'd retire. He was always a very agreeable man, and he said, whatever I felt. And Gladys decided that she'd retire too; we're the same age. Martin had a

---

* Aunt Katie's daughter.

little evening for the two of us, and I ended up with so many bouquets I didn't know where to put them. I was putting them in buckets and everywhere else, all over the place. I was very touched, and pleased, with the treatment I got.

'But it was quite exciting; I didn't regret it. I settled at home straight away. I'd been very happy at work but I was quite happy to be at home. We made a life for ourselves and it was lovely and free and easy. I never got out of the habit of getting up early; the clock still goes off in my head.

'It's only lately that I've had any sense of getting old. And it isn't mental; I don't feel any older mentally.* But when I sit for a while and stand up, or sometimes if I do a lot of walking; up to a while ago, I'd stand up and go out and do the garden or something, but I find now that I have to slow down in that respect. And sometimes it annoys me, but I suppose it's a nudge, to tell me to take it easy and I'll last longer. I never think about my death. When I'm with people my own age, we might mention the subject, but we only laugh at the idea of us being the age we are. We decide that we've better things to talk about than what might happen. My greatest worry would be to be dependent. I'd like to go out in a blaze of glory, rather than be dependent – that, I would hate.

'The biggest change, from our point of view, is the security thing. When we were married, and for years afterwards, we'd go up and down to the shops and never lock the doors; it never crossed my mind to lock the door – we'd no side gate, no double locks, none of these

---

* Rory: 'I won't say a word.'

things. And then myself and Máire used to go out at night; we'd meet in town and window-shop. In those days, neither of us could do a lot other than window-shop, but we enjoyed it. The windows were lit up. We'd meet at Cassidy's, the material shop, in O'Connell Street; we'd just wait there, at the entrance. You couldn't do that now. You'd feel a bit insecure, standing there.* It's not as safe as it used to be.

'I still go into town, but I don't go in very much at night. It's not a case of being afraid to go in; it's just a case of age catching up with you. I'd have to be in a bad way before I'd stop going into town during the day. I love Dublin. I love everything about it.

'Some of the modern things I think are absolutely amazing. Even if I can't fathom them. Even the phone – I think it's marvellous, and the television. It's unbelievable that Clinton or Bush can be over there and we can see them. I'd never miss watching Bush walking out with his arms away from his sides and his leather jacket on. I can't admire the man; I really can't. And the films; I'd miss them. And computers – if I was still working, I'd learn how to use them. The fact that you can stick a page into a machine and press a button and it comes out in England or America – that, I can't fathom. I say to myself, "You don't have to understand them." I enjoy it all thoroughly. I can walk out to the end of the garden and keep talking to people on the phone, or down the hall and into the bedroom. Many times I've said it to myself, "Isn't it marvellous?" All these things are wonderful.

---

* Ita: 'I've never been mugged but I was once accosted by the Legion of Mary.'

'We're extremely happy. Just now and again, you have a certain nostalgia for the times when you could leave the door open, the times when the children could run out and play and you could leave things lying around and nobody would touch them. That happens, now and again, when you're talking to your own contemporaries. But, sure, goodness gracious, the comforts today are unbelievable, towards what we had. And I never get blasé about having things. Even going out for a meal – it's still a treat, no matter how often I do it. We both enjoy the time we are living in. We make the most of it. I just wish to God the taxis were better.'

Chapter Twenty – Rory

'My sister Nancy and her husband, Brendan, arrived on New Year's Day:* my father had died. He'd been ill for quite a while, and rather discontented. He had emphysema; he was smoking cigarettes from the age of nine. And, eventually, it got him. He was lying there; it was sad, because he was a country man, essentially. He used to go fishing, and rabbit hunting, but he had to lie in bed and listen to the country sounds that Tallaght still had, even at that time. He died at home. The poor heart eventually gave out. He was only sixty-seven years old.

'I drove to my parents' home and my mother handed me my father's War of Independence medal, and said, "Your Dada would want you to have that."† Then she said, "I'd like him to have a military funeral." I enquired from the Department of Defence, and was told that that matter was decided by the Old IRA Liaison Officer. I went to his address, in the Tenters, a small area of two-up, two-down houses, near Marrowbone Lane. He was obviously a Mick Collins man; he had a picture of him on the wall, and Robert Emmet as well. He knew immediately who my father was, and his record. He told me he'd make the arrangements, and to call to his house that afternoon and he'd give me the flag, to drape the coffin.

---

* 1961.
† Rory: 'I still have it. It's in the china cabinet, in the front room.'

'After the requiem mass, the coffin was borne by hearse up Tallaght Main Street to St Maelruain's grave-yard. We were met by a file of soldiers, who presented arms. When the funeral prayers were said, I lifted the flag from the coffin, which was then lowered into the grave. The soldiers then fired three volleys over the grave, and the trumpeter played the last post, and then the reveille. It was a fitting tribute to a man who did what he considered to be his duty to his country, asked for no reward, and was totally unpretentious. I am absolutely proud to be Tim Doyle's son.

'My mother died seven years later. In fact, she started dying when my father died. It was just, she wasn't greatly interested in life after he went. She had a stroke, a massive stroke. I was at home. I got a phone call from my Aunt Lil, to tell me. So I headed for Tallaght right away. She was taken into James's Street Hospital.

'It was a shock; it wasn't expected. She was only

sixty-seven, and she didn't act sixty-seven. But she got this massive stroke and I prayed to God to take her. I didn't want a woman like her to be half-paralysed; she would have been in dreadful agony, in her mind. She died about two days after. After requiem Mass in the Dominican church in Tallaght, we laid her to rest with her beloved Tim, in St Maelruain's graveyard.'

'The Apprenticeship Board★ was set up in 1965, to organise and co-ordinate the training of apprentices in different trades. They designated a post for the printing trade, and advertised. And I got the job, mainly because I knew the printing industry and I was a teacher; I had been involved in apprentice training.

'And so, I was away again. I travelled all around Ireland, visiting every printer who had apprentices, and those who had apprentices and shouldn't have had them; generally, setting standards, laying down the rules and regulations for apprenticeships. I liked it immediately. I'd been teaching for thirteen years, and I'd reached a stage where the curriculum wasn't keeping pace with new developments, and I had an uncomfortable feeling that the students were aware of this. It became a dreadful bore, carrying out training which I knew was never going to be implemented. The syllabus was set down to match current practice, but the current practice was disappearing rapidly, with the development of electronics, first the transistors and then the microchip. And therefore I was working with young apprentices who I knew wouldn't use the older processes at the end of their apprenticeships, or even during it. It irritated me, because

---

★ Rory: 'It became Anco in 68 or 69.'

I couldn't jump out of the syllabus – because they had to pass the examination, which was based on the syllabus.

'When I went into the Apprenticeship Board, my first task was to write down all the descriptions and regulations that were unique to the printing trade. Then I set about organising block-release courses. Instead of going to a school or college each day, the apprentices would be released from their jobs for up to ten or twelve weeks. This meant that they had to get digs in Dublin or Cork, so that had to be organised too. But the main part was persuading their employers to release them; that took a job, because they were paying the wages. As far as they were concerned, it was a heavy expense to send the apprentices away *and* pay them. The thing that particularly annoyed some of them was the idea that, when it came to Holy Days of Obligation, the school closed down and the lads were just hanging around the place. And one of the printers from Sligo was foaming at the mouth. There was a mid-term break, two or three days, so the young fellow went home and the printer was up to his neck in work, and he wanted to know why the young fellow wasn't up in Dublin. And he said, "Come in and give me a hand," and the young fellow said, "No, I'm on my mid-term break." That annoyed the printer; he was in there, working under great pressure, and your man was hanging around outside. But all these little problems were part of the job. The block-release scheme was a very good idea, and it worked, but only after a considerable amount of difficulty and persuasion. There was one particularly difficult case in Donegal, where everybody, including the apprentices, felt that the apprentices shouldn't have been paid money at all; it was unfair to the employer to have to pay out good money when they were being fed as well – they'd be spending maybe ten shillings a week on the diet. But the apprentices in this case were happy enough, because they saw themselves setting up little businesses of their own when their time came, and they'd do the very same thing. They were quite honest about it; it wasn't two-faced.

'But it was marvellous. It meant, of course, that I drove around the country. Mind you, it was a different Ireland; all these little grey towns, dreadful hotels. And the advent of the nylon sheet – I can tell you, there's nothing worse than getting into a bed with nylon sheets in the wintertime. I met some tough characters. One of these was Pat Dunne, the boss of the *Leitrim Observer*, a very old man. He told me he was opposed to civil servants telling him how to run his business. Then he produced the biggest Webley revolver I had ever seen. He placed it on his desk, the muzzle pointing in my direction. He said he reserved it for Black and Tans and civil servants. I told him I was a printer, and he said, "OK. Talk," and put the Webley away.

'We were based in Merrion Square, and then the headquarters was moved to Ballsbridge. The technical people, like me, had initial difficulties with the civil servants from the Department of Industry and Commerce, then Labour, who were assigned to the Board; they resented our status in the pecking order. It was an ingrained thing. Some of these civil servants had spent a lot of their time in the lower grades, and they looked upon the men in the higher grades as gods and super-gods. Then, with the surge in industrial activity, they were promoted and they wanted the same treatment themselves, and they couldn't understand why we, the technical staff, weren't

prepared to accord them that privilege. I was called a Senior Training Advisor; I was at a grade comparable to a Higher Executive Officer in the Civil Service. I was entitled to a mat under my feet, and a large table. I was also supplied with a pencil parer, which I immediately recognised as a knife, or scalpel, for cutting quill pens.*
An even higher-grade officer was also entitled to a desk with drawers, a square of carpet and a coat-and-hat stand.

'Eventually, Anco managed to reduce the medieval seven-year apprenticeship. It was now four years, and that was more than adequate. The overall effect of the training scheme was to provide the country's printers and newspapers with young people who were *au fait* with the new technologies, and most were not now turned out after completing their apprenticeships. I felt pleased to be involved in such an improving and radical scheme.'

'Things changed. First, the road outside the house. Suddenly, we *had* a road, and it also became a tennis court, in a sense – because of the lack of traffic. Then there were more houses built. Jim Kenny built more bungalows, and then other builders arrived. All this was happening when Jack Flood's fields were bought and, gradually, a ribbon

---

* Rory: 'They had originally been provided for the British Civil Service, and the Irish Stationery Office had continued to order them. I was very interested in calligraphy, and had tried unsuccessfully to find such a knife myself. The Stationery Office was in Beggar's Bush Barracks. During the War, around 1942, paper stocks ran very low. One morning, an especially large amount of paper was taken away, and there, behind the stack, were two little old men – book binders. They'd been working there and, when the British left in 1922, no one had told them to go away, and nobody knew they were there. They'd been drawing their wages from another office.'

of houses grew up along Kilbarrack Road.★ The changes were radical but, at the time, it was just happening – almost unnoticed by us, the area changed.

'It's hard to explain: a new major sewage system was put in, for all of North Dublin, and it came down the middle of Kilbarrack Road – a major inconvenience. But one of the results of that construction was that, years later, we ended up with a very attractive walking and cycling path, covering up the major sewage pipe which was laid along the seafront. We lost *and* gained. There was a most unsightly pumping station, built at the end of Kilbarrack Road – and people now had a place for swimming, which was very welcome. We didn't appreciate it at the time, the sheer vulgarity of the building. But we learned: it was blocking the wonderful view of Dublin Bay.

'It wasn't a rural place any more and the people who were here first, who were native, were more or less swamped, between ourselves and then the other developments and the Corporation houses that were being built all across North Dublin. All of North Dublin filled in. That was development, and I never wanted to stop it. "Don't put that there; it's my patch." I never saw it that way. Everybody was getting a chance to have improvements in their lives, and these were now being provided. As well as that, although I didn't think it at the time: the more people arrived, the more services were set up. We got supermarkets, churches, and a chipper.†

★ Rory: 'The change from "Lane" to "Road" was considered a good move. "Kilbarrack Lane" would nowadays be considered "posh".'
† Ita: 'And I got plenty of exercise, picking up chip bags, wrappers, empty cans and, on one memorable occasion, ladies' underwear, adorned with little red roses – stuck in the hedge.'

'My cousin Vi* lived in St Lawrence Road, in Clontarf. Her son had gone off to England and married there, and he was thinking of buying a house. He suggested that she might like to live there. So she sold the house and went to England.† But it wasn't working out, so she came back to Ireland, and she stayed with a cousin, another cousin of mine, in Ballymun. But she was the type of person who was best living by herself and, after a while, it began to weigh on her mind and, in desperation, she was wondering what she could do. And she came up with the idea, and asked might she build a small chalet at the end of our garden. Maybe I was used to the idea of having buildings in the back garden, from my living in Tallaght. But I agreed and so did Ita. The chalet went up, and that was it. It was, in fact, a debt paid, because her mother, Mrs Pim, my Aunt Lizzie, had been very, very good to our family – my father was her brother. In fact, because of her husband, who was an engineer with the company, my father and his brothers and brothers-in-law got jobs on the railway, the Dublin to Blessington tram. It had made a big difference, and I felt a kind of obligation to repay. When Vi arrived, she was inclined to give directions – she was inclined to dictate – about what she would or wouldn't expect, but, after the first few weeks, she fitted in to our way of life.'‡

'When Jack Lynch became the leader of Fianna Fáil,§

---

* Violet Fullam.
† Ita: 'We had a lot of her furniture in the front room for a few years. We couldn't get into the room.'
‡ Ita: 'She was here for many, many years. Until she got so old that she herself couldn't manage any more.' Vi died in 2000, aged ninety-eight.
§ 1966.

there was a general uplift of interest in politics. There seemed to be a move towards modernism. Myself and my neighbour, Seán Cleary, went off and joined the Baldoyle Fianna Fáil cumann. We were both former members who'd left their native areas and had drifted out of active politics. We liked Jack Lynch's steadfastness, his straightforward approach, and his lack of what you'd call side.

'I remained with the Baldoyle cumann until we organised our own local cumann, in our new parish of Kilbarrack.★ That was about the time Michael Woods came on the scene. He lived in Kilbarrack; he got involved in the local affairs of people. The new housing estates were going up. Some of the people who had taken out mortgages from Dublin Corporation were suddenly faced with an increase in interest rates; it had been generally accepted that these particular mortgages would not have a variable interest rate. The Corporation broke its word, and many of these people faced great financial hardship, might even have lost their homes. Michael Woods took on the case of the people in this mortgage battle, and he successfully got them a very good deal. We more or less decided that we had a man who could well represent the party, whom we could support, and who could go to a higher level of politics. He was also ambitious, which helped. But how to get him there – that was the problem.

'The constituency stretched from the North Inner City to Howth. There were five seats in the constituency, and Fianna Fáil held three of them, with Charles

---

★ Rory: 'We called it the Kilbarrack cumann. Then our friend Tony Canning died, so we changed the name to the Tony Canning cumann.'

Haughey, George Colley and Eugene Timmons — all party heavyweights. But we now had, as a cumann, three delegates to the constituency organisation and to any convention to select election candidates. Michael Woods was our Secretary and, automatically, one of our three constituency delegates.

'He didn't waste his time and, with his access to the higher echelons of the party, he came under the watchful eye of Jack Lynch, who was always on the lookout for young talent. And then came the General Election of 1973, and off we went to the convention for the selection of candidates. We felt like the Three Musketeers and, at the end of that convention, Michael Woods got exactly three votes. Fianna Fáil lost that election, and we were left kicking our heels.

'And then the new Government threw us a lifeline. In a review of constituencies, usually caused by population changes, our constituency was broken into three new constituencies.★ Eventually, George Colley and Charlie Haughey went their separate ways; Dublin North East was now a four-seater, and opportunity beckoned for local talent. We succeeded in having Michael selected as a candidate for the 1977 General Election. And he was elected. He took the last seat from Conor Cruise O'Brien, in a nailbiting final count.

'Conor Cruise O'Brien was our *bête noire*. He was,

★ Rory: 'The sitting Government organised the extent of electoral constituencies. Under the Proportional Representation system it was important to have balanced electoral areas. It's probable that some governments would be tempted to nudge these changes to their own advantage. The sitting Minister, James Tully, was a bit too drastic in the changes he made, and they backfired on the Government in the next election. It created a new term in politics, the "Tullymander".'

with Justin Keating and David Thornley, one of three brilliant intellectuals who flashed across the political scene. He became a Government minister. To my mind, these people opportunistically decided to use the Labour Party for political advancement. They had a brief success. I disliked Cruise O'Brien's outlook on national politics, essentially because it differed from mine. I admired his work for the United Nations in the Congo, and he was a very distinguished writer and journalist.★ Strangely, he was supported by the Kilbarrack branch of the Labour Party, and I never, ever met any other member of that branch. I'm sure he was a charming man to meet, but I never did meet him, and we took his seat. He is now the Cassandra of Irish politics – we are all ruined and doomed.

'In the generality of politics in Ireland, people like to feel that they are not just electoral fodder. People like to be listened to by the politicians they have elected, and come away from clinics feeling that they are regarded as important human beings. Michael Woods set up clinics and, in addition, he canvassed every area, even in places where Fianna Fáil would not have been held in high regard at that time, Sutton and Howth. People said that we were wasting our time, but Woods was determined to go in everywhere, and he did. The fact that he had a doctorate was helpful, and made him very acceptable to people who had no problems. In other areas, where there were social problems, Michael gave a lot of his time to helping individuals with their difficulties.

'Election campaigns are highly emotional – soaring

★ Ita: 'Joe worked with him, in Washington, and liked him. He liked his brand of humour.'

adrenaline and non-stop hard work. There was postering to organise, publicity to be distributed, and house-to-house canvassing. There was also the usual contingent of well-wishers, who'd waste your time talking of elections long ago, or people who thought that shouting "Up Dev!" or "Up the Republic!" was winning voters.

'I remember the count. I was exhausted from the campaign and got tired of the election-count atmosphere, and came home to Kilbarrack. I was sitting, talking to Margo Woods, when the word came through that Michael had been elected. Then Michael arrived, and the whole place erupted. It was absolutely marvellous. Michael was subsequently appointed a Minister of State and Party Chief Whip. In 1979 he became a Cabinet Minister, and has held many such posts.

'After that, I somehow became chairman of the constituency, and Director of Elections for the next election. And that was an even better elation, and result. Woods topped the poll, with over ten thousand votes. We won two seats out of four – we very nearly made it three. I think that was 1981;* time marches on and the years march into each other.'

'My sister Breda was living in the old home in Tallaght with her husband, George, and three children. She was the nearest to me; she was hardly a year younger than me. And we were pretty close. She'd also worked in Juverna Press for a few years, before moving to the Stamping Department in Dublin Castle. When Breda got married, she moved to London with George, who

---

* Rory: 'I was subsequently National Executive representative for Dublin North East for a number of years.'

was an aircraft engineer. When my mother died, she'd willed the house to Breda. They came back to Ireland, and George got a job in the Potez aircraft firm, near Baldonnell.

'She smoked incessantly. She smoked so much she took to rolling her own cigarettes, and she could roll one faster than the average person would take to get a pack of cigarettes out of their pocket. And, inevitably, she got cancer. Cancer was endemic in the women of my family. My grandmother died of cancer, two of my aunts – so it was probable that the gene was there. So, Breda got the cancer, and died. She was fifty-seven, or so. It was devastatingly sad. She was a very lovable person.'

'My generation first became aware of "abroad" as a destination, apart from emigration, when a few of our better-heeled and prosperous neighbours began talking about the Costa Brava; it was the done thing. I thought, Very nice, and forgot about it. In the course of my work as a teacher, I'd been to a few conventions in Britain and, later, with Anco, I managed to get to Germany and Britain, for exhibitions. But apart from that and the odd trip to Ballybunion – which wasn't foreign travel, but probably should have been listed as such – we never went anywhere. And then, suddenly, we discovered that we now had the means to go on holidays. In fact, it was when Ita went back to work and the kids had finished school. So, off we went to Torremolinos, and enjoyed that no end. Then we went somewhere else in Spain; I think it was Benidorm. We went to Italy, to Rimini, and we saw Venice and Florence – and one of those events you can look back and laugh at – the bus turned a corner, high up in the mountains, and, right up on the hill, a man under a tree, with only the trunk of the tree behind him, making himself comfortable, trousers down around his ankles. All like a camera shot; I can still see him.

'Over to France – we stayed in Cannes, and visited Nice and St-Tropez, and saw all the marvellous sights. We went to Italy again, up beyond Genoa, to Alassio. Then, another time, we went to the south of Italy; we started from Venice, down to Sorrento, and back up to Venice, and home – amazing, even apart from the fact that there were earth tremors, a palpable earthquake, when we were in Venice. When we were in Sorrento, we took a trip over to Capri. On the way back, a tornado or hurricane hit the Bay of Naples. We were tossed up and down by huge waves and we thought we were goners. However, we survived, with a lot of very frightened people.*

'We went to Greece. We had intended going on a nine-day tour but, after a day, when we toured Corinth and Mycenae, the place where Agamemnon was born, and a wonderful open-air theatre, we sat down and said, "Look. If we go on a nine-day tour, it'll be like the rock that St Paul is supposed to have stood on, day after day." So, we said, "No, we won't do that. We can imagine the rest.† So we went to a place, Rafina, about eighteen miles from Athens, a very pleasant place, and ferries coming in and ferries going out; you could spend all day looking at all the different kinds of people, and their attitudes, coming and going on the ferries. On the

---

* Ita: 'I wasn't frightened; all I could do was laugh. Rory sang "Nearer My God to Thee", and a Scottish woman said, "Jesus! The *Titanic*!"'
† Ita: 'We decided to play it by ear.'

Sunday, we got Mass, as everybody else did – it was broadcast to the whole town, and it took about two or three hours. Women who were in the church would come scurrying out, probably to make sure the meat wasn't being burnt at home, and they'd come back; they were coming to and fro. The clergy were all dressed up, in full dress; they really go about it in a marvellous way, and the music was very, very nice. There was no escaping the Mass, orthodox, Greek, whether you wanted it or not.

'We went to Russia in 1982. We landed in Moscow and there was an almighty row because the Customs men found a bundle of Bibles and religious tracts in the baggage of a little get from Lurgan, who was actually a teacher. After a long delay, we were allowed to proceed, and we arrived at the hotel. I ordered some tea, and it arrived in a bucket-sized teapot and it remained in the room until we left. Cold tea is very pleasant. We went into the Kremlin, and saw all the wonderful sights,★ but not Lenin's tomb – there was a queue a mile long to visit him. I discovered the secret of how the ranks of Red Army soldiers marched in perfect step, in ranks of sixteen or more. There were lines painted on the road, across Red Square, and, between the lines, white spots, each about twenty-seven inches apart. If every soldier placed his boot on the spot – and he did – everybody was in line.† We inadvertently

---

★ Ita: 'We walked the legs off ourselves.'

† Ita: 'The people all looked miserable. I don't think I ever saw any of them laughing, and they were all in these badly made suits, what we would have described as Guiney suits, from Guiney's on Talbot Street – good value, but they wouldn't have been the finest workmanship. And anoraks that looked pretty miserable. They all seemed to be dead serious going along, and they had medals on their chests, the best sweeper of the week, the best typist, the best hairdresser – they all seemed to have these medals.'

strolled into a construction site, all soldiers, but the lads with the shovels had Asian faces. We apologised but everybody just smiled.★ And we visited the GUM, the famous department store, just off Red Square, where Mrs McCarthy from Kenmare bought a radio valve for her local parish priest. He'd given her the index number; it was, apparently, one of the few places in the world where a valve for an old radio could be bought. We walked along the banks of the Muskva River in the quiet evening. Men were busy, exercising their dogs by throwing sticks into the river for the dogs to retreive.

'We flew to Samarkand, in Uzbekistan, in Central Asia. The flight was attended by large Russian women, built like Sumo wrestlers, and they had very hairy legs. One of the young girls on the trip with us asked Boris, our Russian guide, why Russian women had hairy legs.'Well,' he said. 'The winters in Russia are very cold, and hairy legs are a great comfort.' The flight attendants handed out plastic cups of water to everybody, and said, "Trink," and everybody "trank".

'Samarkand – another lovely hotel. We visited the observatory built by Tamerlaine, the grandson of Genghis Khan, and the Grand Mosque. We also saw Lenin's bed-room. The guide had warned the women that we were in a Muslim country and to be careful in their dress. However, there were a couple of lassies from Cork who had no intention of being constrained. One of them was particularly well-endowed and was wearing a football jersey and little else. We were in the bazaar when we

---

★ Ita: 'We were warned not to take photographs of bridges, or other things like that. But we always bring cameras and forget to use them. We're like that.'

heard a strange sound, a buzzing noise. It grew louder, and a policeman tapped me on the shoulder and indicated that the young lady was giving great offence. I didn't feel like getting into trouble for something I'd no control over, so I said to the young lady that we'd better get out of the bazaar before there was trouble. "Feck them," said she, but we got out of the bazaar. Later, in a bookshop, we spotted the two girls surrounded by a swarm of the local boys. They were now frightened, and I went to the boys and ordered them away. They just laughed and kept trying to maul the girls. I then had an inspiration, and reached into my shirt pocket and produced my Anco identity card. Why I had it in my pocket on holiday, I don't know, but, when they saw the card, they all took to their heels. They probably thought I was one of the KGB.

'Later, my Ronson lighter was stolen, I suspect by one of the waiters. I had to find matches. None to be had in the hotel. I was directed downtown. None to be had at the tobacco shops. I was waved further downtown. Finally, I discovered that selling matches was a different job and was separately licensed. I found an old chap who sold matches. He looked at me, and said, "Englaise". I shook my head, and said, "Irelanda". He looked puzzled, then said, "Ah! De Valera, Georgie Best." He was delighted with himself and we had a long conversation, he in Uzbek, me in "English". I got the matches, and then discovered that I'd been struck by the curse of Tamerlaine. We'd been warned not to drink the water, but I had; I'd added it to some of my John Powers whiskey – the damage was done. I was desperate to get to a toilet, and was eventually directed to the town jacks. It was built about a thousand years ago and, when I got in, I realised it hadn't been cleaned out since it was built. The business end was star-shaped, with a short wall on each side of each cubicle – and a hole in the ground. The local cornerboys just hung about inside the building, smoking and, no doubt, commenting on my Western equipment. As I applied myself, swarms of metallic flies, gold, silver, green, blue and every other colour of the spectrum rose out of the hole in the ground. There were millions of them. They buzzed all over me. I survived the ordeal, and Boris prescribed a diet of boiled rice and hard-boiled eggs, with green tea. He said it was a three-day treatment. It worked.

'We went by sleeper train to Tashkent, the capital of the region. The plain looked vast and the pervading odour was that of human faeces, the general fertiliser used in the area. In the morning, there was a babushka with a samovar of tea in the corridor.

'Tashkent was newly restored after a dreadful earthquake. Among other things, we were shown the room where Lenin had slept. It had a small wooden table, with an ancient typewriter, small iron bed and a small rug on the floor. It looked very like the bedroom we'd seen in Samarkand, and I should mention that we'd seen the identical room in Moscow, and we'd see it again in Dushanbe and in Leningrad. We visited a junior school, since a lot of people on the tour with us were teachers. It was impressive. The children sang, and we noticed that the senior people were Russians and the attendants were Asian. Whenever women met on the street and stopped to talk, they immediately hunkered down and, when they were finished talking, they stood up and went about their business. We were taken on a tour of the countryside and saw a co-operative farm. It appeared to be very successful and popular, and allowed for individual farmers to sell some of their produce in the bazaars. We saw one old guy sitting beside a pile of watermelons being picked up by a very substantial limousine; a young lady in colourful robes got out of the car to assist him, displaying an elegantly clad silken leg and shoes that Ita said were the most expensive to be had in Europe. Our guide was a Hollywood-like wide-boy with a mouthful of gold teeth. The gold teeth were ubiquitous to the region.

'We went up to a village tea house,* with large double beds on which everybody sat and talked, or lolled, and drank "choy", the green tea. I did some sketching, and a woman came from a little house and joined us. She was a scientist and was recuperating at a dacha which had been provided for that purpose. She wrote a little note on the sketch, and I still have it. She said she was Tartar in origin,† and Ita and herself had an animated conversation, Ita in English and the woman in Russian, and Ita was able to tell me how many children the woman had and all about her business.

'We flew to Dushanbe, in Tajikistan. We were given priority on boarding the plane, over American, British and German tourists, and, finally, the locals.‡ The locals were laden with kettles, teapots and every contrivance, presumably for use in the tea houses. The cabin soon stank with the odour of musk and what we afterwards learnt was hashish, which the men were smoking. The inside of the plane was dire – tattered wallpaper on the

---

* Ita: 'Some of them were rough-and-ready places, and some of them were very elegant.'

† Ita: 'She pointed to horsemen in the distance, and said, "My people."'

‡ Ita: 'For some reason, they always put the Irish in front.'

sides of the cabin. We shot up into the sky and Ita disappeared. I looked around and discovered that somebody had removed the bolts that fixed the seat to the floor and, on our descent, I had to grab Ita, because now the seat was sliding in the opposite direction.

'Dushanbe was a nice city and we saw the usual sights, including Lenin's bedroom. We weren't encouraged to wander the town, because there was some local unrest as a consequence of the Russian war in Afghanistan, not too far away, and a lot of the local Tajiks had relatives across the border. One of the men on the tour told us that he'd been in the park the night before, and a demonstration started up; and police with dogs had made short work of the demonstration. We went for a picnic up in the mountains, the Hindu Kush. We were warned not to dally on the road, as there was a constant stream of lorries laden with soldiers on their way to Afghanistan, and we were told that the lorries would not swerve or stop if we got in the way. So, we didn't dally on the road. We walked down from the pass and, on the way, we were greeted by a couple of Russian generals and their "wives", all roaring drunk in a field off the road. I never saw so much gold braid in my life. They wanted us to join in the fun. We politely declined the invitation and carried on down to where our own picnic was being provided. I had finished my cure, after the curse of Tamerlaine, and I got lucky because a large number of the party were respectable teachers and didn't drink alcohol. I had more than my fair share of the lovely Georgian wine and I started a singsong, to the mortification of some of our party but to the delight of a large group of Germans.

'Then we flew to Leningrad, a very lovely city, and

saw Lenin's bedroom and a circus. The circus had the usual bear, and a large Russian lady in mesh tights controlled the bear.* Then home.'

'My time for retirement came on the 8th of December, 1988, and I was glad to get out. I'd been very enthusiastic about the work and had enjoyed meeting all the people around the country. However, there were lots of new people coming in, as a consequence of the fusion of different agencies, including Anco, to form a new organisation, called FÁS. I began to feel that some of these people had a very hazy knowledge of what the job entailed, as I understood it. So, what's new? They probably saw me as a dinosaur, and I was occupying an office, now in high demand. Subsequently, a new scheme of retraining for the unemployed, called Job Search, was introduced and, as a "very experienced" officer, I was asked to participate. I accepted the invitation, as I reckoned that my main task was complete and I knew I wouldn't be given a serious assignment so close to retirement. I was now out of my office – out of sight, out of mind – and experienced the most stressful period of my working life. The scheme was to cater for long-term unemployed people. Unemployment figures were very high, and there was also a considerable number of people drawing the dole who were suspected of also working in the black economy. Many more were untrained for the new industrial processes that were gradually coming on stream towards the end of the 80s. Many of these

---

* Itá: 'The rain lashed; the roof of the big tent leaked. It was real rough and ready, but great fun. They say that horsey people grow to look like horses, and the circus lady with the bear must have been a long time with the bear; the only difference between them was the spangled tights.'

people were very pleased with the new opportunities but quite a number were displeased – they were being discommoded. Essentially, the participants would be required to attend for interview and would then be assigned to training courses deemed suitable for their needs. I was assigned to do the interviewing in Swords and Coolock, and it was not a pleasant experience. At the end of a day, all the positive feelings of helping people could be swamped by the sheer negativity of the smaller numbers of objectors. The stress arose from the sheer predictability of the objections raised by some of the people who were antagonistic to the scheme. They argued and blustered and produced the most amazing reasons for non-compliance and, of course, held me personally accountable for their plight. Others – most, in fact – were delighted with the opportunity. One particular character who was in the bad books with the Social Welfare Department was called to be interviewed, by me. He came to the office I was occupying and said that he wouldn't be available for interview. I told him I'd no option but to set a date for the interview. That afternoon, as I was strolling down the main street in Swords during the lunch break, I met him face to face – High Noon. He threatened me in a very aggressive manner. I recommended a training course for him. The following Friday, when I was having my lunch in the local hotel with some of my colleagues, he came in, half-jarred, and he assailed me with a litany of bad names and descriptions, and he attempted to physically assault me. He didn't succeed, and was ejected from the hotel by the staff and customers. The next week he declared to Social Welfare that he'd found a job, and he ceased drawing the dole.

'The 8th of December rolled up, and I had completed forty-eight years working, as a printer, a teacher and an industrial-training advisor. I'd been particularly fortunate in my working life, and had moved seamlessly from one job to the next. I was never unemployed for a single day. I never made a fortune but I got my pension, which I've enjoyed, and I've no worries about the rise and fall of stocks and shares.'

'My heart problems started earlier than they were officially recorded. I had a bad spell of not feeling well, and Ita sent for J.J. O'Leary, my doctor. He took a look at me, and said, "Put on your coat," and he brought me up to Beaumont.* I spent about a day and a half there, for assessment, but I didn't show any of the classic symptoms of a heart condition. They told me I had this oesophagus ulcer; I can't remember the exact name of it.† So, I came away; and every time I got this pain across my chest, I was to take Gaviscon, a stomach tablet. I'd go for a walk and, every now and again, the pain would come and I'd take one of the tablets.

'It went on for about two years. Until one famous night, after the Fianna Fáil Árd Fheis. We always had a party, hosted by Michael Woods. This one was in a restaurant in Howth. We were upstairs, and we were enjoying ourselves and, suddenly, I saw spots, shooting stars, in front of my eyes, and then pain across my chest.‡ And I began to perspire, at a terrible rate. In fact, I'd a good

---

* Beaumont Hospital; northside of Dublin.
† Ita: 'It was reflux of the oesophagus.'
‡ Ita: 'The next thing, I looked around, and he went falling over the table.'

suit on me and it was absolutely saturated.⋆ I heard my good friend Noel Leech: "Leave him alone and call a fuckin' ambulance."†

'I was carted by stretcher, down the stairs, and into the ambulance.‡ And I remember, as it turned up Kilbarrack Road, driving along, no siren on, I said, "Every other night, you fellows wake me up with your sirens. And here's me coming up Kilbarrack Road, and not a sound." So the driver said he'd soon fix that, and he let the sirens go.§

'So we arrived in Beaumont, and I was taken to the intensive-care ward. I was put into a bed, and tubes were stuck in me, and various people prodded and tapped me and consulted dials.¶ I passed out, and woke the next morning and looked up at the window, and there was a blue, blue sky. A nurse came in and said, "What are you smiling for?" I said, "I'm looking out at a blue, blue sky that I never expected to see again. And", I said, "that makes me very happy."

'Innumerable tests were done on me for about four or five days. I'd had a heart attack; they agreed on that.

⋆ Rory: 'I'd paid a lot of money for that suit – Maurice Abrahams was the tailor – and it was never quite the same again.'

† Ita: 'And Noel Leech shouted out, "Get the fuckin' ambulance." I can still hear that.'

‡ Ita: 'I can remember putting my hand on his forehead, and it was saturated. People talk about breaking into a cold sweat. He was frozen, and this perspiration pouring out of him.'

§ Ita: 'So, the ambulance driver put on the alarm, and he said, "Now are you satisfied?" '

¶ Ita: 'A nurse came over to me, and she said, "Is your husband in the VHI?" and I said, "Yes, he is." And she said, "Have you got his number?" I said, "I didn't expect this to happen." So, she said, "You'll have to pay a fee, £10." I thought, They don't let you away with much; there I was, waiting to hear was he dead or alive. And I paid her the fee.'

But not one of the standard tests suggested that I had a bad heart – no high blood pressure, no high cholesterol. So they said they'd send me home.* I rang up Ita to tell her that I was coming home that day. Then I went down through the wards, to get a newspaper – to walk through the wards in Beaumont took considerable exercise – and I got the paper, came up, was sitting on the side of the bed reading it, when the sparks started again. So I pressed the button, and everybody came running.† They decided to go a bit further, with probing tests, and discovered that I needed a bypass.

'I remember going to Blackrock‡ on a Sunday, a very pleasant day. And being put into a nice comfortable bed. And that night, a priest came along. He was a Franciscan, and he looked rather solemn. He said, "Do you want to go to confession?" And I said, "No. At this stage in my life, all the sins I'd like to commit, I've neither the money nor the inclination for. So, I don't have anything troubling me at all." And he said, "Would you not like to think of the sins of your past?" And I said, "No. One of the benefits of increasing age is that you can forget the things that you don't want to remember. So, I can't even remember a sin I ever committed." So he said, "Would you like me to anoint you?" I said, "Yes." So he anointed me.

'The next morning, the surgeon, Maurice Neligan, came and took a look at me, and then another man came along and said, "I'm the anaesthetist," and it suddenly struck me: it reminded me of the story of the

* Ita: 'I think he was there a few weeks. Time seemed odd at this time; I can't recollect.'
† Ita: 'I got a phone call to say he'd had a relapse.'
‡ Blackrock Clinic; southside of Dublin.

309

English hangman, Pierpoint, coming to the cell and looking at his client, his height and weight and all, to determine the length and strength of the rope. I said this to the anaesthetist, and he said, "You're pretty close to it; that's what we're doing." He was trying to work out how much anaesthetic I'd need. I was to have a triple-bypass heart operation. I was taken off then, someone gave me a jab, and I remember nothing else.*

'I woke up feeling all clustered with wires, tubes all around me, people looking at me. And I was with the fairies. I hadn't a clue where I was. One of the nurses said, "You've done very well."† They'd opened up my leg and taken a vein from it – "harvested", they called it. This was for the purpose of replacing silted-up heart arteries. I still have the scar; it goes from just above my ankle, up to my thigh. They were rather proud of the job, the sewing-up, a gaping big hole in my chest but no stitches, all very neat. And I was still with the fairies.

'I spent two or three days in bed, and then I was visited by this very large, formidable-looking lady, and she said, "Up! You're going to walk." I said, "I can't walk." "Yes, you can," she said, and she just put her arm around me – I'm twelve stone, not a light-weight – but she hoisted me up on my feet and marched me up and down the corridor several times.‡

---

* Ita: 'The matron took me down, just after the operation. He looked dreadful, grey – wires and tubes all over the place. And I was told that he'd be taken off life-support the next day, and that this was a crucial time.'

† Ita: 'I phoned up at about half-twelve the next day, to find out, and I was told that he was grand. He'd been taken off the support at eleven.'

‡ Ita: 'The anaesthetic affected him badly. I remember, he was talking about being out in the corridor – and this, mind, was before he was walking again – and he said that when he'd been out there, he'd met a crowd of black men. And I remember you saying to him, "They must have been the Harlem Globe Trotters." '

'Everybody who visits Blackrock Clinic says, "Look at the lovely menus." As far as I was concerned, the food could have been dog dirt. I was no more interested. The food was beautifully done, and everybody came in with "oohs" and "aahs". But I wasn't interested.★ It took me quite a while; I only really ate again when I got home. I lost an awful lot of weight. I couldn't sit, I lost so much weight; the hardness of the chair was killing me.

'It struck me later that the anaesthetic had had a lingering effect on me, for some months. I had waves of fuzzy thoughts, and waves of black depression, and I just fought them off. I couldn't concentrate enough to read. It was tough going, but if you make up your mind to fight, you're not going to be overwhelmed by depression, or become a burden. I came through it alright, and I was fine. That was in 1992. I had a minor relapse when I was switched to aspirin, as an alternative to warfarin. It didn't work; I began getting pains again. I had to spend several days in Beaumont, so that I could be balanced out. I now have a fine selection of tablets,† about eleven, to be taken morning, noon and night. They appear to be doing the business. About five months after the operation, I saw an advert for a leather jacket. I liked the look of it, and decided to make a statement of survival. I bought the jacket. I still have it.

'I don't worry about death. It's inevitable. The longer

★ Ita: 'He went to skin and bone; I'd never seen him so thin.'

† Ita: 'My sister Máire was telling me about a neighbour of hers, a very cheerful man who'd had a triple bypass. He was only a month out of the hospital, and Máire asked his wife how he was: "I don't know what it is with him. He's very slow. He comes home and goes to asleep. I can't understand it – he's on the best of tablets." '

you live, the more people you lived with are gone. But I don't regard them as gone; they're still around, somehow. I can still think of them and I don't feel any pain or sense of loss.

'I hope that I don't become a burden. I know that I'm into old age, what some people would call old age, but I don't think it's old at all. I'm quite happy with it. I can't jump over things or climb ladders any more, to clean gutters. I was through the trauma of the heart attack, and thought then that I was going, so I'm quite prepared to go when the time comes, but not too soon. I believe we cross over to another, very pleasant place. I don't know what it is; I don't speculate.

'I'm now living in a totally different world. The availability of space, travel, movement, colour, and people's outlook – it's so totally different. We have much more in the way of material things, much more money and travel. It's a very mobile society today, and a very pleasant one. And the country – every time I go out now, say, to Ennis* – a dreary town has become a vibrant, colourful place. And all the towns of Ireland reflect this lively image. Young people and no dreariness, and good hotels and restaurants. And some idiots go on about how corrupt the country is. There's been corruption since Adam got booted out of the Garden of Eden.

'And Dublin has become a very cosmopolitan, colourful and lively place. The streets throb with the sound of multiple accents and languages, and there's a very obvious presence of different races, and a noticeably large number of young people. I wish our young

* County Clare.

people would get over the current phase of overdrinking, but then I seem to remember episodes from my own past years.'

Chapter Twenty-one – Ita

S he first saw the letters in 1963, after her father's death. *Dear Sister Ellie – I am elated to hear you are going to be married, and if you make your husband as good a wife as your sister Mary made me, he can thank his stars.* 'They were from a John J. Beekman, in Hempstead, New York. I read two of them.' Ellie was her mother, Ellen. 'And I remembered: there were little poetry books in the house when I was a child, with the name John J. Beekman on the covers. And I realised that the wife of this John was my mother's sister, and that her name was Mary.' Another letter was addressed to 'Dear Sister Ellie and Brother Jim'. 'But I'd only barely started the letters when my stepmother came in and told me that I'd no right to be reading them, because everything now belonged to Joe, and to put them away. Which I did.

'Pearl was in a very disturbed state after my father died. I decided, out of sensitivity for her feelings, I'd leave the things as they were, for the time being. I left the letters in the bureau.* There were photographs as well; some of them had writing on the back, and press clippings. They meant nothing to me.

'But I was quite elated. I'd found out that I had

---

* Ita: 'Why I worried about Pearl's sensitivities, I do not know; on leaving Mount Jerome cemetery after the funeral of Uncle Bob Brennan, I clearly heard her say to my father, "Where's your missus buried, Jim?" '

relations in America and that, at least, I had this Mary. They stayed there for many years, but I never forgot them. I knew they were there.'

'I always wondered, it was always in the back of my mind: who was she? I even remember, when I was younger, walking around and wondering, saying to myself, "That person could be related to me!"' She knew very little about her mother. 'Nothing really. Just the few little things I remembered. There was a neighbour on our road, Mrs McGahon, and she used to go walking with my mother, pushing the prams, and she said that my mother was always in good humour. Then there was Mrs McManus, who lived beside us; I remember her saying it too – she was always in good humour. That was all I knew about her.'

She didn't know that her mother's maiden name was O'Brien. 'Not for years and years. It was kind of in the background, a memory of the name "O'Brien". But not for years. Her name was never mentioned. I'm sure this happened for some good reason. Not to cause upset for her children or possibly to avoid upsetting my father, who must have been going through a dreadful time. The awfulness of his situation only really dawned on me when I was an adult myself. I certainly lay no blame on him. The saying "Little children should be seen and not heard" was very much adhered to in 1929, and neither my sister nor my brother nor I would have dreamt of asking questions. And the arrival of a stepmother when I was ten certainly put paid to any chance of questions, or answers.

'All my life I wondered how things would have been if she'd lived. Apart from one photograph which, in the style of the times, made her look a lot older than she could have been, I had no idea what she looked like. My appearance was no help in that regard. I remember, as a young teenager, crossing Enniscorthy Bridge, and an old lady looked at me and said, "Which of the Bolgers are you?" All through the years, I wondered had she brothers or sisters? If so, where were they? Had they children? The only memory I have – it came suddenly to me, only recently – is of a box coming to the house, at Christmas, after she died. I can't remember what was in it, other than it was wrapped in white paper. It was for me. Who it came from, I don't know. Some mention was made that whoever had sent it had been related to Mammy. But it's so vague, I can't confirm it, and it's the one and only memory I had of her family.'*

There are five letters, all written by John J. Beekman. The first is dated February 14th, 1921. The last is dated February 14th, 1929. The others are dated February 16th, 1921, September 10th, 1922, and August 9th, 1925. The first three are typed; the ink is light blue. The remaining two are handwritten; the ink is black. All five letters are in a white envelope, addressed to Mrs James Bolger, 25 Brighton Gardens, Terenure, Dublin – Ireland. The envelope was franked on the 14th of February, 1929, in Hempstead, New York.

'Joe died in 1974.

'If I'd mentioned the letters to him when he was alive, he'd have said, "Take them; look at them." But I didn't,

---

* Ita: 'A few nights ago, it hit me: I remembered what was in the white paper – a child's bright green, patent-leather handbag' (April 2002).

because I didn't want to upset my stepmother. Some years later, after she'd gone into a nursing home, I had a good look at the letters. I glanced through them, and then decided to bring them home. I remember feeling – not sentimental; that doesn't cover it – but, certainly, highly emotional. So, I brought home the small black folder, with all the letters in it. There'd been more letters the first time I'd seen the folder, in 1963. And the paper cuttings; I presumed that they were related in some

way to the letters – but they were gone. The black folder also contained what I presumed was my mother's wedding ring. It was a beautiful deep gold. She must have had a small finger; the ring fitted on my hand, which is quite small.

'There were three photographs. One was of a little girl in a long white dress. The writing on the back read, "Cornelia Van Cartlandt Beekman. Born Feb. 22nd 1909. Parents – John J. and Mary E. Beekman." Another was of a lady dressed in a long black dress. The writing on the back read, "Mary – your sister – taken June 1926 – Cherry tree in the background – which aunt Emily and Mary ate their fill and said it was first real cherry feast they had since they left Ireland." The third photograph is of a young

woman standing in front of the same cherry tree, and, written in pencil on the back, "Cornelia Beekman. Taken June 1926".

'I read the letters. *Dear Sister Ellie* – Ellie was my mother – *I am elated to hear you are going to be married, and if you make your husband as good a wife as your sister Mary made me, he can thank his stars, why don't you come over Mary is anxious to have you and the children are and have been yearning to see you* – I'd say what happened was, Mary would talk with him and he would type it out – *come over for a visit and stay awhile with us and your husband as well, make it a honeymoon trip, you will enjoy your stay, as the spring is coming, and the country will look beautiful, now is the pleasant, season, we wish you a life of happiness and luck, you can make this trip, a honey moon and some time in a few years, we can make a trip over there, I have always, been anxious to go to England and Ireland and France, we expect you to come, let us know when you will sail and we will meet you on your landing, come without fail, as the children are looking to the day, to meet their aunt and uncle* – the children were my cousins – *with love to yourself and Jim – Your loving sister and brother – Mr and Mrs John J. Beekman.* It clicked then, I think, that this was the man who had written the little poetry books that had been at home when I was a child.★ Not one of them remained, but my father never threw a book out in his life.'

The first letter is typed on headed notepaper: 'City of

★ Ita: 'Máire remembers them too.'

New York Insurance Company – Cash Capital $1,000,000.' The company logo is a detailed sketch of the Manhattan skyline. The directors are listed, four on each side of the logo: Eldridge G. Snow, pres.; Frederic C. Buswell, v. pres.; Clarence A. Ludlum, v. pres.; Frank E. Burke, v. pres.; Charles L. Tynor, v. pres. & treas.; Wilfred Kurth, v. pres. & secty.; J. Carroll French, secretary.; Vincent P. Wyatt, asst. secty. John J. Beekman's name is on the left side, below the names of the first four directors, followed by the word 'Agent', and his address, 89 Main Street, Hempstead, N.Y. The letter is dated February 14th, 1921.

The second letter was written two days later, also typed, on 'The North River Insurance Company' notepaper – 'Capital $1,000,000 – incorporated 1822.' The company address is 95 William Street, New York. Again, 'Agent' follows John J. Beekman's name.

'*Dear sister and brother:– Received your letters yesterday –* they must have had letters from Mammy and Daddy the day before – *and wrote you yesterday, Mary says she will do everything she can for you, and I will do what I can, and will be elated to see you, and we think you certainly will like your visit here, as the spring is coming and the country will be at its best, I tell Cornelia, she will have to behave when you come over, she says no she wont –* Cornelia sounded like any other little girl; she was the little girl in white in the photograph – *she is anxious to see you.*

'In those days, myself and some other women cleaned our local church after ten o'clock Mass, every Monday morning. As we cleaned, we chatted quietly and, as we were cleaning *His* house voluntarily and free gratis, we decided He wouldn't object. I was telling the women about the letters, and a friend of mine, Kitty Murphy, told me that she had a cousin in the New York telephone exchange, and she would forward the details to her, the name "Beekman", with special reference to the Hempstead area. *Joe and young Joe, spent Saturday and Sunday with us, he and I went to the show (and in Lent, too) but I go to Mass every morning during Lent, so you see, that is my lenten portion this year, and then Sunday afternoon Joe and one of my brothers went to the show-Movies and Vaudville, Mary was there Saturday night, she goes often, it seems to be all the vougue in this country, I don't know whether its effects are good or not I doubt it, but it prevails nevertheless, I must confess I enjoy them myself . . .*

'After a few weeks, Kitty presented me with a list of around a dozen people named Beekman, with their addresses. I was delighted. I wrote to them all, telling them who I was, and asking them could they be related to me. I waited impatiently for weeks. A strong part of me was optimistic.

'. . . *you will have quite some visits to make after you get here awhile, we will meet you, if we should not be there on the arrival of your boat sent us a telegram collect, and we will go down and meet you, you better do that if possible, I called the British Counselate on the phone and he said I could do nothing in regards securing you a Passport only write you a letter, as I done yesterday the 15th* – with the situation in Ireland, the War of Independence, it must have been difficult for Daddy to get a passport, with his Sinn Féin involvement* – *you and Mary and Jim will have a great time, and we have room for you and will be glad to have you with us until matters change* – I wondered would they have come back, if they'd gone over – *if you need money let us know how much and I will send it by postal money order, come over as soon as possible so*

---

* The new Provisional Government took over the administration of the country on the 16th of January, 1922.

you will enjoy the spring season, before it gets too warm, with fond affection, be here by Easter and before if possible, we are anxious for your coming – with love and blessings – your loving sister and brother – John and Mary.

'I got two replies. One was from a Howard Beekman. He thanked me for the letter and said that he wasn't related to me, but that his cousins on his father's side were related to me, and he'd spoken to them. That gave me great hope. The second letter was from Jack Beekman. Jack said that he was my cousin; he was Mary and John J. Beekman's son. He was delighted to hear from me, but was no good at writing letters, and had handed my letter on to his sister, Connie, and that she was going to write.

'I was absolutely thrilled, and wild with excitement; I couldn't believe it – I was sure New York was full of people with the Beekman name.★ I felt pleased with myself; I felt I'd accomplished something. Then Connie's letter arrived the following week. Connie was Cornelia Van Cartlandt, the little girl in the photograph. She was now Mrs Fred Reimor, a widow, with one son, Dirk. As well as Connie and Jack Beekman, I had two other cousins, Euphemia, called Phemie, and Robert, called Bob – all the children of Mary and John J. Beekman.†

★ 'As Terry crossed Beekman Street near Park Row two men jumped from a butcher's cart and approached him. One knocked him down with a slung-shot, while the other snatched the satchel. Both then sprang into their vehicle and whipped up the horses, easily making their escape. In recent years this method of robbery has been used extensively by automobile bandits, and by the hi-jackers, who specialize in liquor' (from *The Gangs of New York* by Herbert Asbury, 1927).

† Rory: 'Over the years, I'd been aware of Ita's feeling of, almost, a sense of loss at the fact that she knew nothing of her mother's people and, indeed, little enough about her mother. When Kitty Murphy's information bore fruit, and Ita was elated, I was more than pleased.'

It was a long, long letter – she was as pleased as I was – and she gave me a good part of our family history.★ There were a lot of holes but at least I knew why they were there.

'My great-grandmother, a widow named Hyland, travelled from Ireland to America before the turn of the twentieth century. She settled in a place called Roslyn, on Long Island, New York. She was accompanied by two sons and two of her daughters. Connie remembered our great-grandmother, and described her as small and thin and good-humoured. The two daughters, Mary and Emily, eventually married two brothers called Daly, but neither of them had families. The fate of the two sons, Peter and Mike, was a bit vague. The Hyland family seemed to prosper. Connie put that down to the fact that, when they started out in America, they were employed by Quakers, and the Quakers were good, kind employers. I'd imagine, myself, that they were servants, but Connie didn't say this. She did say that it was economic need that sent them to America.

'My grandmother, Bridget,† another Hyland, was married to John O'Brien, and had remained in Ireland when the others emigrated. She had three daughters: Mary, Connie's mother; Ellen, my mother, and Emily. The O'Brien family lived in Ballydonnigan, in Wexford.

'My grandmother died – Connie had no idea of the year. My grandfather, John O'Brien, travelled to America, to join the Hylands. I don't know what family he brought with him; I don't recall – perhaps I never knew. But he couldn't settle there, and he came back to Wexford. When

★ Ita: 'Unfortunately, I lost this letter, and this I bitterly regret.'
† Ita: 'I'm Ita Bridget.'

I read that bit of news, I decided that I'd been destined to be born in Ireland, and from two Wexford grandfathers. Grandfather Bolger went to Australia, and came back. And Grandfather O'Brien went to America, and came back.

'In time, Grandfather O'Brien remarried. There was no mention of a second family. Although her mother seldom spoke about her home in Ireland, Connie felt that the three girls were not happy. Mary, Connie's mother, travelled to New York, to join the Hylands. Emily eventually married a man called Cleary, in Wexford. I know nothing of where my mother lived, or what she did before marrying my father.'

The third letter is dated September 10th, 1922. It is typed on 'City of New York Insurance Company' notepaper; the company address, '56 Cedar Street, New York', has been added, below the skyline logo. John J. Beekman's address is still "89, Main St." but with "cor. of Bedell St." added to the line. *'Dear Sister Ellie and brother JiM: – Received your welcome letter last evening and was elated to hear the good news, Mary will send baby over something in the near future –* Máire was born in May; her full name was Mary Johanna *– that is the name I wanted one of my girls named but Mary wouldn't hear it, I love the name of Mary – Joe's oldest is Mary also, I told Mary this A.M. that you and Joe both had Mary's, Well, Ellie I feel sorry for poor Joe, this is why – some four years ago little Joe was playing on the ice with his sled and fell and went in the house with a bij bump on his head the applied home reme-dies, and thought no more of it, in about a week the little fellow went to sleep and slept for six weeks the doctors pro-nounced it the sleeping sickness, he recovered they sent him to school but he could learn nothing, recently they had him exam-ined like they did many times before, the Specialist found that*

when he fell over four years ago he fractured his scull and the
bone grew together crooked and is now pressing on his brain,
and at times he is not himself at all, all the New York news-
papers carried the story, he will have to operated on, but it is
a delicate operation, Joe asked us to pray for him Mary had
him remembered in a Mass, so you too pray for him, that is
all we can do, we were at Joes about two weeks ago, but did
not see Joe he had just left before we got there, its to bad he
was a fine boy until that time, I am so glad you got along so
nice – Could they have gone to America after all, in
1921? Or was he referring to Joe, the father, before he
emigrated? And who was he? Was he my mother's
brother? My own brother was John Joseph, Joe, but there
were no other Joes in the Bolger family – *I just received*
Holy Communion this morning, my baby is here with me now,
she is over five and goes to the Kindergaren – that must have
been Euphemia, Phemie – *that is the baby class at school*
they learn deportment only, and have a general good time the
teachers read them stories and .C. – it's as if they switch;
Mary is talking, then John talks – *we were at Roslyn Friday*
evening we out for a ride and stopped there on the way home
saw your aunt Emily – my great aunt – *and had a long talk*
with your uncle Mike we were speaking of you, thought some-
thing might have happened you, not having heard form you
in such a long time, and this time especially – was that a reference to the Troubles here; the Civil War? They were
worried about Mammy and Daddy – *we were at your*
aunt Marys one evening last week she was ill, throat trouble
but is not out of bed so aunt Emily said she was over there,
your cousin Emily Hyland was in the store last night – I was
fascinated with all the Marys and Emilys; they really
handed down the names.

'About a year after I'd contacted the Beekman cousins,

Connie visited Ireland. I was at the Royal Dublin Hotel in O'Connell Street to welcome her and her friends. Rory and Máire were with me. I knew her, and she knew me. We hugged and kissed. She was a tiny little woman. She was smaller than even my five feet. She was bright and friendly. We had dinner with them that night. They had landed in Shannon and had travelled by tour bus up through the country. They were very happy with the trip, but I noticed that Connie was very quick in recognising the tourist traps, and wasn't at all interested in buying shillelaghs or shamrocks as souvenirs. We had a lovely evening. That was the 27th of August, 1977.

'*. . . your cousin Emily Hyland was in the store last night, she and her husband do not get on good it is his fault, she made a grave mistake in her marriage, its too bad, she is a good looking good disposition girl, your cousin Mary Hyland expect the Stork, she had three nice children, Well, I see Mike Collins has made the sacrifice, God rest his soul, I trust before many moons peace will again come to poor war ridden Ireland may God be merciful to her, let us hear from you soon . . .*

'That was Saturday, and they all came to us for lunch on Sunday. There was Connie, and her friend Violet, a very tall woman; she had red hair piled on top of her head. And a bright-green trouser outfit; she was a lovely woman. And there was Frank McManus, whose parents had emigrated to America from Queenstown,★ when he was a year old, "a baby in arms", but his parents had come from Fermanagh; and his wife, Henrietta, who had left Bremen, in Germany, when she was six months old. Connie told me that they'd all been friends since child-hood. And my cousin, Bob Beekman's wife, Jean Epp,

---

★ Today, Cobh, County Cork.

who was also of German extraction. And I was told that Jean was more Irish than the Irish themselves; she was big into Irish music and Irish everything, and she collected Belleek china. So, they came in and, first of all, Frank said, "Hey Henrietta, this guy has a bigger TV than we have." Connie gave me a paperweight, a brass American eagle, which her mother had given to her the day she started work. She also gave me a painted stone, a lighthouse, from Long Beach, and a piece of planking, cut from the barn of the Reimors' farm, her husband's home, in Cooperstown, Long Island. There was a painting of a red cardinal bird on the wood; Connie's sister-in-law had painted it. They all sat down to the meal.

'I had planned this lunch beforehand, and I'd planned on Irish smoked salmon to start with. But when we were having our dinner in the Royal Dublin the night before, Henrietta, reading the menu, had said, "Irish smoked salmon?" And Frank turned to her, and said, "No, Henrietta, that's sheenie food." I didn't know what he meant, but I knew that it was rather a derogatory description,★ so I decided against smoked salmon. And I'd bought tins of soup. I served the soup, and Frank, who seemed to do a lot of the talking that day, said,

---

★ Ita: 'Connie told me that she remembered Great-Granny Hyland; this Jewish lady or gentleman called to the door, and said they were looking for a Jewish family that lived on the same street. And Great-Granny Hyland said she didn't know any Jewish family but there were some sheenies up at the top of the street. Connie said that she wouldn't have hurt anybody's feelings, but she just didn't know that the word meant Jewish; she'd been told that the people at the top of the street were sheenies. The same as she would probably have said that the people at the other end were Prods. One thing that Connie's mother used to say, when she'd drink anything very hot, soup or something, was "Oh my God, that would scald a Protestant." There was no harm in it; it was just a saying.'

"Henrietta, there is nothing like good home-made soup."
At which, I went to the kitchen and said to Pamela,
who was helping me, "Dump the tins. Quick." I told
Connie, in private, later, and we had many a laugh over
it. It was Campbell's soup.

'. . . *I wrote Emily some time ago I will soon get an answer,
she like Mary very much, I mean she seems very fond of her,
she too has a young daughter, I hear nothing from Peter, why
dont you write Joe, if you don't care to, let Jim, I feel for him
in his trouble – Address – Mr Joseph O'Brien – 157 Dikeman
Street, Brooklyn, N.Y. – U.S.A. I wished he was near us in
the country the city here is no place to live, the air is so different, no one care for you there, everyone for themselves, but
I don't think his wife will ever come near any of his relatives,
trusting to hear from you soon love to yourself and baby and
Jim, before I close, There is a Henry Bolger Working in one of
our banks and his father came here many years ago from vinegar
Hill section,★ his name is James ask Jim if he ever had an
uncle James Bolger, I think he is some relative to Jim he has
red hair, a fine fellow, I had him Henry ask his father what
part of Ireland he came from, he came to America many years
ago, write soon – John and Mary.*

'I think it might have been the following year that
we went to America; I can't remember exactly.' It was
in March. We were there for Patrick's Day. Jack and
Connie met us at the airport and, from then on, it was
like a pilgrimage. We visited Roslyn, where the Hylands
had settled, a beautiful little town on Long Island, very
picturesque, quite touristy in its look. We saw, and prayed
in, the church where Great-Granny Hyland and her sons
and daughters had attended Mass. We saw the graveyard

★ Vinegar Hill, scene of a battle in 1798; Enniscorthy, County Wexford.

where they are buried. The funny thing there was, knowing we were coming to America, Jack and Connie had gone earlier to the Great-Granny's grave; they wanted it looking its best. But the day we arrived, we hunted and hunted in bitter cold, but we could not find the grave. Connie said, "Knowing Great-Granny Hyland, I can imagine her sticking her head up and saying, 'Gotcha.'"

'Two tall wooden houses were pointed out to me. These had been the homes of the two Hyland daughters and their two Daly brother husbands. The Beekmans, as children, had visited them regularly. They told me that their Beekman relatives were very nice people, but rather staid and serious.* They much preferred their visits to their mother's relatives, where they had lots of fun. I don't know how an Irish family ended up with the surname Beekman; I have absolutely no idea. It never crossed my mind to ask. Connie never mentioned how her parents had met. She wasn't a secretive woman. It was just, I didn't ask, and she didn't say.'

The fourth letter is dated August 9th, 1925. It is handwritten, in black ink, on 'City of New York Insurance

---

* 'For nearly twenty years I lived at Barrytown on the east bank of the Hudson, upriver from the villages of Hyde Park, Rhinebeck, and Rhinecliff . . . The area entered our American history when the Dutch patrons, centred upon New Amsterdam, began to build neat stone houses north of their island city. Of the Dutch families, the grandest was called Beekman . . . The Dutch Roosevelts of Hyde Park were fifth cousins of President Theodore Roosevelt (of Long Island). They had also intermarried not only with the Beekmans but with the Delanos. In fact, for Franklin Delano Roosevelt, his Beekman heritage was a matter of great pride, rather like an Englishman with a connection to the Plantagenets, the one true, legitimate, if fallen, dynasty' (from 'Love on the Hudson' by Gore Vidal, *New York Review of Books*, 11 May 1995).

Company' notepaper. In the list of directors, J. Carroll French had been replaced by Ferd. Ermisch, asst. secty. John J. Beekman's address is now 151 Front Street, Hempstead, NY. '*Dear Sister Ellie – I wrote you several letters perhaps they did not reach you at your old address.* My parents had had a flat in Castlewood Avenue, in Rathmines; but, to my knowledge, Máire was the only one born there. I'd been born by the time this letter was sent – *In cleaning my desk I found your present address. I have not much news to relate thank God, we are all well at this writing. I hope and trust you are the same. I reckon your children are able to walk and talk by now –* I was only seven weeks old. They obviously hadn't heard about me yet – *Uncle Mike, Pat, aunt Mary and Emily are all well. I drove over about a week ago with Mary and Robert and Euphemia and took aunt Mary and two of her children Alice and Gordon to the beach we had a real good time, we go several times a week it's only a 1/2 hours run from our place Long Beach. I haven't saw Joe in some time. The last time he was up I brought him to aunt Marys uncles Pat and Mikes and aunt Emilys to all of his relativis here in Nassau County.*

'*In your letter Ellie you say you were knocked about a bit, how come, in moving about. Cornelia is working – typist and stenographer. Jack is away. Cornelia and Euphemia, we seem quite lonesome today, I cleaned my desk and found your last letter Mary and I received Holy Communion this morning. We often hear from Emily. I and aunt Mary just send her 1 Pound each – she never complains, but says only for us would have to put the children away. she certainly seems very grateful, in a few years the children will be able to help her a little. You asked how Joes boy was. I believe Ellie there is no improvement. I am glad to learn you have your own home –* that's Brighton Gardens. Maybe the letters had been sent to the wrong address – *it adds so much to life, give our love to Jim, thank you for the invatation to Ireland, some day, if we live, in many years to come we might possibly pay you a visit. but not for a long while yet as our children are so young, would wonderfully like to, write soon, always glad to hear from you, with love and best wishes from all to all your sister and brother – Mary and John.*

'Connie, Jack and Bob lived in Hempstead. My other cousin, Phemie – Mrs Seaman – lived further up Long Island, in Stoney Brook, which looked like a Hollywood-style village. Her kindergarten lessons in deportment hadn't been wasted on her; she was a tall, slim woman who held herself very well. We were shown the greatest love and affection. We were wined and dined* and, I'd swear, if the fatted calf had appeared, he would have ended up in the oven. I felt that the void created by my mother's death had almost been filled. I didn't feel like I was going home, meeting these people, but I suppose I was closing a chapter. The one unfortunate part of it was that my mother's sisters, Mary, Connie's mother, and Emily, who had been living in Arklow,† had died only a few years previously. If I'd just been that little bit sooner, I could have met them. And Mary had actually visited Emily in Arklow. So that was a pity. But, at least, I got my own generation.

'I came home to Ireland in a high state of delight. While nothing could make up for the loss of my mother, I felt I knew the type of person she'd been, as mirrored

---

* Rory: 'On Saint Patrick's night, we went to an Irish club. Everybody there was very welcoming; I couldn't pay for a drink. Every time I tried, the bar staff said, "We don't take confederate money here." I liked Ita's cousins; they were very easy people to like.'
† County Wicklow.

by all her relations. From that time on, we corresponded regularly. Connie wrote long, newsy, witty letters – *Dearest Ita – my lovely cousin –* and I answered in my own style. Jack visited us on three occasions. Bob and his wife, Jean, came over. Aunt Emily's granddaughter, Breda Key, who lives in Toronto, also visited us a few times.'

The fifth letter is dated February 14th, 1929, exactly eight years after the first. It is handwritten, in black ink, on John Beekman's own headed notepaper; 'John J. Beekman'. The words 'You Always Need Insurance' are above the name, and 'estb. 1908' below it. There is a phone number, 'Phone 2693-W', in the top left-hand corner. Four services are listed below the name, two on each side of the paper; 'Fire and Auto Insurance' and 'Real Estate' on the left; 'Mortgage Loans' and 'Notary Public' on the right. There is no address. The day and month are handwritten. The first three numbers of the year – 192 – are printed; the '9' is done by hand. '*Dearest Sister Ellie – Was mighty glad to hear from you and learn you were all in good health, after all, that is the greatest blessing as far as worldly blessings go.*

'*You spoke of the flu, well Mary had it and Pneumonia was real bad, but was spared to us Thank God, she is mending but her heart is yet weak and will be for some time –* my mother died a month later, of pneumonia – *it's been an extremely mild winter here. but I see Europe is under a severe cold climate at present. The coldest in years. well Lent started yesterday, so fish will come in to its own, not so well liked as meat.*

'Jack was very funny. I remember thinking of my brother Joe; he was a very funny, witty man, and I'd often wondered where he got it from. And, having met

Jack, I realised: a kindred spirit, and a lover of the gee-gees, like Joe. And I thought to myself, what a pity they didn't know each other when Joe was in America. One of the times when Jack was over here, and I was working, Rory brought him to the zoo. And they were roaming around; it was a lovely, sunny day. There was a big gorilla lying in a corner, stretched out, with his stomach up to the sun, and Jack said, "I guess that guy has it made."★ He was full of these sayings; they tripped off his tongue – although he was a very serious-looking man. And Connie wrote very witty letters. Unfortunately, I didn't keep them all; there wouldn't be room in the house, because she was a great writer of letters. Bob was into music in a big way. He was a great admirer of Hank Williams. And, of course, Irish music; he followed that all over the place. The others really didn't. They were happy enough that they were Irish, but they weren't Irish, Irish, Irish.

'*Aunt Mary and Aunt Emily will be with us tomorrow to spend the day. Never see Joe anymore, he is now on the N.Y. Street cars, not with Butler anymore. we used to see him frequently when he was with Butler, he came this direction with the truck often and would call in for a few minutes, but we haven't saw him in over a year* – I never found out who Joe was. He might have been my mother's brother; his name was O'Brien. I didn't ask enough when I had the chance – *uncle Pat Hyland was confined to the bed several days with cold, and uncle Mike O'Brien wrenched his back. both are back at work. Aunt Mary has trouble with her back. not serious but enough to annoy her (Do you remember the time Aunt Mary and you gave Grandfathers trousers to the*

★ Rory: 'I can still hear him saying it.'

old woman for some apples?) I guess you and aunt Mary had some real great times well, Ellie, time goes bye fast, if we ever come to Ireland, (May be we will some day) we will sure call on you, We often hear from Emily. Aunt Mary and Emily uncle Pat sent her a pound each for X mas, and I sent her two since then, aunt Emily and I, each, sent her 1 pound, she must have it hard enough, God help her. it won't be many years before her children are a help to her, then she will have it a bit better I hope, but you cant count so much on children, but then some of them might be good to her, I feel they will. I see you met aunt Emily's old sweet heart. she married a brother of Uncle Pat's wife. a very steady man. remember us to Jim, well, Ellie, I suppose you have a motor car, we get a lot of enjoyment with our small car, soon we will get the Spring, and pleasant days . . .

'That meeting with my cousins happened over twenty years ago. Bob is the only remaining cousin. Connie died first, then Phemie, and her husband, Anson Seaman. Jack died on Christmas Eve, 2000, aged ninety. From the time we'd met him, Jack phoned every two or three weeks. Early last year, four of Bob Beekman's children came out to us for lunch – an all-day lunch. I hoped that the three O'Brien sisters, Mary, Ellen and Emily, were looking down on us, along with all the other O'Briens who might have been related to me.

'*Easter comes early this year. Do you ever hear from Peter? write soon, we always like to hear from you and dont forget, if we ever go to Ireland, we will sure see you, and pay you a visit. we are expecting the Photos of the children, write soon, Mary and I go to the movies and Theatre once a week at least. we like shows, write soon, closing with love to all from your loving sister and brother, John and Mary.*'

Afterword by Ita Doyle

The trouble with reminiscing is that, while events occur in chronological order, memories don't. This applies particularly in old age, when one might remember an incident that happened seventy years ago, and yesterday's dinner is a complete blank. Memories are triggered by sights and smells and sounds, and even certain gestures.

Blue taffeta for sale in Henry Street, and I remember the blue taffeta of my party dress when I was seven or eight. It was my birthday, and about ten little girls were gathered in our garden. We all had our party dresses. Mine had puff sleeves and three deep frills in the skirt. We were eating strawberries and ice-cream. The garden was small but strawberries and ice-cream were a rare treat; we could have been in the Garden of Eden.

I smell lavender and I remember my Aunt Una. She

was beautiful, and she always smelled of lavender. My cousin Maeve told me that it wasn't lavender water; it was her soap. A bar of lavender soap was one of the first things I bought when I started to work. I might never be as beautiful as Aunt Una but I would do my best to smell like her.

Last year, I saw an advertisement on the television for Bacardi Breezer. Gay young things twisted across the screen. The word 'breezer' was the trigger. I saw my brother, as a cheeky, bold little boy: 'Julius Caesar let a breezer, Off the coast of France, Napoleon tried to do the same, And did it in his pants.' This, to Joe, was the height of daring boldness.

The songs 'The Boys of Wexford' and 'Boulavogue', particularly if sung completely off-key, will for ever remind me of my father. He loved Wexford with an abiding love. I phoned my cousin Jim one day. He asked me to hold on for a few minutes, and I was delighted to hear 'Boulavogue' on the other end of the line. Let others stick to 'Greensleeves'; Jim Bolger Senior would have approved of Jim Bolger Junior.

A few years ago, in December, President Clinton visited Ireland. Banner headlines boasted of the President's third visit to us. But we were also told, for some strange reason, that he had only once visited the American state of Nebraska. 'Nebraska' was the key to the memory of my late brother-in-law, Jimmy Peoples, sitting in our kitchen, strumming Rory's guitar and singing: 'Take me back to old Nebraska, And if anyone should ask ya, I'll be waiting where the cornfields grow, In a tumble-down old cottage, Where a humble bowl of porridge, Is the most delightful meal I know.' He sang it so beautifully, and with such sincerity, that you would have sworn that he was born and reared in Nebraska.

It could be mid-June, in the sunshine, or any other time of year, and I get the whiff of cigar smoke. I am back in Terenure, in our sitting room, on Christmas Day, and my father is smoking his annual cigar. The cigar was taken carefully from his breast pocket, both ends were rolled carefully and gently between his fingers. The gold paper band was removed. When I was very young, I wore it as a ring. As one cigar per year did not merit the purchase of a cigar clipper, he used his small folding scissors. He opened it slowly, and snipped the top from the cigar. A match was lit, and placed to the cigar. And, with one or two puffs, the top glowed. My father lay back in his armchair, with an expression of all-this-and-heaven-too on his face. How I loved that smell, and still do.

Last Sunday, at Mass, the reader spoke of Jeremiah, the prophet. He lost me there. I was back in Kate Dempsey's little cottage, outside Kilmuckridge, in Wexford. Kate is blowing the fire with her bellows. 'Jeremiah, blow the fi-ah – puff, puff, puff.' Over and over we say it, both laughing until the kettle boils and I am sitting down to my special tea.

Kate Dempsey helped my Aunt Bessie on two or three mornings each week. I would stand and wait at the back gate until I saw the little black figure make her way over the brow of the hill, and down through the fields, a short cut to the house. I always went to meet her. I first met her when I was ten. She seemed old then, but she seemed no older when I last saw her, at age twenty-five. I walked the fields with Kate when we brought in the cows. I helped her spread the washing on the hedges and lawn, to bleach. We went to the market in Kilmuckridge to sell the chickens. Bessie allotted me two chickens each year, for holiday pocket money, and Kate fought my corner for me. 'There's something wrong with that scales. You're robbing the child. Ah, give her another few pence for sweets.' Each year, I visited Kate for a 'special' tea. Scones with jam, apple tart and some 'shop-bought' cake. These were lowered. But best of all was the chat. I loved to hear the life-stories of the neighbours, the farms they occupied and, sometimes, the farms they should have occupied if the world had been fair. Kate told me of people who were long dead, and the places where some of them are said to appear, 'God rest their souls.' On my first visit to Kate's cottage, she gave me a little dish made of a scalloped shell. I still have it. I loved Kate Dempsey and I still love her memory.

There are other memories, of course, that are not so pleasant. If at all possible, these are best forgotten. Bad memories, when dwelt on, can only make you bitter. Bitterness is no good for man or beast.

Of course, there are the memories I wish I had. Memories of the mother who died when I was three. All I can remember of her are hands, doing chores, turning the gramophone handle, holding me, and, finally, lying still and white. I have a photograph of her, but can never conjure up the living face. Memories of a baby who died after one day and one night. 'You have a little angel in heaven,' said a neighbour, by way of comfort. I wanted him out of heaven and tucked up in his pram.

C'est la vie.

FOR THE BEST IN PAPERBACKS, LOOK FOR THE

In every corner of the world, on every subject under the sun, Penguin represents quality and variety—the very best in publishing today.

For complete information about books available from Penguin—including Penguin Classics, Penguin Compass, and Puffins—and how to order them, write to us at the appropriate address below. Please note that for copyright reasons the selection of books varies from country to country.

In the United States: Please write to *Penguin Group (USA), P.O. Box 12289 Dept. B, Newark, New Jersey 07101-5289* or call 1-800-788-6262.

In the United Kingdom: Please write to *Dept. EP, Penguin Books Ltd, Bath Road, Harmondsworth, West Drayton, Middlesex UB7 0DA*.

In Canada: Please write to *Penguin Books Canada Ltd, 10 Alcorn Avenue, Suite 300, Toronto, Ontario M4V 3B2*.

In Australia: Please write to *Penguin Books Australia Ltd, P.O. Box 257, Ringwood, Victoria 3134*.

In New Zealand: Please write to *Penguin Books (NZ) Ltd, Private Bag 102902, North Shore Mail Centre, Auckland 10*.

In India: Please write to *Penguin Books India Pvt Ltd, 11 Panchsheel Shopping Centre, Panchsheel Park, New Delhi 110 017*.

In the Netherlands: Please write to *Penguin Books Netherlands bv, Postbus 3507, NL-1001 AH Amsterdam*.

In Germany: Please write to *Penguin Books Deutschland GmbH, Metzlerstrasse 26, 60594 Frankfurt am Main*.

In Spain: Please write to *Penguin Books S. A., Bravo Murillo 19, 1° B, 28015 Madrid*.

In Italy: Please write to *Penguin Italia s.r.l., Via Benedetto Croce 2, 20094 Corsico, Milano*.

In France: Please write to *Penguin France, Le Carré Wilson, 62 rue Benjamin Baillaud, 31500 Toulouse*.

In Japan: Please write to *Penguin Books Japan Ltd, Kaneko Building, 2-3-25 Koraku, Bunkyo-Ku, Tokyo 112*.

In South Africa: Please write to *Penguin Books South Africa (Pty) Ltd, Private Bag X14, Parkview, 2122 Johannesburg*.